Chief of the Pilgrims

Or the Life and Time of William Brewster, Ruling Elder of the Pilgrim Company That Founded New Plymouth, the Parent Colony of New England, in 1620

By Ashbel Steele

PANTIANOS
CLASSICS

Published by Pantianos Classics

ISBN-13: 978-1-78987-542-3

First published in 1857

Embarkation of the Pilgrims, engraved from Wier's painting at the National Capitol, D.C.

Contents

At a meeting of a number of the descendants of Elder William Brewster, held in Norwich, Connecticut, September 13, 1853, chiefly to take measures for procuring a suitably written life of that eminent and revered ancestor, the following resolution, among others, was adopted: —

"Whereas no Biography, containing even all the marked incidents of Elder Brewster's life, has ever yet been written; and, whereas, additional facts have been lately brought to light, and faithful research may bring forth others, as materials for the purpose; therefore,

Resolved. That James Brewster, Esq., New Haven, Conn., Chairman,
William Brewster, Esq., Rochester, New York,
Austin Brewster, Esq., Preston, Conn.,
Samuel C. Brewster, Esq., Syracuse, New York,
Sir Christopher S. Brewster, Paris, France,
(With ten other gentlemen named, of the connection,)
be a Committee to devise a plan, and provide means as they may deem best for securing such Biographic History."

In accordance with this resolution, arrangements were entered into with the present writer; he having previously made preparations for the work; while to the Committee, the Author is much indebted for means wherewith to extend his researches in all directions, and to all supposable sources, on both sides of the "Atlantic," for the desired information.

Commendatory

"Whatever skill and diligence can do will be done by the Rev. Ashbel Steele, to whom has been assigned the duty of preparing an ample account of the Life of Brewster."

Founders of New Plymouth, p. 144. By Rev. Joseph Hunter, Fellow of the Society of Antiquarians, Assistant Keeper of her Majesty's Records, &c. London, 1854.

From Sir David Brewster, LL.D., &c., Scotland.
"To Rev. Ashbel Steele, Washington, D. C, United States.

"I shall look forward with much interest to your Life of your distinguished relative — the history of so interesting a person as Elder Brewster.
Believe me to be, dear sir,
Ever most truly yours,
D. BREWSTER.
St. Leonard's College, St. Andrews.
February 4th, 1854."

Introduction

Significant were the words of Governor Bradford, when, after more than thirty years' intercourse with Elder William Brewster, he declared, in his History, "I should say something of his life, if to say a little were not worse than to be silent. But I cannot wholly forbear, though haply more may be done hereafter." [1]

To say a little, then, the governor confesses, could give no just idea of Elder Brewster's varied, self-sacrificing, and not uneventful life; nor indeed of the movements of the period with which he was connected. Therefore, while yielding to the constraining impulse to *say something* for that present purpose, in terms not to be mistaken did he announce that a more full and worthy delineation of the character and deeds of this noble Christian pioneer ought, in due time, to be given.

That full and just delineation, however, did not appear. And that generation passed away, and the next; and with them perished valuable letters and records, with the knowledge of many things which would give life and freshness to the history. Still, no other hand undertook the task. A brief and worthy sketch, indeed, along with sketches of other worthies, was afterwards drawn by the pen of Dr. Belknap; yet the life or biography proper was never written.

The causes of such neglect or delay at the time were, doubtless, the cares, labors, and incessant occupations of mind and body, incident to the settlement of a country strange and new; where, in the presence of savage foes, the first means of living were to be provided, wildernesses were to be converted into the abodes of civilized man, highways from settlement to settlement to be constructed, temples for divine worship to be reared, and the school-house and college to be erected. Tradition, too, was then fresh and credible. So that, while the narratives of the deeds and trials of their fathers, their fathers' fathers, and their fathers' neighbors, could, from memory, be repeated at their labors by day, and for entertainment at night, there was not felt, as now, the need or importance of the accurately written personal histories, even of those most distinguished. In after years, other causes operated to deter those best qualified from the undertaking.

But that state of things no longer exists. Tradition has long since become deceptive. The time has arrived when, along with mental culture, and more abundant means and leisure, public attention is awakened, and awakening more and more, to subjects of original inquiry. Historic facts and incidents, as far as they can be obtained, are now demanded. Records are searched, libraries are ransacked, remains of long neglected, worm-eaten scripts, and registers in time-honored Bibles, as well as oldest cemetery inscriptions, are now sought for with an avidity in this country before unknown.

In the case before us, the interest is becoming equally evident. And, to meet the demand, though parts of the materials for such a life connected with the time of Elder Brewster as might at first have been written, have perished — though, in addition to the waste of so many years, sad has been the havoc wars have made with manuscripts, public and private, yet the chief facts were put upon record; others, also, of much interest, have been lately brought to light. In place of those lost, we have what, if not equally life-like and romantic, are even more important. We can now trace most valuable *results* that have been developed, which our forefathers could not know, and most precious *principles* that have been evolved and reduced to practice, which at no early period could have been so clearly presented, or, if presented, would have been so generally appreciated.

As, therefore, this portion of biographic history was not then written, no period since could have been so favorable for its execution as the present.

As to the manner of its present execution, the writer has felt and acted on the principle, that, to bring out the individual character truly and impartially, he must lay aside prejudice, if he had any; must enter understandingly into the views of the person or persons concerned; must examine candidly their honestly declared motives; must, as far as practicable, place himself in the scenes, and sympathize with them in the trials and sufferings, which they passed through, whatever he may think of some of their opinions. All this must he do and feel, or he cannot be fitted to write of them, nor make allowance for the infirmities of even good men, or for the errors and customs of the age, not fitted to discern, delineate, or even appreciate the character of the fathers of New England, or especially of him who was a father of those fathers, and the subject of this narrative.

For himself personally would the writer add that, being connected in marriage with a descendant of the Elder, [2] and being himself descended from a granddaughter of the pilgrim governor, Bradford, and having for years desired to see such a work, and labored long to collect from all sources, far and near, the scattered materials, at length, by loss of voice, laid aside from the active duties of the Christian ministry, and called upon by many of the Brewster name to undertake the task, he yielded to the call, and the result is before the reader.

The purpose has been to present *facts, not theory,* not facts mingled with philosophical disquisitions, but in connected narrative, and in style suited to the nature of the work.

And here would the writer express his grateful acknowledgments to kind friends who have favored him —

To Peter Force, Esq., of Washington, D. C., for free access to his extensive and unrivalled collections in the department of early American history:

To Professor Joseph Henry, LL.D., Secretary of the Smithsonian Institution, Washington, D. C, for the use of valuable sets of books from the library of that Institution:

To the librarians of the State Department and Congress Libraries; also of the American Antiquarian Society at Worcester, Massachusetts; of the Mass. Historical Society, Boston; and Mr. Moore, librarian of the New York Historical Society:

Likewise to the Rev. Joseph Hunter, one of the Vice Presidents of the Society of Antiquarians, of London, and assistant keeper of the Queen's Records; and

To Cardinal Brewster, Esq., of Halstead Lodge, Halstead, Essex, England, for valuable communications, the results of long continued researches in the Fatherland.

Also to all those other kind friends who have made valuable suggestions in reference to the work.

Washington, D. C., June, 1857.

[1] Bradford's "History of Plymouth Plantation," lately recovered and published by the Massachusetts Historical Society, Boston, 1856, p. 409.
[2] Mrs. Clara Brewster Steele, by whose zeal in collecting family history, and at whose earnest suggestion this work was first commenced; — a daughter of the late Jacob Brewster, Esqr., of Otsego Co., N. Y., who was son of Stephen (one of eight brothers), son of Joseph Brewster, of Preston. Conn., near the Thames, son of Jonathan Brewster, of Preston, Conn., son of Benjamin Brewster, of Norwich, Conn., son of Jonathan, the oldest son of Elder Wm. Brewster.

ix

Chapter One – 1560-1584

He that of greatest works is finisher,
Oft does them by the weakest minister:
        Great floods have flown
From simple sources.   Shakespeare.

From smallest beginnings, which appear to most men at the time unworthy of notice, often issue the most important results. Some most precious principles, which now guide communities and governments, have had this origin. And in the history of fallible men, the progress of these principles is shown to have been often marked by the fiercest struggles and contests of the age; while yet in another age the descendants of the contending parties have united in their adoption.

In these struggles and conflicts, the resistance of those in power has generally issued in acts of violence and tyranny; and the assaults of the weaker as they grew stronger have led to rebellion or bloody revolution. In these ways, and at this dear rate, has much of man's wisdom been learned.

When Elizabeth, in all the conservative pride of prerogative which marked the race of the Tudors, sternly rejected further reforms in some rites and ceremonies in the Church of England, and adopted the policy which her successor, James, endeavored to follow, she little imagined what would be the contest then begun; a contest that was to carry one king from his throne to the block, and send another to live in exile; — a contest which was to result in the establishment of broad popular principles in her own kingdom, and to plant on this distant continent a hardy race, whose claims of legalized liberty would at length be satisfied only with a republican form of government, and the right to worship God in such order as they alone should choose.

Yet we live at a time when we can look back with some degree of calmness upon the contest and the results. The age of Elizabeth and James, of Cartwright and Hooker, of Laud and Baxter, with that of Charles and Cromwell, has passed away, and with it, for the most part, the bitterness of the contest.

And we claim, now, since the tempest is over, and the sympathizers with each party are living peaceably together under good governments, that we can begin to estimate justly the sincerity and zeal, the heroic endurance and chivalrous course, then manifested as traits of our common ancestry.

Great principles were indeed at stake. We speak not here of the right or the wrong at the first, or of the right or the wrong in the sanguinary revolution that followed, or in the counterrevolution. We ascribe not to the acts of any one party all the peculiar blessings since enjoyed. We notice not the faults of one side only. But we speak historically of the facts. And we trace with deepest reverence the marks of an Overruling Hand in *bringing good out of evil,* while we deeply regret the mistakes, the bitterness, the misdeeds of men as earnest, as zealous, as courageous as the world ever saw. And we speak thus in reference to another fact: that, among the persons early and deeply affected by the contest, was an *individual*, then unknown to fame, yet destined to lead that *band*, which, in the New World, and on the shore of New England, was to lay one of the foundations for these mighty results. That individual was Elder William Brewster, the subject of this narrative.

"This William Brewster," says an English antiquarian, "was the most eminent person in the movement, and who, if that honor is to be given to any single person, must be regarded as the Father of New England." "And independently of this movement, there is enough in the connections which he had formed in England to make him an object of interest." [1]

Of the immediate parentage of William Brewster no satisfactory information has been preserved, though there are grounds for very probable conjecture.

Among the old English families inhabiting the northeastern parts of Suffolk County, and the adjoining parts of Norfolk, on the eastern coast of England, were the ancient Brewster family and their connections located, ranking among the early "English Landed Gentry." As early as the forty-eighth year of Edward the Third, or in the year 1375, *John Brewster* was witness to a deed in the Parish of Henstead, in Suffolk, and not long after, in the

Wrentham Hall, England

reign of Richard the Second, a John Brewster was presented to the Rectory of Godwich, in the county of Norfolk. In the list of the gentry of Norfolk, returned to Henry the Sixth, was Galfridus Brewster; and the Norfolk branch became connected by marriage with the distinguished Houses of De Nar-

11

burgh, Spelman, Gleane, and Coke, of Holkham. But in the county of Suffolk, we find, further, that Robert Brewster, of Mutford, possessed also lands in Henstead, and that Wm. Brewster, of Henstead, and Robert Brewster, of Rushmere, died possessed of these estates, prior to the year 1482. This Robert had married the daughter and co-heiress of Sir Christopher Edmonds.

Not fifty years after, Humphrey Brewster, of this connection, purchased the Manor and Living of Wrentham, not far distant, and in 1550, built Wrentham Hall, where his descendants continued to reside until 1810, when this venerable mansion was taken down, and the estate sold; the income of the proprietors being derived from more than twenty parishes in the two counties.

To this family belonged the lordship of the Manors of Wrentham and the advowsons of the parish church. In this parish church repose the remains of Humphrey Brewster, over which was placed a monument to his memory on his death, in 1593, with an effigy in brass, retained therein to this day. [2]

From this Suffolk connection, a branch became established at Castle Hedingham, in Essex, near the time with that at Wrentham, and formed connections with the knightly families of Corbel, Clopton, Seckford, Quarles, Wentworth, of Nettleshurd Hall, and others of similar rank. In this vicinity, have descendants of this branch continued to reside, and the name of William generally kept up, to the present time, now more than 300 years. Of it is the present Cardinal Brewster, Esq., of Halstead, Essex. [3]

Both the Wrentham and Hedingham branches were families of the same coat-armor, bearing a chevron ermine between three silver étoiles, on a sable field, viz: stars breaking through the darkness of night.

That our William Brewster was most probably of this connection, seems to be indicated by the fact that an old copy of the *same coat-of-arms* (and it appears to be a very old copy) has been preserved from time immemorial in one branch of the Brewster family in this country. [4] Other indications, in addition to something of tradition, favoring the idea of this relationship, will be noticed in the course of this narrative.

Of other branches of the original family, one was settled in Barking, Essex County, and possessed the manors of Withfield and Condovers; one settled in Lincolnshire, about the year 1560; one in Kent, in the time of Elizabeth, and owned lands in Luddenham, Linstead, Linham, and other parishes.

Of the original stock, it is highly probable, was the Scottish branch, of which is that distinguished philosopher. Sir David Brewster. And such was probably the case in respect to Sir Francis Brewster, Lord-Mayor of Dublin. [5]

But that "other branch," with which we are now concerned, "was established," says Burke, "in the United States of America by William Brewster, the ruling Elder and spiritual guide of the Pilgrim Fathers, who, in 1620, went out to America, and were founders of New England."

From the summary thus presented, of principal connections of the Brewster name at that early period, we pass to the chief subject of our history.

12

William Brewster, called also subsequently Elder William, was born, according to the most reliable records and dates, about the year 1560, a little more than a year after Elizabeth came to the throne. [6]

Of the place of his nativity, no record has been discovered. And respecting his education, very brief, indeed, is the statement preserved; but, though brief, it is clear and explicit. First was his preparation for the University; though at what school, or under what masters, is not specified. Yet among his preparatory "attainments," were "the knowledge of the Latin tongue, and some insight into the Greek." [7] And his *knowledge* of the Latin, as the term was then understood, was the being able not only to read and write that language, but to speak it readily, and even more grammatically, than the then native English.

Of Brewster's mastery of Latin in all these particulars, we have full evidence in his ready use of it afterwards in Holland, as well as from the character, and large number of Latin works retained to the last in his library. This knowledge of it was the requirement of the *time* at the Universities, and was especially needful for one designed for that course of life for which he was apparently intended. [8]

He also acquired "some insight into the Greek." The fact that Greek literature was then less cultivated than at subsequent periods, accounts for the less attainment in it here mentioned.

Corresponding with these preparatory attainments in the languages, must have been his progress in mathematical and other branches required.

Thus prepared, he entered the University of Cambridge. It is not known into which of its then fourteen colleges or halls (now seventeen) young Brewster was received, yet in whichever it may have been, no privileges or opportunities of advancing in knowledge, classical or scientific, we are well assured, were suffered by him to pass unimproved. Nor could his feelings while at Cambridge, be uninfluenced, or his tastes uncultivated, amidst its gathered specimens of art, its noble gardens, its verdant lawns, its venerable shades, and refreshing walks by the slow winding "Cam."

But the highest attainment, that which moulded his character, and became the moving principle of his subsequent life, was his imbibing there the spirit of the Christian religion, in the words of the historian, "then being first seasoned with the seeds of grace and virtue." [9] Nor in this respect, was Brewster's case at all singular. Many and eminent were the examples of like religious influence at the time in the universities; of which, history and numerous biographies of that period bear ample testimony.

How long Brewster remained at Cambridge University is undefined; but considering the many years usually passed there, and his probable age on leaving, the *time* indefinitely expressed in his friend's memoir, may imply a period sufficiently long, though not longer than to take his first degree.

Thus qualified, he left the University "for the Court," where he entered the service of one of the Queen's ambassadors, Mr. Wm. Davison, afterwards one of her principal Secretaries of State. And henceforth for a time we must trace Brewster's course almost wholly by that of his patron, and through a most eventful period of that statesman's life.

[1] Rev. Joseph Hunter, Fellow of the Society of Antiquarians of London, &c., and of the Mass. Hist. Society, and an Assistant Keeper of Her Majesty's Records; author of Collections concerning the Founders of New Plymouth; also Mass. Hist. Coll., 4 series, vol. 1st, 64, 65.

[2] English paraphrase of an old Latin inscription to the memory of Humphrey Brewster: —

> "Sculptor, why gravest thou marbles, or why rear
> Thy useless structures to his memory here?
> Hath he not made himself a monument
> More lasting far than brass or adamant?
> This house, his gift, where through the coming years
> The word of God shall bless his people's ears,
> This temple for a sepulchre he hath.
> And holy prayers shall be his epitaph.
> Wouldst thou aught else to represent his fame?
> Take the strange bird, that from his funeral flame,
> With life and youth renewed, is said to fly,
> For emblem of its immortality."

[3] Burke's Landed Gentry of England and Ireland, 2 vols., London. Articles, Brewsters of Wrentham and Hedingham, and Supplement, Corrigenda, &c. Also communications of Cardinal Brewster, Halstead Lodge, Halstead, confirmatory of the foregoing statements, and containing many interesting particulars of the Brewsters of England.

[4] This old copy of said coat-of-arms is now in the possession of Dr. George G. Brewster, Portsmouth, New Hampshire, U. S., who has also furnished particulars respecting his branch of the family, from the year 1629.

[5] Thurloe's State Papers and Whitlaw's Dublin, vol. ii., Appendix.

[6] See note, Chap, xxxiii., on the date of his death.

[7] Bradford, 409, 412.

[8] Much of the conversation and epistolary correspondence among the learned of this period was in Latin. Many of the most important works, in literature and science, were still written in that language. To a large extent it was the language of the court, and of diplomatic intercourse, as well as of the universities. Of the state of learning generally at the universities, at this period, and also of its encouragement at the court of Elizabeth, we have a favorable view in Hallam's Literature, and Sir Roger Ascham's Treatise on the same subject.

[9] Bradford's History of Plymouth Plantations, 409.

Chapter Two – 1584-1585

Call some of young years, to train them up in that trade, and so fit them for weighty affairs. — Bacon.

We are to glance at the time and the general state of things when Brewster entered the scenes of public life. He was now in the service of Mr. Davison at the "Court." To be placed in this position, he must have had family influence, or have been recommended by peculiar qualifications, perhaps both. At what particular time he entered the service of that statesman, can now be determined only by other concurrent facts and dates, which, compared, prove it to have been at one of two periods — either in the autumn of 1584, or early in the summer of 1585. If at the former period, which seems more than probable, it must have been in accordance with the following recorded facts: —

On the last of September, 1584, after an embassy or continuation of embassies of about two years in Scotland, Mr. Davison returned to the court of England. [1] Here, then, was an opportunity (and it was the first that had occurred in these years) for Brewster to become engaged in his service at the court. [2] On this supposition, however, his stay here, at this time, was but short. Two months had scarcely elapsed after this ambassador's return from Scotland, when he was called to enter on another mission to the Netherlands: a confidential mission, preparatory to a succeeding one, in which Brewster is known to have been engaged. And this preparatory mission, important in its results, and of no little historic interest, not having been noticed by any historian here known, merits, in this place, a more particular attention. [3]

There had now arrived one of those eventful periods in England's history, which attracted the special attention of surrounding nations then, nor has it ceased to do so even to the present time; to Queen Elizabeth, it was one of the most critical of her whole reign.

Throughout Western Europe, jealousies and embittered feelings, between so-called Catholics and Protestants, existed to an extent scarcely kept within control. In England, the excitement and danger were much increased by the long-continued imprisonment of Mary, Queen of Scots, the fruitful source of party intrigues and plots, and of hopes and fears depending on her life. As to France, the awfully thrilling sensation caused by the never to be forgotten massacre of St. Bartholomew's Eve, had scarcely yet subsided; nor were there wanting, in the ruling party at that court, the readiness and will to strike some other kindred blow. Pope Pius V. had also issued his "Bull," pronouncing Queen Elizabeth a heretic, and absolving her Catholic subjects from their oath of allegiance to her government. [4] In Germany, after some cessation from internal conflicts and so-called religious wars, now again were aroused the hatred and passions of kindred against kindred, ready for deadly strife. [5] Spain, watchful and suspicious of Elizabeth's course, provoked and provoking, and ready to arm against her, was, at the time, the most powerful kingdom in Europe. Under the stern, intolerant Philip the Second, were held almost the entire commerce of the East, and the control of the gold and richest possessions of the New World.

Over the Low Countries, of Holland, called also the United Provinces or Netherlands, he claimed by inheritance absolute sway; and here, in violation of long established rights and privileges, he had introduced, and by his agents had exercised, the bloody atrocities of the Inquisition. In these states, now mostly Protestant, had the Prince of Orange headed a confederacy of defence against this long continued persecution and tyranny. Here had been awakened a spirit of religious liberty, maddened, at times, indeed, into anarchy, but at length merging into patriotic efforts for independence, which could not easily be crushed. And now there was a struggle, as for life, to cast off the Spanish yoke. In this, the states at length found themselves contending single-handed against the whole power of the Spanish monarchy. Spain's veteran troops, that had before spread devastation over city and country, under the cruel and butchering Alva, were again assembling in force against them under the more politic, but not less skilful and determined Duke of Parma. [6]

At this critical conjuncture, and to the consternation of the confederated states, their great leader, their country's hope, William, Prince of Orange, fell — basely assassinated by a supposed emissary of Spain. [7] Almost in despair, they cast their eyes abroad for help. And foul deeds like this ever excite an interest and sympathy for the sufferers, wherever selfishness and bigotry have not closed the heart against them.

Elizabeth had aided them, but only cautiously and covertly. They applied to France, but were refused.

Elizabeth and her council, sympathizing with them, and sensible of her own exposed condition should the Spanish arms there again prevail, resolved on offering protection.

Such were the circumstances, such the views and feelings that prompted the present mission. And Mr. Davison was selected for its execution.^ He, had much experience, first as a diplomatic agent at the Hague; next in a mission and residence at Antwerp; afterwards in an embassy to the Low Countries, where he became well-known and highly esteemed; lately he had returned from one of much difficulty in Scotland. "With great prudence and skill had he negotiated important treaties, giving unusual satisfaction to all parties concerned. And now to him was committed the present trust; one in the wise and discreet execution of which, a worthy and patriotic people might be preserved from despair and despotism, their numerous Protestant churches from desolation, and Elizabeth and her people's position strengthened; but in failure of which, the whole might be involved in inextricable difficulty and danger. Hence the importance, as well as the object of the mission.

Accordingly, even before the close of the year, the ambassador proceeded to the Netherlands. Among the objects claiming his immediate attention was the condition of the Elector of Cologne, Gebhard Truchsis, or Truxis, who was also the archbishop. Entertaining Protestant views, he had influenced many others in the same way. For this, and the crime of marrying, he had been deposed, and forced to seek protection in the Confederated States. [9] In this emergency, a warrant from the Queen authorized Mr. Davison to take up and deliver to the Elector, 6000 pounds towards the relief of his troubled estate, and the furtherance of the common cause." [10] On the 12th of the following January, the ambassador reported his conference with the States Delegates; [11] and on the 9th of March received further special communications respecting the matters to be transacted. [12] On the 10th, at the Hague, he communicated the welcome intelligence of the Queen's intention, under the circumstances, to support the oppressed people of the Netherlands. [13] Before the close of April, the States General proposed to offer Elizabeth the sovereignty; but she, on hearing it, declared to the ambassador through the Earl of Leicester her marked displeasure, supposing that he had sought this offer from the states; but her ministry justified him, and satisfied her, on the ground that it was only rendering to her the same honor that before had been proffered to the French King. Now also was suggested the Earl of Leicester's project of an expedition to the Low Countries. [14]

Thus, the way being made clear, and the preliminaries settled for the needed aid, a warrant from the Queen of the 24th of April authorized the ambassador's return. [15]

Accordingly having been the bearer of aid to the needy, having met the States General, or Delegates in council, ascertained their purposes, condition, and resources, made known to them the mind of his sovereign, procured answers to the propositions presented, and treated of all the matters to be transacted in accordance with his instructions, he returns again to England, and in due time reports at court the results of this mission.

And supposing, as we have done, that young Brewster was with him, this constituted his first experience in connection with diplomatic life. And the view here given, presents more clearly than could otherwise be done, the first steps in the important movements soon to follow, in a portion of which he is known to have acted, though a subordinate, yet an honorable part. Something may yet be discovered in the Harleian, or other manuscripts, to confirm our supposition. If so, born about the year 1560, and coming to the court in the autumn of 1584, he was in his 24th year when he entered the service of Mr. Davison.

In either case Brewster came into the active scenes of life, not when all around was as the calm unruffled sea, but when the broad surface of all Europe was as the heaving ocean; and ere long he must himself feel its surging billows, and taste its bitter waters. And deeply engraven upon his mind must have been the apprehensions, as well as effects of tyranny and religious intolerance now manifested in the Netherlands, and which called forth the sympathies of England, in view of the threatening contest.

[1] Saddler's State Papers, vol. iii. vol. i. 166, and Catalogue of Harl. MSS., p. 156, No. 291 and Nos. immediately preceding.

[2] Unless Brewster's entrance upon service with the Ambassador commenced thus early, Bradford's expression, "divers years," would be restricted to a term of about two years, a restriction which these words will scarcely admit.

[3] Even in the Life of Secretary Davison, by Sir N. H. Nicholas, where we should surely expect to find this mission noticed, we not only do not find it, but we find an attempt to alter dates from manuscript documents which relate to it, so as to make them conform to a mission in the next year. (See Life of Davison, pp. 19, 20, 21, and notes.)

[4] Turner's Eng., xii. 300, 340, 350, 371. See the document in Burnet's Hist. of the Reformation, Record 309.

[5] Kohlrausch's Germany, p. 307.

[6] Brandt, Holinshed and Rymer, at this period, Strype's Annals, iii., part i., 304, 306, and 317; Malte Brun, iii. 1094 and 1106. Ranke, 143.

[7] The Prince of Orange was treacherously assassinated at his own house, at Delft, July 10th, 1584 (N. S.), by Belthazar Gerrand, a Burgundian, and a supposed Spanish emissary. The King of Spain had offered a reward of 25,000 ducats to any one who would take the Prince's life. Strype's Annals, iii., part i., 304, 306, 309, 417.

[8] Biographia Britannica, article Davison; and Strype, as referred to before.

[9] Catalogue, Harl. MSS. i. pt. 126, 156, with Strype's Annals, iii. pt. 11, 275, and Leicester Correspondence, 15, 134, 373, 376.

[10] Catalogue, Harl. MSS. vol. i. p. 126, and 156: Dec. 29, 1584.

[11] Catalogue, Cott. MSS. Galba C. viii. 2, p. 222.

[12] Catalogue, Harl. MSS. i. 126; 285, 47.

[13] Catalogue, Cott. MSS. Galba, C. viii. 16, 35, p. 303, &c.

[14] Catalogue, Harl. MSS. i. 126, p. No. 285, 49.

[15] Catalogue, Cott. MSS. Galba, C. viii. No. 46.

Chapter Three - 1585

Great honors are great burdens. — Jonson.

We have spoken of the "Court." The court of Elizabeth, it is well known, was at this time one of distinguished eminence. *There* was the Queen of strong mind and lion heart — quick to discern, though at times imperious — passionate, and not always without guile. *There* were her chief Officers of State, consisting of not a few of the noted men of the age — a Cecil, now Lord Burleigh of the Treasury; a Walsingham and a Smith, now Secretaries of State; Mildmay, Sadler, Hatton, Bromley, with the lords of the household, and ladies of the court, and others that have left their marks upon the age. There also assembled, at her majesty's summons, the Privy Council, consisting of twelve of those principal officers of state, with an undefined number of the lords, all of royal choice; whose duties were, under oath, to advise the sovereign according to their best skill, knowledge, and discretion, without partiality or corruption, and to observe, keep, and do, all that good and true counsellors ought to do for the sovereign's honor and the public good! [1]

As to *place*, "The Court" was wherever the Queen was at the time resident; whether at Westminster, Whitehall, Greenwich, Richmond, Windsor, Nonsuch, or other royal residences; and at each of these were the offices and apartments, for all state purposes and attendants, as well as for the royal household." [2]

Of the Privy Council, then eminently the great Council of State, Mr. Davison appears to have held for the time the office of Clerk — an office of high trust, usually committed to tried statesmen, of whose diligence and discretion as well as abilities, there had been full proof Such proof had he given in more than eighteen years of responsible service. [3] And at this period, Brewster is clearly *known* to have been in his service. It is the only *other* period in which he *could have been* connected with Mr. Davison "at Court," previously to going on a specified embassy to the Low Countries. [4]

What then, it may be asked, was now and here young Brewster's position? We say not that it was such that he became particularly acquainted with the princely and the great; but that he was at least an active observer behind the scenes; also (what was matter of much greater interest to himself), that he had all the advantages, and the accompanying influence not only of the acquaintance, but of the esteem and marked friendship of his honored patron. [5]

Thus situated, and qualified with solid and classical attainments, no doubt he was engaged with mind and pen, in duties relating to Mr. Davison's position in connection with the Council, Here, all would be calculated to call forth his mental energies, to excite his youthful curiosity, and prompt to the most circumspect deportment.

Here for the time were opportunities for advancing in the knowledge of men and things, and of the operations of Government, in matters civil, political, and ecclesiastical, equal to his utmost capacity to improve.

But what, among other subjects, now engaged the special attention of the Queen, Court, and Council? What other than the subject of the late negotiation and still further action in respect to the Low Countries? [6] Daily was the condition of the Confederated States waxing worse and worse. Town after town was falling into the hands of their stern and cruel enemy. The noble city of Antwerp, the great emporium of the States and of Western Germany, was besieged and in danger. In the pressing emergency, deputies, with full powers to act, had hastened to England. [7] Met by the Queen at Greenwich, at her feet they plead their cause. They brought to view her former favors — their present danger — her assurances of anxious care for their defence and preservation, lately signified to them by her ambassador; the mutual interests of the two countries; the threatened overthrow of their Protestant faith; their hopeful prospects if further aided; but desperate condition if unaided;

and, waiving all former objections, they again proffer to her the sovereignty. On the terms specified they urge its acceptance as a work most royal and magnificent — acceptable to God, to Christianity all helpful, and worthy of immortal commendation. [8]

Elizabeth heard with deep interest their plea. She declined the sovereignty; but on due deliberation assented to an alliance. Accordingly commissioners were deputed from the Privy Council to treat with the Deputies. [9] The eyes of all Europe were fixed upon her. It was a bold and daring step. The King of Sweden said: "Queen Elizabeth has now taken the diadem from her head, and ventured it upon the doubtful chance of war." [10] Some of her Council were for declining the hazardous connection. She had herself at first hesitated; but at length concurring with those in its favor, she determined upon the heroic act. [11] At the magnificent palace of "Nonsuch," was the treaty negotiated, the Queen herself being often present at the conferences. Here also, for most of the time, was Mr. Davison — officially concerned and well qualified to act. [12] And here doubtless was Mr. Brewster also occupied in his Patron's service.

By the 10th of August the treaty was concluded, [13] and Davison was soon clothed with powers as her majesty's ambassador to carry its stipulations into execution. [14] Five thousand foot, and one thousand horse, were to be dispatched to the aid of the States, to be paid at first by the Queen, while the port of Flushing with the fortress of the Ramikins, in Zealand, and the Brill, with its forts in Holland, were to be put into the hands of the English, as precautionary sureties, until the repayment of the incurred expenses. Hence were they called the "Cautionary Towns."

Scarcely, however, had the treaty been concluded, when the startling news arrived of the fall of Antwerp. This unexpected intelligence, causing despondency in the States, and fears in England, hastened the departure of the embassy and a portion of the military force. [15]

In this embassy was Brewster. In the quaint old style of our historian it is recorded: "He attended Mr. Davison when he was sent in embassage by the Queen into the Low Countries, in the Earl of Leicester's time, as for other weighty affairs of state, so to receive possession of the Cautionary Towns." [16] The embassy was to proceed to the Hague, by the way of Flushing, to counteract there and elsewhere, as quickly as possible, the sad effects of the fall of Antwerp, and the wily policy of the conquering enemy. All along, as might be expected, had Spanish agencies been at work, in every practicable way, to undermine the efforts of the States, and to oppose the influence of the English. [17]

Assertions were confidently made that the Spanish arms would now again prevail. Slanderous reports were put in circulation respecting the acts and purposes of Elizabeth. Artful insinuations were uttered that, on getting possession of the important towns, as stipulated, the very keys to the heart of the country, the Queen would hold the States in complete subjection; or else,

20

that she would desert, and leave them to their fate, or make a selfish treaty with Spain, without their knowledge, whenever it would serve her private ends.

Efforts were also made to destroy confidence, and cause dissatisfaction among the people themselves, in respect to their own rulers, as well as between their rulers and the English queen. Attempts there were, too, and at times threatening to be successful, to awaken jealousies between their leaders — to estrange them from each other, and thus to break their strong bond of union. Others, again, who could be reached by more base and sordid motives, were stealthily appealed to on the score of interest: as heavy taxes, the expenses of the war — even the sacrifice of their estates, if conquered — all of which would be saved by submission.

These influences were to be met, and met they were successfully. The ambassador's well-known character, his sympathizing interest in their behalf, his wise counsels, gentlemanly deportment, and prompt action, aided powerfully in checking opposition, dispelling fears, strengthening their hopes, and calling forth all the combined energies of the patriotic.

Here were lessons for Brewster, in the school of diplomacy, and in conferences with chief men and rulers, as the embassy journeyed from Flushing to the Hague. [18]

From the Hague, the ambassador reported the success of his negotiations for the execution of the treaty and the delivery of the Cautionary Towns. In the mean time, instructions had been forwarded to him from the Queen, with authority to receive and take possession of those towns in her majesty's name. [19] Accordingly, on returning to the Briel, he thus reported again: —

"In the evening I received the keys, which I this day have committed to Mr. Henry Norris, with the government of the place by provision, till her majesty shall otherwise dispose thereof." [20]

But at Flushing was the transfer in which, from Brewster's known connection therewith, we are most interested. While at the Briel, the ambassador received possession, and placed its government in the hands of another; at Flushing, he was not only to receive possession and take upon ^himself the civil government, but to take command also of its fortifications, until the arrival of its future governor. And this transfer appears to have been attended with something of an imposing ceremony.

On the morning of October 19th, 1585 (Count Hollock, or Hohenloe, and the young Prince Maurice, son of the lately assassinated chief, being present and assenting), the English troops marched forth from their quarters, in good and quiet order, to the principal church. There, in solemn manner, was administered to them the oath of fidelity in respect to the present peculiar trust. This solemn act, in this sacred place, being performed in the presence of all assembled, they next marched to the fortifications, and took armed positions and possession, while the troops of the States quietly retired; "and, in token and sign" of the transfer and possession, the keys were also delivered

21

to the ambassador in due form, and accordingly received by him in her majesty's name. And thus, all concurring, was concluded, in quietness and peace, a transaction which was evidently one of great delicacy — to both parties a matter of no little anxiety." [21]

Connected with this, was the further occurrence, that the ambassador, after keeping the keys for some time, "committed them to Brewster;" and he, as deputy, and as indicating his sense of the responsibility and of faithfulness to the trust, slept, the first night, with them under his pillow. [22] Thus early appears the position which Brewster held in the ambassador's confidence, while engaged in this special mission.

How long William Brewster kept the keys of Flushing is not stated; but, from various sources, we learn that Sir Philip Sidney, one of the noblest of England's worthies, and, for his years, one of the wisest, was commissioned on the 9th, and arrived to take command on the 18th of the following November, when to him were the keys of this important military post transferred by the ambassador, probably from the hands of Brewster. [23]

The main purpose of this mission being now accomplished, the embassy is anxiously looking for permission to return. Private considerations induced a request for it, which, however, was not yet granted. [24]

From the first movement in the preparatory mission, through the whole course of the negotiations to the final carrying of the treaty into effect, had Mr. Davison been the main responsible agent.

Great wisdom, discretion, and tact, were required amid all the conflicting interests, in avoiding the jealousy of neighboring neutral states, and in provoking as little as possible the threatening wrath of Italy and Spain. And "in this, which was without question one of the most perplexing transactions of that whole reign, the ambassador conducted things in such a happy dexterity as to merit the strongest acknowledgments on the part of the States, at the same time that he rendered the highest service to his royal mistress." [25]

In such a service, under such a patron, was Brewster acquiring enlarged views, and acquaintance with other manners, customs, and conditions of society, civil and religious, and laying up in store practical wisdom, of no small advantage to himself and others, in his future life.

[1] Records of the Time, Blackstone's Com. The Privy Council became afterwards gradually changed, and was for the most part merged in the Ministerial Council; and this again in time to the present so called *Cabinet Council*. Hallam's Constitutional History, ii. 347.

[2] Beatson's Political Index, i. 398.

[3] Strype's Annals, iii. part i. 420, and Life of Davison.

[4] Brad. 410. The chronological order of Bradford's statements, to accord with historic facts and dates, must be made to stand yielded thus: 1st. Brewster went from the University to the Court, and there he entered the service of Mr. Davison; 2d. He attended Mr. Davison on the embassy to the Low Countries, as specified; and last, he was with that statesman, when he was Secretary of State.

[5] Brad., 409.

[6] Strype's Annals, iii. part 363.

[7] Rymer's Foedera, xv. 802.

[8] Speech of States' Deputies to Queen Elizabeth at Greenwich, June 29th, 1585; the original in Old French. Holinshed, iv. 416, 419, and 619.

[9] Cottonian MSS. Galba, C. vii. 55.

[10] Campden's Elizabeth, folio, 321.

[11] "Threw herself into the present war for their sakes, with the greatest Prince and Potentate in Europe." Cabala, part ii. 34.

[12] Leicester Correspondence, letter xviii. 126, xliii. 117.

[13] Corps Universale Diplomatique, tome v. partie i. p. 454, and further stipulations on the 18th of the same month.

[14] Strype's Annals, iii. part i. 436. Murdin, 783. "Life of Davison, 15."

[15] See references in preceding note 14. Antwerp surrendered August 7th, 1585 (Sup. N. S.); Sir John Norris was appointed to the command of the forces Aug. 12th; this, and the ambassador's urgent instructions, indicate that the embassy must have left England by about the middle of this month. Burleigh's treasury entry was: "Aug. 1585. Mr. W. Davison, sent of special message into the Low Countries, with 40 shillings diet." Murdin's State Papers, 783.

[16] Bradford, 410.

[17] Davison's instructions in Strype's Annals, iii. part ii. 363, and his letters to the court of this date in Cabala and Leicester Correspondence.

[18] Letters, &c., last referred to.

[19] Cottonian MSS. Galba, C. viii. 69 and 73, and Cabala, part ii. 34, Sept. 24, 1585.

[20] Extract from the MSS., kindly forwarded by Mr. Hunter, of London.

[21] Cabala, part ii. 3 and 34; Cottonian MSS. Galba, C. viii. 73, 75, 78; Leicester Correspondence, 61 and 74.

[22] Bradford, p. 410.

[23] Rymer's Foedera, xv. 802, and Sir Philip's Report; Harlein MSS.; Lodge's Memoirs, iii. 9. Sir Thomas Cecil, son of the Lord Treasurer, was commissioned at the same time Governor at the Brill, but did not arrive until after the 12th of January following; Leicester Correspondence, 38, 51.

[24] Cabala, ii. 3, 34.

[25] Biographia Britannica, article Davison; and Cabala, with Leicester Correspondence as before quoted.

Chapter Four - 1585

Knights, with a long retinue of their squires,
In gaudy liveries march, and quaint attires. — Dryden.

Between the time when William Brewster kept the keys of Flushing, just mentioned, and that of the next incident recorded respecting him, were other occurrences too marked to be omitted. To pass such unnoticed here, would be to pass over much that throws light upon this part of the narrative. Connected with these, there comes before us another personage as the chief actor — the Earl of Leicester. Our historian's allusion to him specifies the time, and the fact of Brewster's continued connection with the embassy.

The earl, at the time high among the highest in the Queen's personal favor, had been commissioned on the 2d of October, as her General-in-Chief and Counsellor in the Low Countries. [1] After many hindrances, and one mortifying detention by the Queen, he assembled on the 6th of Dec. his numerous and splendid train, at Colchester, in Essex, all zealous for this famed expedition. Moving onward, they arrived on the 8th at Harwich, and, the day after, embarked for Flushing in Zealand. [2] On the 10th, with a numerous fleet of ships and transports, they entered that noted port. There landing, the gallant band, in which was the Earl of Essex, with "lords, knights, captains, and choice soldiery," was greeted with shouts of welcome, displays of banners, ringing of bells, and roar of cannon — all evincing the gratitude and joy of the people of Zealand, for England's aid in their time of need.

The Earl of Leicester, received and entertained by Prince Maurice, and Sir Philip Sidney, now the governor, was lodged at the residence of the ambassador; who, with Sir Philip, bore to him the relationship of cousin. Here the ambassador, attended by Brewster, became connected with the civic and martial train, to aid and counsel the earl in his diplomatic intercourse with the States. Here also commenced a splendid pageant, in the manner of a triumphal progress, from Flushing through the States of Zealand and Holland even to Amsterdam.

The next day, after a large assemblage and discourse at the principal church, followed by a banquet, the earl and a large body of attendants, with the embassy, embarked for Middleburg. Passing the fortress of the Ramikins, a demonstration greeted them, limited, but not less signal than that of the day previous at Flushing. Landing at Middleburg in grand procession, they entered its gates amidst gorgeous display and presentations of national standards, roar of artillery, drums beating, trumpets sounding, and every practicable demonstration, civic and military; the best estates of the country attending. Amidst all this, conspicuous on every side, were numerous and expressive mottoes. Underneath the arms of England, emblazoned, and linked by chains to the arms of the States, and as most strikingly significant of the hopes of the present alliance, was this: "Quos Deus conjunxit, homo non separet;" "Whom God hath joined together, let no man put asunder." [3]

It was the season of Christmas, according to the old computation; and the hospitalities were without limit. The authorities of the States first feasted the earl and his train in the States House, where most sumptuous was the fare, and grotesque the devices; castellated structures of crystal, emitting silvery streams; animals prepared in full size and very form, of every eatable description, from earth, sea, and air, served up with all their varied accompaniments, in true olden Dutch style, amid speaking representations of England's aid — distress relieved, and of gratitude to the Great Giver. In short, in the words of the accurate old chronicler, "There were devices of all kinds, music of all sorts, variety of all things, and wondrous welcomes."

In return, the earl entertained the authorities and others most royally after the English manner; and then, less publicly, the widow of the late Prince of Orange, and her youthful son Maurice, and their train. Thus were mingled associations of deep sad interest in the past, with grateful acknowledgements of the divine mercy, in the aid proffered for the future. [4]

The earl having passed seven days here, and "dispatched his weighty affairs," again embarked with his train, upon the waters of Lake Bies-Bosch, or Bugersveld, [5] and for the next four days, wended his way through mists, over a country deeply submerged, his course impeded by the old foundations of houses, churches and castles, until at length, saluted by numerous Dutch ships-of-war, he arrived on the 22d at Dort. Here also was he greeted with joyous welcomes, displays, and bountiful entertainments, too numerous to be here described.

Passing on thence, a varied and equally imposing reception awaited him at Rotterdam. In the midst of demonstrations in this noted city, as characteristic, and most conspicuous, was the newly-erected statue of the great Erasmus, in a pulpit, holding forth the word of truth, with his own paraphrase of the Gospel in hand, and the peculiarly appropriate motto, "Erasmus, Rotterdam."

Onward he moved the next day; and on arriving at night, illuminations [6] and other modes of reception equally marked, met the train at Delft. The earl was here conducted to the very house where, the year before, as we have already noticed, the Prince of Orange was assassinated.

Here, too, the States feasted the guests, and they in turn the States. There were present chief men and ladies, with orators, setting forth with glowing tongue, both in Latin and native Dutch, the grounds of the English alliance, and the expected results in withstanding the conquering enemy, and in securing their dearly cherished liberties and rights.

Three days having passed here, the train again moved onward, and at night entered Donhage, or the Hague, illuminated with torches and fireworks, connected with still other curiously devised modes of expressing their country's joy in their country's style.

At this celebrated place, long the princely seat of the House of Orange, the earl resolved to keep his standing court. From it, he reports to the Queen his progress and prospects.

Respecting Brewster's patron, the ambassador, the earl's declarations were that without his continued presence and aid, rueful indeed would be his own condition: "Without Mr. Davison, I confess myself quite maimed; his credit is marvellous great here. He is, I assure you, the most sufficient man to serve her majesty that I know, of all our nation; for he knoweth all parts of these countries, and all persons of any account, with their humors, and hath great credit among them all." [7]

In diplomatic conferences and discussions, where the French only could be spoken, the ambassador answered for the earl in that language.

Such being the case in respect to Brewster's patron, we have some further idea what must have been his own condition in all this course of splendid receptions, magnificent entertainments, and military pomp, himself discreet, modest, retiring, yet an observer, and in some respects a partaker, while "attending" upon his appropriate duties.

Omitting the notice of other demonstrations in the earl's further progress, or excursions from the Hague, passing by even the fantastic devices at Amsterdam, we give a passing glance at but one more, that at Leyden. It was now the 3d of January, 1586, three weeks from the commencement of this gorgeous pageant, when the earl, attended by 300 horse commanded by many of the elite of England, proceeded to this ancient city. Met on the way and escorted thither by Burgomasters, Marshals, and chief citizens, in their robes and gala dress, they enter and pass along its decorated streets, lined on each hand and overhead with hangings and adornings of costliest material, while over the earl moved a splendid canopy. Amidst such, and corresponding modes of reception, he arrived at his munificently prepared lodgings. But of all the demonstrations and tokens of welcome here, we mark one peculiar to the place and most expressive.

Eleven years before, this city had endured, from the Spanish forces, one of the most terrible sieges on record. And now were set forth before their guests, as in drama, the successive events and scenes in that memorable siege; the battles and slaughter; the progress of the enemy; the failure of food; the hunger, thirst, and famine; the soldiers in frenzy seizing upon children in their mother's arms; the pestilence, burials, even the hardened Spaniards beholding them from beyond the walls with pity; then messages from the enemy to surrender, but promptly rejected; at length, signs of their utter extremity, and for speedy help, made from the highest tower, and discovered by the Prince of Orange, at Delft, and answered favorably by the device of a carrier dove; then, along with commotions discovered in the camp of the enemy, are heard the crash of falling walls and dykes, and the sound of inrushing waters; and presently are seen coming on the spreading flood, with a favoring gale, at the opportune moment, boats with men and provisions for their full relief. Then followed the quick dispersion of the enemy; and all is closed with spontaneous acknowledgments of God's providential hand in this their great deliverance. [8] And this was Leyden; a place again to come under notice as the residence of Brewster and his friends in years to come.

These pageants passed; affairs at the Hague demanded the earl's and ambassador's attention.

The States having lost their own distinguished leader, were in consultation about placing Leicester in the chief command — not stopping short of conferring upon him the vice-royalty. To this the ambassador, not being informed of the Queen's injunction to the contrary, appears to have tacitly assented. [9] And soon, on the part of the States, was the plan matured.

On a set day, authorized deputies met the earl and presented to him, in set form and speech, their proposals. With some show of hesitation, he accepted the overtures, and then, with almost regal pomp and ceremony, was he invested with nearly absolute authority (under Elizabeth) over the States of the Netherlands; a proceeding that provoked the Queen's highest displeasure.

This done, the ambassador and suite must hasten their return to England. Already had he been detained too long by the earl, while the Queen and her council were impatiently awaiting his arrival home, to learn by him the true state of affairs, aside from the gorgeous receptions and pageantry, which of late had been the burden of the earl's communications. Another and higher place, also, had the Queen in view for the ambassador. [10]

On the eve of departure, about the 1st of February, occurred the next incident recorded in respect to Brewster. The States would not have the ambassador depart without some token of their high appreciation of his official course. Accordingly, says Bradford, "at his return, the States honored him with a gold chain, and he committed it to Brewster, and commanded him to wear it when they arrived in England, as they rode through the country, till they came to the court." [11] Aside from the honor bestowed upon the ambassador, what did his committal of the chain to Brewster signify, but a mark of honor and a token of his high estimation of the ability and faithfulness with which Brewster had executed the duties assigned him during the mission.

And what did the ambassador's *commanding* him to wear the chain signify, but that the latter would have modestly declined the honor, unless thus commanded? An honorable testimony, surely, from him who bestowed to him who received!

The embassy now left for England. From the direction, as above given, it would appear to have been their purpose to pass, by the way of the Brill (the usual course), over to Harwich, and thence to *ride across the county* of Essex, 70 miles, to London. [12] Yet whatever may have been the ambassador's intention, their return finally was otherwise. Their passage from the Brill to London was wholly by water. He thus writes to the earl: "After my departure from your lordship, I was detained at the Brill, some five or six days by the wind and weather." "The Friday following I put to the seas, and by God's goodness had so happy a passage, as the next morning, by ten or eleven o'clock, we anchored at the Receivers, within Margate, and the same night, about midnight, came to Gravesend, and from thence immediately with the tide hither, where I arrived the next morning early." [13]

Arrived in London, the ambassador, having signified to Mr. Secretary his readiness to report himself at court, had access to the Queen the same evening.

We pause not here to describe this agitating interview with the Queen, nor those that followed, nor the stern conflicts of opinion between her and her chief counsellors, respecting the course to be pursued with the Earl of Leicester. Sufficient is it to say, that it was not until after strong contests, in which

Mr. Davison expressed his readiness to retire to private life, and even Burleigh, that able man of the age, and the Queen's long tried and most trusty counsellor in extremities, declared lie would resign his place and leave public service, unless her majesty would yield to their united counsels in the present emergency. It was not until this had passed, and the Queen had gradually yielded, that matters were again amicably arranged. [14]

On the settlement of this strongly contested and sorely agitating question depended Brewster's continued position. Thus he remained with Mr. Davison, ready for any future service to which he might be called. [15] He had seen much of men and things in this year and a half's embassy abroad, and had doubtless profited by all that he had passed through.

[1] 2d, and 22d Oct. Rymer, xv. 799, 802.

[2] Admiral Burroughs' Journal, in Appendix to Leicester Correspondence; and Holinshed, iv. 640, &c. The dates here given being according to the Old Style, ten days must be added for the New Style. This will be the case throughout the work, unless otherwise specified.

[3] Holinshed, iv. 640, and Leicester Corres.: a part of the marriage ceremony.

[4] It should be remembered that the Prince of Orange, while living, feeling that his life was in continual danger from the hands of assassins, had solicited the protection of Elizabeth for his daughters in case he should be taken from them. For this Elizabeth gave her pledge; which, when the time came, she promptly and generously redeemed. Strype's Annals.

[5] This was a lake of about 12 square leagues in extent, caused on the 19th of Nov., 1421, by the rupture of several dykes; in consequence of which 72 villages and a population of 100,000 souls were submerged. Malte-Brun, vol. iii. 1093.

[6] Holinshed, iv. 643 and 645.

[7] Holinshed, iv.; also Leicest. Cor., 33, .59, 64, 69, 77. Here would the writer point out an error in the Catalogue of the Harlein MS., No. 285, fol. 171. It is an error which might occasion great injustice to Mr. Davison's character as a statesman. It erroneously attributes to the ambassador what the earl said, not of him, but of another person, viz., of Dr. Bartholomew Clerk, of the civil law. Compare said No. of the Catalogue, with p. 33, and note 75 of Leicest. Corres.

[8] Ranke, p. 146, Brandt, &c. It was by the cutting of the dykes, and letting in of the waters, and a high wind blowing most providentially from the direction of Delft, that the boats were wafted direct to Leyden, with men and ammunition, &c. The Spaniards seeing this retired. Malte Brun, note Leyden. In the extremity of the siege, their noble magistrate, Adrian De Ver, when appealed to by citizens to surrender, such was the awful havoc of the famine, answered: "Friends, here is my body; divide it among you to satisfy your hunger, but banish all thoughts of surrendering to the cruel, perfidious Spaniard." Taking the advice, they answered the enemy — they would hold out as long as they had one arm to eat and another to fight. London Encyclopedia, article Leyden.

[9] In all this matter the earl acted according to the promptings of his own ambition, and most deceptively towards the ambassador, concealing the queen's injunction, and urging other considerations. Leicester Corres., pp. 121, 168, 175, 333, 335.

[10] Leicester Cor., 111, 77, 123.

[11] Bradford, 410. Some writers have, indeed, understood Bradford to say that the chain was given by the States to Brewster, but they evidently misunderstood the passage.

[12] This would accord literally with the words of Bradford.

[13] Letter to the Earl, Feb. 17th, 1586, Leicester Cor., 117.

[14] Leicester Correspondence, 124, 197, 193. It was one characteristic of Elizabeth, that she was slow — very slow — in adopting any important course of action; but when she had adopted it, she was imperative in enforcing compliance. The keeping of this in mind will help to explain many of her acts as a sovereign. It was her own declaration to Parliament: "My manner is, to deliberate long upon that which is but once to be resolved." [Hansard's Parl. Hist., i. 843.] In the present case,, the Queen was doubtless right in regard to her displeasure at Leicester's acceptance of supremacy in the States. Her honor was at stake. Consistency was to be maintained in the eyes of the Princes of Europe, to whom she had issued her manifesto disclaiming all idea of rule in the Netherlands. Leicester had concealed and gone contrary to her injunctions. Therefore, said she, "I may not endure that a man shall alter my commission, and the authority that I gave him, and without me." Again, "It is sufficient to make me infamous to all princes, having protested to the contrary." On the other hand, the counsellors were right, in continuing, in this extremity, the pledged aid to the States. This was the prior concern. With this nothing should interfere. Leicester had disobeyed; but he could be privately dealt with, or recalled in time, or the matter be settled in some other way. The States also, had, it was true, miscalculated, and had taken a false step. But they should not therefore be made to feel rebuke and discouragement, or any fear of England's desertion. The safety of the Queen's own kingdom even forbade this. For other particulars, and further specimens of Elizabeth's keen perception, and masterly seizing, and setting forth of the gist of a complicated argument, see particularly in Leicester Cor., 173, and 175.

[15] Bradford, 410.

Chapter Five - 1586

Modesty winneth good report. — Tupper.

After several weeks of retirement at his country place, in Stepney, Mr. Davison, at the desire of the Queen, appeared again at court, and was soon after made one of her majesty's principal Secretaries of State, and also a member of her Privy Council. [1]

And Brewster having "continued with him," had now a further appointment in his service. [2] What his new position and duties were, we are again to learn chiefly from those of his patron.

"The Secretaries of State having under their management and direction the most important affairs of the kingdom, were therefore obliged to attend constantly on the sovereign. They received and dispatched whatever came to hand either from the crown, the church, the army, or whatever related to private grants, pardons and dispensations. They received petitions to the sovereign, which, on being read, were returned to them. All was executed according to the sovereign's direction. They had also authority to commit persons for treason and other offences against the state. They were members of the Privy Council, which was seldom or never held, unless one of them was present. Business and correspondence within the kingdom were managed by either of the secretaries without distinction. But of foreign affairs, all was divided into two provinces or departments, Northern and Southern, comprising all kingdoms and states having intercourse with Great Britain; each secretary receiving all letters and addresses from, and preparing and forwarding all dispatches to the several princes and states included within its province." [3]

Placed in this high position, Mr. Davison was contemporary with the far famed Sir Francis Walsingham. "And these offices, it may be affirmed" (says the learned Dr. Kippis), "were now as well filled as in any period that can be assigned in our history; and yet by persons of very different, or rather opposite dispositions; Walsingham being a man of great art and intrigue, and not displeased to be thought such; whose capacity was deeper than those who understood it best apprehended it to be. Davison, on the other hand, had a just reputation for wisdom and probity; and though he had been concerned in many intricate affairs, yet preserved a character so unspotted, that to this time, nothing he had done could draw on him the least imputation." [4]

And not only had he this high unblemished character as a statesman, but his "virtue, religion, and worth," in the words of the Earl of Essex, "were taken to be so great, as that no man had more general love than he." [5]

With such a Christian statesman, and in the high duties of the secretary's office, it was Brewster's privilege now to be employed. Already has it been specified as the duty of a secretary of state, *to attend constantly on the sovereign.* [6] For this purpose, "in all the royal houses, the Secretaries of State had each his apartment as well for his own accommodation, as his office, and those who attended upon it. They had each of them two undersecretaries and clerks, attending the office, and of their own choice, without any dependence upon any other; and those places were of considerable profit." [7] Consequently, now, at whichever of the royal residences the Queen might be, Secretary Davison was present with those holding appointment under him; all attending upon their respective duties.

Which of those positions, specifically, Brewster held, it would be gratifying to us to know: but we must be content with Bradford's statements, which designate, not, indeed, the office by name, but, what is of far more consequence, the confidential nature of his duties, and his rare qualifications for their performance.

First, "the secretary found him so discreet and faithful that he trusted him above all others that were about him." Next, "he only employed him in all matters of greatest trust and secrecy." In a position of such trust, and employed in matters of state thus confidential, a position at all times important, but especially so in the critical circumstances in which the Queen and her kingdom were now placed, Brewster stands before us, a person of no little interest.

In addition to this, in social intercourse, "the secretary esteemed him rather as a son than as a servant," or official subordinate; "and, for his wisdom and piety, he would converse with him in private more like a familiar friend than as a master." [8] Discretion, faithfulness, wisdom, and piety, not favoritism, then, won for him the place and this high confidence.

But it is not only on the outward position and duties of his high trust, putting his rare qualities to a test, that we here look; but we are enabled to look within, to see something of the *inner man*. We mark the principles and qualities in the youth, which, developing more and more, became, in after life, the prominent characteristics of the matured man.

It was now the summer of 1586, and Brewster was in about his 26th year, and his patron in his 48th. We have already remarked upon this period as one most critical and trying to the Queen and to the kingdom. This and the following year were years of peculiar perplexities. No one can read the Parliamentary debates, in either House, during the time, and the addresses and messages between them and the Queen and Council, without being made sensible of this fact. [9]

Philip of Spain, aroused by Elizabeth's alliance with the United Provinces, and the aid she had sent them, was secretly preparing immense armaments, naval and military, not only to reduce those States again to submission, and punish them for their so-called rebellion, but to carry, with all energy, the war into England. Hence the mighty "armada," ere long to hover in terrific power as over one vast scene of prey and plunder, over the whole southern coast of the kingdom. In concert with this mighty armament, had a league (as was believed) been entered into in France, Italy Spain, and Germany, to put down Protestantism in Europe, and dethrone Elizabeth, or at least to provide a Roman Catholic successor to the English throne. [10] Plots to this end had been formed, and were believed to be still forming, in England — plots even to assassinate the Queen, as the Prince of Orange before had been.

To discover and foil these attempts, to forestall the movements of her powerful and combining enemies, called for all the penetration, activity, and skill of Elizabeth's wisest statesmen. For the first of these tasks, the other and more aged secretary, Walsingham, was peculiarly fitted, and in these he chose to take the principal part. But the affairs connected with the Earl of Leicester, the providing against the disappointment felt in the Low Countries, as well as in England, in consequence of his humiliating inefficiency, mismanagement, and the inglorious results, after his pompous beginnings, these fell to the share of Secretary Davison. Adding to the great perplexity and danger, the fate of the Queen of Scots was now to be determined. She was believed to be, at this very critical period, in secret correspondence with the enemies of the Queen and of the Protestant faith. [11]

To name other particulars here would be needless. Sufficient is it to have alluded to these, in connection with the current duties of the day, to indicate what must have been a portion, at least, of those "matters of greatest trust and secrecy," in which Brewster was "employed" in the office of Secretary Davison.

But before proceeding further, we will bring to notice two persons, one of whom is about this time received into the secretary's office, and the other becomes afterwards Brewster's valued and efficient friend.

Some fifteen years before, or about the year 1571, two truly Christian Bishops, Jewel and Sandys, who had once, for their Protestant faith, been in long and dreary exile together from country and home, in the time of the Roman Catholic Mary, and had there formed a stronger than earthly friendship, met often in affectionate intercourse after their return; the former incidentally, near the time of the above date, made mention of a young Richard Hooker, of whom he had been the patron. And such an account of his learning, life, and manners did he give, that Sandys, though educated and having strong attachments at Cambridge, resolved that his son Edwin should be sent to Oxford, and "by all means be a pupil of Mr. Hooker." "For," said he, "I will have a tutor for my son that shall teach him learning by instruction, and virtue by example; and my greatest care shall be of this last; and (God willing) this Richard Hooker shall be the man to whose hands I will commit my Edwin." Scarcely had two years passed when the resolve was carried into execution. [12] Hooker, now in his 19th year, and, for his age, one of the maturest scholars in the university, had under his tuition other pupils, among whom was young George Cranmer, grand nephew of the martyred archbishop of that name. With such a teacher and such pupils, most happily passed the years of their preparatory, and most of their university course, to the great advantage of all, "but especially," says Walton, "of his first two, his dear Edwin Sandys and his as dear George Cranmer."

In the mean time, there grew up between the pupils and their tutor a friendship, so founded on religious principles, and so free from selfish ends, a friendship so blessed and spiritual, matured through many years in that university, until it became, says Walton, "so improved and perfected, that it even bordered upon heaven." The time coming when they must leave the halls of learning for the active duties of life, Sandys and Cranmer, still united, travel together on the Continent; together visit France, Germany, and Italy; together search out the state of religion in each, and gather stores of knowledge for future use; and together, after three years' absence, they return to England.

And here we have reached the point for which, and what follows, this notice of them has been introduced.

Cranmer enters the service of Secretary Davison, and becomes an associate in office with Brewster. Sandys, Cranmer's endeared friend, might now, if he had not before, become acquainted with Brewster. Cranmer, henceforth Brewster's companion in office, is engaged with him in its responsible, and to their chief, most hazardous duties.

Edwin Sandys becomes the author of the "Europae Speculum," or "View of the State of Religion in the Western Parts of Europe," and in time, *Sir* Edwin Sandys, and an eminent statesman; "a man (says Fuller), right-handed to any great employment, with a commanding pen, corresponding with Hooker respecting his great work, also a member of Parliament, and as constant in attendance as the speaker himself, a patriot advocating legal rights at home, and colonial settlements and rights abroad; and though sometimes displeasing to King James, yet after all faithful to his country without being false to his sovereign." [13]

But his friendly and Christian correspondence with Brewster it was, and active efforts for him and his people, hereafter to be noticed, that will cause his name to be handed down with gratitude and honor, by the Pilgrims' descendants to the latest posterity.

Cranmer's name stands connected with one of the most critical transactions of Secretary Davison's life. [14] That period being past, he becomes secretary to Sir Henry Killegrew's embassy to France. Aids or counsels Hooker also in respect to his "Ecclesiastical Polity;" of which his epistle or treatise, addressed to him in 1589, is ample evidence. [15] But ere long his career, and with it the great hopes entertained of him, were brought to an unexpected close. Having been solicited by Lord Mountjoy, he accompanied that personage as his secretary to Ireland; where, at the battle near Carlingford, he fell mortally wounded, and soon after expired.

But William Brewster's course, less marked and brilliant at the time, indeed, than were those of his two associates, especially that of his friend, Sir Edwin, was yet, as the event will show, of much longer duration and more eventful, far more trying to flesh and blood, and of immensely greater interest in its far-reaching results.

[1] Camden's Annals, 488, and Leicester Cor., 142, 343, 451, 455.
[2] Bradford, 410.
[3] London Encyclopaedia, article Secretary.
[4] Biographia Britannica, article Davison, v. 6.
[5] The Earl's Letter to King James, in article Davison, v. 6. do.
[6] To this end, Mr. Davison had "a house in London," from which he "went to the court continually," as the case and daily duty required. Life of Davison.
[7] Beatson's Political Index, i. 398.

[8] Bradford, 409, 410.
[9] Hansard's Parliamentary Debates, and Simon D'Ewes' Journal, during the years 1586 and 1587.
[10] Ranke, 153, 160, 187. Acta Regia, and Turner's History Eng., in the same years.
[11] Life of Davison, and Leices. Corres.
[12] Walton's Life of Hooker, and notes prefixed to his Ecclesiastical Polity. Oxford ed., p. 66.
[13] Fuller's Worthies, article Sandys, also Chalmer's Annals of Virginia. Bancroft's United States, i. 156, 158, 191.

[14] The execution of the Queen of Scots. "The next morning I received a letter from Cranmer my servant, whom I left at court, signifying to me her majesty's pleasure, that I should forbear going to my Lord Chancellor's, until I heard from her." Davison's Apology. Biog. Britannica, v. 10.

[15] Introduction to Hooker's works, 64, 72.

Chapter Six – 1586-1587

True dignity is never gained by place,
And never lost when honors are withdrawn. — Massinger.

Let us enter the official apartments of Secretary Davison at court, and try to ascertain, as far as we may, the spirit or governing principle by which affairs were there conducted.

A little examination enables us to discover, underneath and mingling with all the multifarious plans of business, anxious consultations, and intercourse with the Queen, with the several departments, and with other nations — a powerful element, which no political combinations, no arts, or crooked policy could overcome; a firm principle, not officiously or obtrusively, but mildly pervading all. It was none other than Christian principle. Of its pervading influence in the manner mentioned, the correspondence of the office, and the well known character of the secretary, bear ample testimony. And that in this there was united action, as far as we can discover, appears from the character of Cranmer, as developed in his college life with Hooker and Sandys, and in his continental tour, the influence of which was now brought into the office. Equally evident is the fact from the character which Brewster brought with him from the university and from his service in the Netherlands.

Thus far, at least, amidst the ambitions of the court, the intrigues and base acts of such as Leicester, the wiles and craft of Walsingham, in *this* office was felt, and from it went forth an influence grateful to every Christian patriot. Here was a green spot (we trust there were others) on which the eye of every real lover of his country could rest with elevated and cheering satisfaction.

And we may here reiterate how in hours of retirement, and apparently in his family, the secretary conversed with Brewster, not only upon affairs of the office and of state, but upon the concerns of religion. A rare privilege surely it was to the young man, to be permitted in free social intercourse, thus to gather instruction from the experienced Christian statesman. Nor can we doubt that a similar privilege was enjoyed by Cranmer, and that probably there were occasional visits from Sandys.

And on the Lord's day, and in the house of prayer, how must it have been"? and also, as Christ's disciples and as Christian friends at the Lord's table, [1] the elevated in station with the more humble in position; the Lord himself being the maker of them all?

34

Who can estimate in all this the amount of influence for good, at home and abroad, discreetly exerted"? Who shall estimate the strengthening influence upon the mind of Brewster'?

But the summer of 1586 was drawing to a close. Great questions agitated the court and the nation. These could not but absorb the chief attention of the secretary and all in his employ. On the 5th of October, Mr. Davison had been appointed on the commission to try the Queen of Scots; but he appears not to have been present at the trial. If he approved of it, it is more than we can discover; he seems at least to have left the responsibility to others. Yet the trial took place; the fearful sentence was passed.

It is not for us to examine here the reasons, the justice or injustice, policy or impolicy, of that transaction. It has been matter of discussion and of divided opinion from that day to the present. And that Queen's pitiable condition and end have awakened sympathy wherever the sad tale has been told.

It is due, however, to historic truth, to say that, after the trial and sentence, both houses of Parliament, after a long discussion of the question, unitedly petitioned, nay, importunately urged Queen Elizabeth to have the sentence put in execution. Elizabeth, delaying long, apparently in great doubt and perplexity, answered: "That, moved with some commiseration for the Scottish Queen, in respect to her former dignity and great fortunes in her younger years, her nearness of kindred, and also her sex, her highness could be well pleased to forbear taking her life, if by any other means to be devised by the great council of the realm, the safety of her majesty's person and government might be preserved without ruin and destruction." To this, after "many speeches" and "debates," both Houses, by their committees, replied, "all with one consent," that "they could find no other way than what was set down in their petition;" "that the sentence be put in speedy execution." "And if the same be not put in speedy execution, her most loving and dutiful subjects shall thereby, so far as man's reason can reach, be brought into utter despair of the continuance among them of the true religion of Almighty God, and of her majesty's life, and the safety of her faithful subjects."^

Elizabeth, still hesitating and delaying, sends to them, again, one of her answerless answers: "If I shall say unto you that I mean not to grant your petition, by my faith I should say unto you more than perhaps I mean. And if I should say unto you I mean to grant your petition, I should then tell you more than it is fit for you to know. And thus I must deliver unto you my answer answerless." [3]

During all these proceedings, the unhappy Queen of Scots had not one advocate in either House that would or durst plead in her favor. The current against her was so strong that it would have overthrown all opposers, and involved them in the same ruin. Nay, there was evident fear on the part of the Commons that some method might be proposed, or foreign influence exerted, to prevent the execution. Therefore, many of them were for taking measures to cut off all attempts at such interference. On the 2d of December,

Parliament was adjourned, and the Queen and court were left to act on their own responsibility in the approaching crisis.

Reports of leagues abroad, and plots at home, and of the threatening Spanish invasion, were the topics of the day." [4] But *how* the sentence against the condemned Queen was to be put in execution, became the absorbing theme. Some were for putting her out of the way privately. This course was proposed or advocated by Leicester (now returned from the States) and was concurred in by Walsingham. Davison, if the execution was to take place, was for the legal course only. Long and decidedly did he argue with the Queen in the council chamber, and in more retired interviews, on this point. [5]

The year closed, and that of 1587 opened with fearful forebodings. For more than six weeks was the public mind held in suspense.

At length the time arrived. It was the time of peril to Secretary Davison, and a turning point in the life of Brewster.

Elizabeth resolved on the long delayed execution. She had tried, in various ways, to shun the responsibility, and to escape from the odium of the final act. Walsingham escaped it, having declared himself sick.

In the turn of affairs, on Secretary Davison was made to rest the chief burden of attending to the legal process. Her majesty summoned him to bring the warrant for her signature, and having signed it, she directed him to bear it to the Lord Chancellor, for the great seal; still pressing the idea of its execution privately. Borne to the chancellor, and the seal being affixed, and her majesty informed of the fact, she seemed to blame the haste of the secretary, still suggesting some other way of proceeding, yet giving no counter-direction. Davison, as directed, informed and consulted with Walsingham, and there being no hint to stay proceedings, and he, not willing to assume the responsibility of acting alone, advised with the chief members of the Privy Council, and left with them the warrant. They sent it to the named officials to proceed therewith. The execution soon followed — that act which Bishop Burnet pronounces the "greatest blemish of this reign." [6]

Two days had passed, when information arrived of the execution. The Queen, at first quiet, at length broke out into the most violent expressions of grief, blaming and threatening the chief members of her council. As an evasion, and to disarm resentment abroad, she pronounced the act, "that miserable accident." But there must be a victim; and, as if to confirm her assertion, and shield herself, the able, upright, noble-hearted Davison must be sacrificed. Committed to the tower, and soon after brought to trial before the Star Chamber Court, and charged with revealing the Queen's counsels to her privy counsellors, and with presumption in having executed her majesty's order, he finds himself in this dilemma: that, to prove himself to have been faithful and upright, he must prove his royal mistress to have been unscrupulous and false. This he would not do; but, with a noble purpose of soul, he committed himself to the court and the Queen's clemency, resolved to suffer all for his country's and her majesty's sake, trusting that in the end her sense of right, and consciousness that he was suffering for her sake, would cause her to make all honorable amends.

The court, though pronouncing him to be a good, able, honest man, yet influenced by state policy, and to shield the Queen, fined him 10,000 marks, and committed him to the tower, during her majesty's pleasure. [7]

The effects of all this upon the mind of Brewster may be easily conceived. Sharing largely, no doubt, in the secretary's sentiments, day by day, and step by step, must he have marked the whole proceeding. With pained heart must he have felt its blighting influence. The generous and patriotic impulses of youth must have been chilled in him, on discovering such ungrateful returns, from the highest in power, for the most devoted service. While to see his loved patron sacrificed, his estate ruined, his good name apparently blasted, his noble form and fine voice almost paralyzed at the unexpected blow, [8] must have produced upon his mind — wrought in upon his inmost soul, an impression which no circumstances could remove, no time obliterate.

[1] That the Secretary, and these his assistants in office were thus communicants in the established church, is evident, not merely from the fact that this was required by law, but from what is known of their lives.
[2] Hansard's Parl. Hist., i. pp. 838, 839, 841, 843, 844. As an illustration of the state of the public mind, and the causes then operating, see also Ranke's Hist. of the Popes, p. 167. Also Hallam's Const. Hist., vol. i. pp. 154, 155, &c.
[3] Hansard, as before.
[4] See the last and preceding references, and Mr. Davison's own argument with the Queen, in his Apology; Davison's Life, Appendix.
[5] See preceding note.
[6] Burnet's History of the Reformation, vol. i. p. 592.
[7] Camden's Annals of Elizabeth; State Trials, article Davison; Rapin's Strictures on Camden, and the Court's Decision, ii. 302, 303, 358, 359; Dr. Kippis' Vindication, of Davison, in Biographia Britannica; and Sir Nicolas H. Nicholas' Life of Davison, p. 158.
[8] State Trials, art. Davison, i. p. 1230.

Chapter Seven – 1587

The gloomiest day hath gleams of light. — Mrs. Hemans.

We left William Brewster, last, in a sorely trying condition. Hitherto his course had apparently been one of prosperity; but now, the patron with whom he had been so intimately and honorably connected being thrust from his high office, and committed to the Tower, his own cherished plans in life were broken up, and his fair prospects blighted.

What was he to do'? Shall he, as the world in general does, and as perhaps many friends may have advised, desert the fallen, shun such intercourse as would connect himself with him, and, joining the general current, push his way to office under some other chief? Such is not Christian friendship—such was not Brewster's. The historian records it, and it was worthy of record: "He remained with Mr. Davison some good time after that he was put from his place, doing him many faithful offices of service in the time of his troubles." [1]

Thus is presented another trait in Brewster's character, a nobleness of soul, readiness to make sacrifices for others' good, especially in aiding and comforting the depressed and afflicted, and that too, not merely from the impulse of the moment, which soon ends, but (as in this case) by many offices of service, faithfully continued.

Precisely what these many offices of service were, we are not told. Yet, from the circumstances, we may well suppose them to have been: visiting him often in his prison, unobtrusively sympathizing with him and offering all personal attentions, and aid in securing valued papers and scattered remains, if any, of his ruined estate.

To the Tower, then, to which Davison had been committed — that far-famed Tower of London, the varied history of which, and the strangely contrasted and thrilling scenes within which, would fill volumes with facts "stranger than fiction" — to that vast pile on the bank of the Thames — not, indeed, to its regal apartments, but to its drearier halls and cells, Brewster evidently went, following his revered friend, seeking, by all the acts which faithful friendship could devise, to alleviate his trials.

Specifically how long these many offices of friendship were continued by Brewster is undetermined. The recorded expression, "some good time after," though of value, like many others equally tantalizing in the writings of Bradford, conveys but a very indefinite idea. To suppose it to have been until all hope of Mr. Davison's release and restoration to office was at an end, would seem, indeed, at first thought, to be reasonable, yet it is found to be improbable. There was hope of his restoration, even strong hope, long continued.

No sooner had the Lord Chancellor Burleigh, chief among counsellors, heard of the committal, than he wrote to the Queen most urgently in his behalf. "I cannot in duty forbear to put your majesty in mind that, if Mr. Davison be committed to the Tower, who best knoweth his own cause, the example will be sorrowful to all your faithful servants, and joyful to your enemies." "Sure I am, and I presume to have some judgment therein, I know not a man in the land so furnished universally for the place. [2] Neither know I any that can come near him." And if this did not reach the Queen, the following did: "What your majesty minded to him in your displeasure, I hear to my grief; but for a servant in that place, I think it hard to find a like qualified person: whom to ruin in your heavy displeasure, shall be more your majesty's loss than his." [3]

The Earl of Essex also put forth his powerful influence with the Queen to the same end. And so encouraged was he of success, that he informed Mr.

Davison, "he dared promise himself it would be done;" or even "a better state" or office provided. [4] And lest the Queen should object on account of her official declaration to James of Scotland, the earl addressed that prince in relation to the deprived Secretary — a "man beloved of the best and most religious of the land; of whose sufficiency in council and matters of state, the Queen confessed she had not in her kingdom such another;" adding, "If, to a man so worthy in himself, and so esteemed of all men, my words might avail, I would assure your majesty you would get great honor and great love, not only in England, but in all parts of Christendom where Mr. Davison is known, if you would now be the author of his restoring to his place." And this bears date more than two years after the committal. Even in 1590, more than three years after that event, this earl, with other chief men of the council, made another strong effort. [5]

The veteran Secretary Walsingham had died; and even the place made vacant by Davison's removal, appears, through this earl's influence, to have been kept vacant. The effort, therefore, now was, that Davison might succeed Walsingham. Indeed, it is stated that he was in some way employed in performing the duties of that place during Walsingham's long sickness, though not appearing in the presence of the Queen.

But Sir Robert Cecil, son of the Chancellor Burleigh, was now the rival candidate. At length, after a strong contest, the place was refused to Davison, and given to Cecil. [6]

The Queen informed the earl, "he must rest satisfied, for she was thus resolved;" though she had confessed to him that, on the former occasion, Davison had been "the man of her own choice," and "that which was laid to his charge, was merely for her safety both of state and person." [7]

Thus, it was not until after three years of expectation, and strong hope justly entertained by Davison and his powerful friends, that the prospect of his restoration was cut off and the hope relinquished.

What influence this long continued expectation had finally upon the plans and movements of Brewster, or whether he was induced in any extent to await the movements in the case, we are left to conjecture. Yet who, in the prospect of that restoration, was so likely to receive some prominent position under him, as the tried, highly qualified and confidential Brewster? But we have said thus much on this point for the further purpose of bringing out facts, and showing in what estimation Secretary Davison was held by his contemporaries, even by the highest and ablest in the land. This is but justice to his character, justice to historic truth.

Whatever idea we may form as to *how long* Brewster continued with the fallen secretary during his troubles, the time at length came when he must leave.

No longer officially connected with any one, but left free to form anew his plans in life, we are now to trace his course as he leaves the great metropolis for the retirement of the country.

Bidding adieu to the scenes of the court, and its lately absorbing, but now painful associations; bidding adieu to him whose confiding friendship and official favors he had so worthily and long enjoyed, and to whom he had now made grateful returns; disappointed in his expectations in public life; taught thus many painful but salutary lessons, he goes forth, not to be a recluse, but, with the energy of maturing manhood, to be the means of good in some other field, wherever his lot might be cast.

[1] Bradford, 410.
[2] That is, the Secretaryship.
[3] Strype's Annals, vol. iii. p. 372, or Oxford ed., vol. iii. part i. p. 542.
[4] Cabala, part i. pp. 213, 215.
[5] Camden's Annals, p. 621, and Cabala.
[6] Aikin's Court of Elizabeth, ii. 230.
[7] Earl of Essex's Letters, Cabala, part ii.; also A. Strickland's Queens of Eng., vii. 113. Sir Robert was appointed in full at Nonsuch, 2d of August, 1591.

For the reader whose interest has been so far awakened as to call for something more respecting Mr. Davison, a few additional facts are here subjoined. First, his ability and skilfulness as a statesman. After the full, clear, unbiased statements of his great worth, acknowledged ability, tried skill and wisdom, declared by Burleigh, Leicester, and the Earl of Essex, though differing from him in many things, also by the Queen and the council generally, it is with no little regret that we are obliged to impute to court influence, or prejudice, the derogatory intimations in Camden's History. Says Dr. Kippis, "Whatever motives those authors might have had who lived near those times, to palliate or conceal the circumstances of that action which proved the cause of Mr. Davison's fall, we lie under no temptation, and are free from any inclination to hide or throw a shade over truth. Bringing into open day these singular and interesting points, we not only rectify partial accounts contained in private memoirs, and supply the deficiencies in general histories, but apply to their proper use, and bring to public view, in an agreeable light, these remains of those stirring times, which might otherwise lie hid in studies, and be at most known only to very few."

As to further particulars. On the rejection of his last appeal to the Queen, in 1590, he gave up all hope of further public life. How long he was confined in the tower we know not, but there are intimations of his being at liberty after about two years. As to his depressed condition, from loss of place and property. Lord Arthur Gray reports that when the Queen was applied to by Lord Burleigh, "to relieve his low estate," the objection was that, "though he was in tolerably good favor with her," yet, "in respect to *her begun course,* she might not, with honor saved, make show of it." And when urged to do it privately, she replied, "Her court was so fraught with lynxes' eyes that the motives of her doing so would be discovered." (Catalogue, Harleian MSS., vol. i. p. 155.) A proof of her persevering determination (cruel as it was to him) to maintain consistency before the world. No relief, therefore, could he obtain, except, probably, a pension of £100 per annum, during the Queen's life. It was not until James, her successor, came to the throne — James, whom every consideration respecting his mother's execution might have urged to the contrary, yet who knew Davison and the circumstances well — not until his accession that there was granted the full relief. And grateful, indeed, to his wounded spirit must the boon have been — a testimony to the world of his deserts and innocence. But the boon came too late to be long enjoyed. His end was near. He died in December, 1608, and on the 28th of that month was buried in Stepney, Middlesex, probably over 70 years of age.

That he was a man of learning as well as a statesman, his numerous writings testify. They have been preserved, for the most part, in the Harl. and other collections in the British Museum. Highly connected in marriage, he and his lady were both cousins to the Earl of Leicester and Sir Philip Sydney. He had also an interesting and intelligent family. One son became an author of note. But, what is most of all, his life, his writings, his public services, all testify that, in all circumstances, in high prosperity as in deepest adversity, he was the enlightened, noble-hearted, consistent Christian. — Life of Davison; Aikin's Court of Elizabeth, ii. 166, 167. Miss Strickland's Note, in vii. p. 63, needs correction.

Chapter Eight – 1588-1590

'Tis a goodly scene —
Yon river, like a silvery snake, lays out
His coil, i' th' sunshine lovingly; it breathes
Of freshness in this lap of flowery meadows.

Sir A. Hunt.

And whither did Brewster go as he left London and his former patron? It is recorded "he went and lived in the country, amongst his friends and the good gentlemen of those parts." [1] But *where* in the country were those friends and good gentlemen'?

On this point, many had been the inquiries, great the curiosity excited, vague the conjectures (and all to little purpose) until the discoveries during the last few years. Morton, Cotton Mather, Hubbard, with Belknap and others, had left to us little more than that most indefinite expression, "in the North of England." It is to the untiring researches of an antiquarian of London [2] we owe it, that facts, dates, and circumstances are brought; to light so numerous and particular as to enable us to point out with fullest confidence, not only the county and district, but the very village and house where our William Brewster resided.

Extracts from Bradford's history specified that the religious company of emigrants who assembled around Brewster "were of sundry towns and villages in Nottinghamshire, and of Lincolnshire, and Yorkshire, where they border nearest together." [3] This defines the district of country to be *in* and *around* the northern part of Nottinghamshire, where, and where only, these three counties and the villages "*border nearest*" to each other. But it was "not," says he to whom we owe the discovery, "until I found out another condition of place in another part of the writings of Bradford, and then brought some historical and topographical knowledge to bear on the question, that I ascertained, as I conceive, beyond all possibility of doubt, the actual village, and the very house."

It was this: "They ordinarily met at his (Brewster's) house on the Lord's day, which was a manor of the Bishops." [4] A bishop's manor, or *manor house,* is no vague expression; it is something fixed, notorious, and remarkable, and is, moreover, rare in any district, "and I," he adds, "who have some acquaintance with the whole country which can be said to be near the adjoining borders of these counties, can affirm with confidence that there was no episcopal or archiepiscopal manor in that part of England except one, which one, in Brewster's time, appertained to the Archbishop of York; this one was at the ancient village of Scrooby, in the Hundred of Bassetlaw." [5]

Confirmatory of the above, was the further discovery, on the assessment roll of that period for Scrooby, of a William Brewster, older than our William, who may have been a relative, perhaps his father, and also, on the church records, near by, of a Rev. Henry Brewster and a Rev. James Brewster, who were successively rectors, and may have been his relatives. And close by was Austerfield, the known birth-place and residence of Bradford; while other names of emigrants were from the same portion of country.

Still more to the purpose, we shall find Brewster holding an office under the Queen, until the very year and month when the future "elder," with his people, left for Holland, and when his connection with that office ceased.

And yet more specifically, we shall find on record, "William Brewster," with two others, "of Scrooby, Brownists or Separatists" (the terms then applied to them), fined £20, each, for non-appearance on an ecclesiastical citation. All of this will appear, as we proceed, with accumulating evidence from a variety of other circumstances too numerous to admit of doubt. Well might Mr. Hunter add, "No reasonable doubt, therefore, can ever arise, that the seat and centre of the religions community, which afterwards planted itself on the shores of New England, was at this *Nottinghamshire village of Scrooby.*'"

In the northern part of Nottinghamshire then, near a mile and a half south of a projecting point of Yorkshire, and but a short distance from the verge of Lincolnshire, and at the small village of Scrooby, was evidently the place where our William Brewster went. Here were his friends, and "the good gentlemen of those parts." Here was the bishop's manor, afterwards called by Bradford, Brewster's house; and here are we to trace his course for some seventeen, perhaps nineteen succeeding years.

As to Scrooby itself, though with the exception of its being on the great northern road from London to York, and thence by Berwick to Scotland, it has scarcely been noticed in modern times; yet such was not the case anciently; nor from the interest now manifested, is it likely to be so hereafter.

"Scrooby Manor," even as far back as William the Conqueror, if not earlier, was a possession of the Archbishops of York, and was to them a place of frequent sojourn, as well as a convenient resting-place in their journeys. Noted for field game, and the easy access to the Hatfield chase, it had long been on these accounts a favorite resort.

Here slept Margaret, Queen of Scotland, daughter of Henry Seventh, on her way to that kingdom. Here Cardinal Wolsey, when dismissed by his imperious master to his northern diocese, passed weeks "ministering many deeds of charity, attending on Sundays in some neighboring parish church, and then dining in some honest man's house in the town, causing great alms to be distributed to the poor:" and who is said to have uttered soon after, those memorable words: "Had I served the God of Heaven as faithfully as I did my master on earth, He had not forsaken me in my old age as the other hath done." [6] At this manor house lodged Henry the Eighth himself, on his northern progress in 1541. This same year the tourist Leland, in passing, gives of the manor, church, and neighborhood this description: "From Mattersy, I rode a mile in low wash and somewhat fenny ground, and a mile or more further by higher ground to Scrooby." "In the mean townlet of Scrooby I marked two things, the parish church, not big, but very well builded of square polished stone." "The second, was a great manor place, standing within a moat, and belonging to the Archbishop of York, builded in two courts, whereof the first is very ample; and all builded of timber, saving the *front* of the hall, that is of brick; to the which, one ascends by steps of stone." "The inner court building, as far as I marked, was of timber, and was not in compass past the fourth part of the outer court." Northerly, "a mile or more is Bawtry; a little beyond Scrooby manor place, I passed by a ford over the river, and betwixt the palings of two parks belonging to Scrooby." [7] Very much in accordance with this description doubtless was the appearance of the place in the time of Brewster.

At the Reformation, some kind of title to the manor seems to have been in the crown; for the Protestant Archbishop Holdgate purchased of the King the mansion, lordship, and manor, with the appurtenances, to himself and Barbary his wife, and the successors in the see. [8] Great, however, was the change which took place as to the future prospects of Scrooby and its manor, in the time of Elizabeth.

To this "See" was Archbishop Sandys (father of Sir Edwin and five other sons) promoted in 1576. Some six years later, Elizabeth desired of him this manor for the Earl of Leicester. The archbishop declined giving the desired lease, specifying as reasons, the heavy expenses he had incurred in repairs and improvements, the deprivation of residence to himself, and the great loss it would be to the see (£60,000 including Southwell); [9] "too much," says he, "most gracious sovereign — too much to pull from a bishopric inferior to many in revenue, but superior in charge and countenance." Yet before the close of the same year (1582), he leased the manor, two parks, mills and Lound Woods to his eldest son. Sir Samuel Sandys. And this resulted finally in the alienation of the manor from the see. Perhaps he thought it better (for he had the power) thus to place it under lease, than that it should be transferred to such an one as the Earl of Leicester. Here accordingly for a time appears to have been the residence of Sir Samuel. In the church stands a monument to Penelope, one of the Sandys family, who died in 1690. [10]

View of Scrooby, Nottinghamshire, England

Under Sir Samuel it was, as appears some few years later, that the manor was held by Brewster: not, indeed, "a district of country, throughout which were enjoyed certain feudal privileges, but the manor place," [11] including, doubtless, its lands and parks. And this suggests not only an acquaintance, but business transactions, between Brewster and the Sandys family.

Tracing the history of this manor-place a little further, we find, that after William Brewster's occupancy some fifteen, perhaps nineteen years, it was at length gradually neglected, and finally suffered to go to decay. One hundred years later — while the park still remained, the house had nearly fallen to the ground. In 1813 nothing remained, marking the ancient abode of splendor and hospitality, but some small part incorporated into a farm-house, and in the garden, an old mulberry tree, planted, tradition said, by the haughty Wolsey. [12] Finally, as seen and described by a tourist's eye and pen, [13] in the summer of 1853, Scrooby presents to view one of those rich pastoral districts, common in England, which with no marked features of hill and dale, the hand of industry has covered with such exuberant crops of grain, in fields neatly divided by green hedgerows, as it is delightful to behold. On the lowest level, lower than the surrounding cornfields — where once were *fenny wastes* — the retreat of abundance of wild fowl, and other varieties of game, justifying its celebrity as a hunting seat, now are seen rich reclaimed marsh lands of vivid green, whereon are groups of grazing cattle, and where the glassy "Idle" (viz. stream of the cornfields) [14] winds its slow and mazy coils through the plain, between Scrooby and Austerfield — Austerfield concealed among the trees, and Scrooby marked out by its gracefully constructed church, rising above the green level, with its gray sky-pointing spire, and where the bridge over the Idle adds beauty to the view. And divided from the gardens of the village by what was evidently once a *moat* (but now dry), and bounded on one side by the river, and on the other by the railroad (the church in the background), is seen the large inclosed area or square, and, nearly in its centre, a group of sycamores, marking, as understood, the ancient site of the manor buildings. Here is now pointed out to the visitor, taking a nearer view, a farmhouse, and a row of willows, as occupying the place where stood the old hall. Evidently discernible as is the site, it is not so with respect to any part of the structure once upon it. Only some fragments of richly carved work, which doubtless anciently adorned the halls of state, could now be found, put to the ignoble use of propping up the roof of a cowhouse. Beyond these insignificant relics is no trace of the "great Manor-House of the Bishops." Such was Scrooby once, and such is it now.

[1] Bradford, 410.
[2] Hunter, to whom we have occasion to refer often in these statements.
[3] See Bradford, in his recovered History, p, 9, where the language is still more express than in Young or Prince.
[4] Bradford, 411; in Young, 465.
[5] Hunter's Founders of New Plymouth, 15, 18, and Tracts.
[6] Hunter, and Life of Wolsey.
[7] Leland's Itinerary, vol. i. p. 36.
[8] Strype's Ecclesiastical Memorials, iii. 250.
[9] (Query— £6000).
[10] Biographia Britannica, article Sandys, and Strype's Annals, iii. pt. ii. 64-70. Hunter, 18, 22, 139, and Bartlett.

[11] Hunter.
[12] Beauties, &c., of England and Wales, vol. xvi. 324, and Hunter.
[13] Rev. W. H. Bartlett's "Pilgrim Fathers," pp. 35-40.
[14] Id, or yd (says Thornton speaking of this river) signifies *seges* [Latin] *corn*, or grain in general: ydlan signifying the place where corn is stacked, ydle, a *granary*. The river Idle had its name then from *the grain* with which its bordering fields *abounded* even from the earliest times. Thornton's Nottinghamshire, 414.

Chapter Nine – 1590-1606

Do good for good's own sake, looking not to worthiness or love. - Tupper.

Returning to the time when Brewster became a resident in Scrooby, we trace next his course here in comparative retirement. It is interesting to find that he came not hither as a disappointed, useless dependent upon friends; but with fixed Christian principles and purposes, and with experience in the influential walks of life, and in the strength of young manhood, to do good, to devise plans, and meet the calls of the time and place for benevolent exertion. And ample was the field before him.

Here "he lived in good esteem among his friends and the good gentlemen of those parts." This was their voluntary tribute to his life and character.

But next, in quaint style and few words, we have summed up for us his individual efforts for nearly twenty years. "He did much good in the country where he lived in promoting and furthering religion, not only by his practice and example, and provoking and encouraging others, but by procuring good preachers to the places thereabout, and drawing on of others to assist and help forward in such a work, he himself most commonly deepest in the charge, and sometimes above his ability." "In this state he continued many years, doing the best good he could, and walking according to the light he saw." [1]

As a counterpart, and most strikingly illustrative of this brief statement, and of the "great need" of these very exertions, we have the following from Archbishop Sandys himself in a discourse before the Queen only a short time previous. "The mother City of the Realm" (London) "is reasonably furnished with good preachers. Certain other cities, not many in number, are blessed too, though not in like sort. But the silly (that is, ignorant) people of the land otherwhere, especially in the north parts, pine away and perish for want of this saving food. They are much decayed for want of prophecy. [2] Many there are that hear not a sermon for seven years, I might say seventeen. Their blood will be required at somebody's hand." [3] Such was the state of things, and such the call on every hand, for vigorous exertion. Hence in his own sphere were the exertions of Brewster; by personal example, self-sacrificing efforts, influence with others in ways and modes ever most effective; and all was in clue order and consistency "with the requirements of the Established Church.

But who were the active ministers in this portion of the country? And who were those whom Brewster and his friends were instrumental in procuring for the needy churches around them?

For a period of about twelve years, ending in August, 1588, had Archbishop Sandys been the ecclesiastical superior — a truly learned and distinguished divine, also faithful, laborious in his Master's vineyard, and a favorer of timely reforms in the established ceremonies — had his life been longer spared, or had his immediate successors been of like views and spirit, doubtless some, at least, of the difficulties that followed would have been avoided.

Already have we noticed the Rev. Henry Brewster as the Vicar of Sutton-upon-Lound, to which Scrooby was ecclesiastically annexed. [4] He had continued in that station for more than thirty years, ending with the spring of 1598. To him succeeded the Rev. James Brewster. That either of these was related to our William, or that this James succeeded to the vacant charge aided by any influence of William, we have no reliable evidence. The only direct indications of relationship are the *name*, their residence at the time in the same vicinity; and in respect to James, nearness of age, and resemblance of signatures, which is indeed striking. [5] And this James had married a Welbeck; and the Welbecks appear to have been from Suffolk, the original location of the early Brewsters. Presented, some years before, by Archbishop Sandys to the mastership of the richly endowed Bawtry Hospital, but having surrendered the same to the crown, under the claim of the commissioners *for concealed lands, he*, with others, afterwards received it back from the crown for private possession. A long contest in law ensuing, both the surrender and transfer were declared to be illegal. Our William must have been acquainted with these transactions respecting his namesake, and perhaps brother; and also with the further fact of James Brewster's presentation to the additional Vicarage of Gringley-on-the-Hill, near at hand. [6]

One minister, whom Brewster and friends may perhaps have been instrumental in procuring for the vicarage of Worksop, a neighboring parish, south of Scrooby, was Richard Barnard. He had been educated at Cambridge by the aid of two eminently pious daughters of Sir Christopher Wray, Chief Justice of England, and was appointed to that vicarage in 1601. Eminently successful as a minister and writer, wavering, and at one time declining to conform to some of the prescribed ceremonies, but at length conforming, he became a close observer of the movements of the times, and especially at Gainsborough and Scrooby. One of his esteemed treatises was the "Faithful Shepherd." Others have been reprinted even in our own day. At length presented to the Rectory of Batcome, "as a minister who, in the opinion of the patron, would best discharge the duties to the edification of the parishioners," he there became best known as "Barnard of Batcome, in Somersetshire." [7]

To Gainsborough, on the border of Lincolnshire, came, during this period, as a minister, a Mr. John Smith, whether as rector or not is uncertain. Bradford describes him as "a man of able gifts, and a good preacher, eminent in his time, but whose inconstancy, unstable judgment, and being suddenly carried away, soon overthrew him." [8] He gathered, after some time, a separate congregation, and removed to Amsterdam, in Holland. Whether he came to Gainsborough through any influence from Scrooby, or whether there was at this time any particular intercourse, other than acquaintance, between him and the Scrooby people, we find no specific evidence. Bradford's statements, and Mr. Smith's own language towards brethren who differed from him, lead to the conclusion that his uncharitable temper and course, could not long be congenial with the spirit of Brewster. But of him more will appear hereafter.

Of the Rev. Mr. Clifton, for years a laborious, effective, and fervent preacher, and Rector of Babworth, near Scrooby, and of the time and cause of his separation from the established church, we shall also have occasion to speak in another place. Other names might be added of ministers in this vicinity at this period; but whether any of them could be included in the terms of our last inquiry, needs further evidence.

But whence had Brewster the means for such active exertions, such liberal expenditures, as have been mentioned'? His was no old Nottinghamshire name, connected with landed estates, the usual source of income of the time and place, nor have we indications of his having: extensive wealth in any other form. [9] The inquiry becomes still more pertinent, since he had in the mean time entered the married state, an event ever one of the most important and memorable in life; yet, as in his case, calling for additional sources of income.

In what year this marriage took place, or with what family, no record has been discovered. The Christian name of Mary, and the other designation, "Mrs. Brewster," are the only ones left us of the partner of his life. Probably their marriage was before the year 1594; since at, or before that time, we may, from all circumstances, suppose them to have become the occupants, and Mrs. Brewster the lady of the manor-place.

But had Brewster no particular *secular* engagements, no regular *business transactions,* making large demands upon his attention, and as a means of increased income'? Bradford's memoir, unintentionally doubtless, would lead us to suppose he had not. Yet, what was long unknown, late discoveries enable us to state: that not sacred studies and Christian efforts and devotion alone occupied his time and thoughts. He held, under the Queen and her successor, a responsible office.

Among the earliest accounts of the post department, commencing in the year 1594, wherein were entered the names of the officers on the great post roads of the realm, William Brewster is found to have held the office of post of Scrooby. [10] It was then, however, an office of the court or government; and not, as afterwards developed, a department for the accommodation of the public. Not until more than thirty years later was it, that provision was made for the conveyance therewith of private correspondence; nor until the time of Cromwell that private passengers were thereby accommodated." More varied, however, were the duties, requiring greater responsibilities and capacity in those beginnings of the postal system, than those of the postmaster of the present day. When recently established by Elizabeth, few were the offices or posts, "dotted here and there about the country" on the great routes, and with no cross routes. Each post, therefore, must provide in his own district for all special dispatches, and distant deliveries, as well as for government messengers or privileged passengers, at certain rates of charge. Being a court appointment, Brewster must have had influence at court to be placed in this office. To perform its various incumbent duties, required the services of employees under him, and suitable accommodations, livery, and attendant servants. And this accounts for his occupancy of the manor place; where had been the residence of archbishops, the stopping-place of royalty and its train; a place not suited for a private gentleman, but well calculated for Brewster's official position.

Respecting his office, in the early accounts of the postmaster general, are found entries in his name for five terms and part of a sixth; three of them for three years, two for two years each, and six months of the succeeding term; in all, thirteen years and six months. The first entry is —

"April, 1594, to April, 1597.— (Old style.)

"William Brewster, post of Scrooby, for his ordinary wages, serving Her Majesty all the time aforesaid, at 20 pence per diem, £91 6s. 8d."

Similar are the other entries, except that in the third term, the wages were advanced to two shillings sterling, per diem, and in the last his connection with the office closed on the last of September, 1607, when one Francis Hall succeeded for the completion of that term. [12]

Very pertinently has it been remarked, that, had the names of the posts or postmasters been entered a few years earlier, we could then have ascertained the precise date of Brewster's first appointment. This would have shown how soon, after the fall of Davison, he was provided for by this office. What we now know is, that on the 1st of April, 1594, he was in full possession of the office; and that on the last of September, 1607, he resigned or was removed, just six months after the commencement of a new term. [13] Evidently, therefore, was the resignation or removal for some cause. It was at the very season when he, and a portion of his people, were on the point of leaving for Holland. So exactly do the dates and facts on record in England, correspond with those (when given) in the history of Bradford.

From the view now taken of this period of Brewster's residence at Scrooby, we have brought before us, not only his continued course of life, public and private, but a further insight into the principles by which he was guided, and by which he influenced the movements of others.

Advancing to the maturity of manhood, we see developed in him more and more, readiness to do good, persevering firmness, characteristic liberality.

Here, too, were developed the affections of the married relation, the tender assiduities of the father, and the kindliness of the Christian neighbor. Here evidently, were born his five children; and these are all of whom we have any information. And here amid the agitation and troubles of those trying times was he, according to his convictions of right, faithful in the service of his country, and in his duty to his God.

[1] Bradford, pp. 410, 411.

[2] See this term fully explained, note, p. 124.

[3] Strype's Annals, iii. part ii. pp. 69, 70.

[4] Hunter, pp. 58 and 73.

[5] Facsimiles —

[6] Hunter, 73, 86; other facts, lately discovered by Cardinal Brewster, Esqr., relative to James Brewster's residence at Chelmsford, near the seat of the Sandys in Essex Co., seem to confirm the connection stated, or intimate acquaintance.

[7] Hunter, pp. 36, 40.

[8] Bradford, in Young, pp. 22, 450, and Hunter, 38.

[9] Hunter, p. 38.

[10] Hunter, p. 71.

[11] English. Quarterly Review, or, the Eclectic, for Oct. 5, 1855; also, "The Post-office," London, 1842, pp. 7, 8, 9, and 17. One of the earliest advertisements for conveyance of passengers is in the "Mercurius Politicus," of April 1, 1658, as follows: "Passengers by stage coach to Bawtry, in three days, for 30 shillings."

It should he added, that while at first the post department was for the court, there was a pre-established and comparatively efficient system among merchants and others, for private purposes. — "P. Office" as above, pp. 8 and 9.

[12] Hunter's Founders, &:c., 66-69.

Note. — Are any surprised at the apparent smallness of the salary in these entries? let such bear in mind the difference, 1st, in the value of the currency, between   that day and this; and next as to the salaries generally, for instance: The salary of the principal Secretaries of State was then —

£100 per annum.

Of Clerk of the Council, £50 per annum.

Of a Clerk, £5 per annum.

While the rate of a Master Mechanic's wages was 1 shilling per day. — Johnson's Life and Times of Chief Justice Coke, ii. p. 149.

[13] Hunter, p. 67.

Chapter Ten – 1559-1606

"Differences of opinion may continue to exist; but when was it otherwise? Never, while men are permitted to think freely. It is not difference of opinion that makes the difficulty. It is the effort to enforce our opinion on somebody else." — Dr. S. Bowman.

We have now arrived at a period in the life of Brewster when a change took place in respect to his connection with the established church, of which, up to this time, he had been an active member. And the question comes up, what were the causes, or influencing and attending circumstances of this change'?

If we look back to the first days of Elizabeth, we find a controversy early commencing; the effects of which, from the way in which it was conducted, were at length sorely felt throughout the kingdom; nor is its sad influence entirely gone even at the present day.

It was not, however, a controversy respecting Christian doctrines; for in these the English reformers were very generally agreed. Under the capricious and dogmatically imperious Henry VIII. the opportunity for a reformation had been afforded, and was so continued and improved under the youthful Edward VI. and again under Elizabeth, that Protestantism, in its clear development of Christian truth, had become established. Nor was it a controversy respecting a uniformity of worship to be established by law. On this point, says the constitutional historian Hallam, "Both parties agreed too well in asserting the necessity of a uniformity of public worship, and of calling in the sword of the magistrate for the support and defence of their several principles." "Neither party were for admitting the liberty of conscience, and freedom of profession, which is every man's right, as far as consistent with the peace of the government." [1]

Nor did this controversy relate to church endowments; no small portions of which had already gone into the possession of the State; and of which many a royal favorite, or grasping nobleman, or unrewarded partisan, was allowed to make still further spoils. On this point, the general voice of the reformers now was for securing and faithfully applying all that remained, to promote the restored faith of the reformation.

Not in respect to any of these — was this controversy, but in respect to the further reforms in church *ceremonies* and *discipline*. This was a subject on which, from the nature of the case and of men's varied modes of thinking, differences of opinion might be expected; not only as to the *extent,* but as to the *rapidity,* with which such reforms should be effected. [2]

Besides, special difficulties attended this question. It was one great object of the Reformers to unite the largest portion of the people practicable, in one reformed national church; while not a small part of the nation still adhered to the old system; and not a few who favored the reformation were yet, from custom, strongly attached to some ceremonies, which others would at once discard. [3] In this state of things, there were those, and they were among the most efficient, who were for giving themselves first, and in the ways most effectual, to the work of enlightening with scriptural truth the great body of the people, leaving these further reforms to follow in more favorable times. [4]

But there was another and still greater difficulty. The church, as a church, could not legislate for itself. By general consent and acts of Parliament, the sovereign was, to an extent by no means clearly defined, the head of the Church, as well as of the State. [5] Changes, or further reforms, therefore, must have the concurrence of the sovereign, and the sanction of Parliament.

But, notwithstanding all these difficulties, a numerous and increasing portion of the nation, including at first a large number of the bishops, with perhaps a minority that finally grew into a majority in Parliament, were decidedly in favor of some further change.

In the year 1562, or fourth of Elizabeth's reign, the matter was regularly and ably discussed in the National Convocation of Clergy. Among the points debated, were propositions: —

"To discontinue holidays, except Sundays and the feasts that related to Christ."

"That the minister, in officiating, should always turn his face towards the people."

"That the ceremony of the cross in baptism be omitted."

"That kneeling at the communion be left to the discretion of the ordinary."

"That it be sufficient for the minister, in ministering, to use the surplice."

"That the use of organs be removed."

The chief reasons given were on the ground of superstitious use and abuse. Other points of reform were debated. On taking the votes upon the reform propositions, *forty-three* were for them, and *thirty-five* against them. But the proxies being counted, there were *for* the propositions *fifty-eight, against* them *fifty-nine*. Thus, says Burnett, "while there was a majority £or them of eight, of those who were present and heard the debates, these were outvoted by a majority of one proxy of an absent person." And what is not a little remarkable, it is noted on the record, "that those who voted against the propositions, seemed to do so on the ground that to vote for them would be to act contrary to what had been authorized, or assuming authority to alter what had been settled by the legislature." [6]

To all such reforms, however, though most of the bishops then favored them. Queen Elizabeth was decidedly opposed. "Loving magnificence in everything herself," claiming under the act of supremacy almost absolute power, urging on the archbishop and others inclined to her views, she presented to every such movement an effectual resistance.

To the Queen were the consequences chargeable. Says the same constitutional writer: "It is inconsistent with veracity to dissemble that the Queen alone was the cause of retaining those observances to which the great separation from the Anglican establishment is ascribed." [7] The immediate consequences were that, whereas great liberty in these respects had been previously allowed, conformity to all the prescribed ceremonies was soon rigidly enforced; and many were the suspensions, and not a few of able and highly esteemed ministers, for non-conformity. [8] There were but two lines to be taken when things had been brought to this pass, says the same authority, "either to relax and modify the regulations which gave offence, or to enforce a more punctual observance of them." And "far more probably would the former course have prevented a great deal of that mischief, which the second manifestly aggravated. For in this early stage, the advocates of a simpler ritual, had by no means assumed the shape of an embodied faction, but numbered the most learned and distinguished portion of the hierarchy." [9]

But now, the controversy became more and more earnest and bitter from year to year. Notwithstanding the efforts of many clergy and laymen to prevent extremes; notwithstanding such statesmen as Burleigh, Walsingham, Mildmay, and others of like mind, labored to influence the Queen, and those who sided with her, to more tolerant measures; notwithstanding all efforts at home, in connection with counsels of learned men abroad, for unity and peace, extreme measures were resorted to, party lines were drawn, those who plead for forbearance were overborne, passion in many took the place of reason, while there was a still more rigid enforcement of compliance on the part of the Queen and court, attended with provocations unwarrantably exasperating on the part of extreme opposers. [10] Nor was this all. To enforce conformity in extreme cases the powers of the High Commission Court were brought into exercise in a manner before unknown. Designed, when reconstructed under Elizabeth, to restrain those who adhered to the Roman sway, its power was now turned as a keen-edged sword against nonconforming and separating Protestants. By means of this court chiefly were effected the fines, suspensions, deprivations, imprisonments, and even executions, for non-conforming. "This mode of procedure," says Hallam, "was wholly founded on the canon law, and so repugnant was this to the rules of our English law, and to the principles of natural equity, that no species of ecclesiastical tyranny seems to have excited so much indignation." [11]

From various parts of the kingdom now came remonstrances and appeals to members of the Privy Council, in behalf of censured as well as deprived ministers, expressing deep concern for the cause of truth, of the Church, of the State, and of humanity. Of these most earnest appeals, that from the magistrates and gentlemen of the county of Suffolk, in the year 1583, preserved in the Annals of Strype, may be taken as a specimen. [12]

Even Lord Burleigh declared to the Queen, in relation to those ministers, "I am bold to think that the bishops in these dangerous times take a very ill and unadvised course in driving them from their cures." [13] More pointed was his letter on the subject to Whitgift, to which was returned a long, but to that statesman by no means a satisfactory, answer. [14]

Years passing on, increasingly bitter, and often most grossly personal on both sides, did the controversy become. Some redeeming examples there were, some praiseworthy exceptions.

That noble declaration of *Hooker*, the very announcement of which comes home to the heart of every unbiased reader or hearer, deserves to be emblazoned in letters of gold on every book of controversy: "There will come a time when three words, uttered with charity and meekness, shall receive a far more blessed reward than three thousand volumes, written with disdainful sharpness of wit." [15]

But other consequences followed. Truly, says Hallam again, "When these obnoxious rites came to be enforced with unsparing rigor, and even those who voluntarily renounced the temporal advantages of the establishment, were hunted from their private conventicles, they began to consider the national system of ecclesiastical regimen as itself in fault, and to transfer to the institution of Episcopacy that dislike they felt for some of the prelates." [16] At length, the opposition became fixed. The hour for liberal concessions was suffered to pass away. Intolerance "taught men to question the authority that oppressed them, till the battle was no longer to be fought for a tippet and a surplice, but for the whole ecclesiastical hierarchy, interwoven as it was with the temporal constitution of England." [17]

Would that we could here end this necessary view of the relative circumstances of the time, but no! Toleration in respect to religion was then by *neither party* understood, advocated, or apparently known. [18] Nor had history, from the commencement of the Romish sway, with two exceptions only — and those by laymen — furnished any other example. [19] How strange that Christians, disciples of the same Divine Master, should ever, for any conscientious differences, persecute or shed the blood of Christians! Where had been hidden that Master's stern rebuke to his disciples, on their suggestion of commanding fire from heaven upon those who would not receive him? "Ye know not what manner of spirit ye are of. The Son of Man is not come to destroy men's lives, but to save them!" Where was concealed that counsel, standing out in such bold relief on the Gospel page? "Take heed! If this counsel or this work be of men, it will come to naught; but if it be of God, ye cannot overthrow it, lest haply ye be found even to fight against God!" Where was that inspired appeal of St. Paul to those who would judge their brethren, though differing in minor matters? "Who art thou that judgest another man's servant? To his own master he standeth or falleth: Yea, he shall be holden up; for God is able to make him stand!" Where were those truths so specific, of such high obligation, uttered as by the voice from heaven! [20] How had they been buried in darkness so deep that even the light of the Reformation had scarcely yet disclosed them to the eye, or fixed them upon the conscience! Alas! they were to be learned, like some other most precious truths — in bitterest conflicts, from scenes of deepest agony. They must be wrought in upon the judgment, burned in upon the souls of men by their revolting consequences; even by victimized fellow-beings in imprisonment, on the rack, or at the stake. Such had been the course under the Romish sway. Would that there were no similar cases under Protestant rule; of Protestant subjects, even under a Protestant princess; that as to Copping, Thacker, Dennis, Penry, Barrow, and Greenwood, whatever were judged to be their legal offences, the Protestant cause of England might have been free from any responsibility of their blood. [21]

But there is one brighter spot amid the dark shades of this dark picture. If it be true, as Bradford relates, it presents an example (and there are many) of Elizabeth's quick apprehension of justice and right, when unbiased by passion or predetermination,

"Asking the learned Dr. Reynolds, what he thought of those two men, Barrow and Greenwood, who had some time before been executed; and seeing him loth to answer, she charged him upon his allegiance to speak. He answered, that he was persuaded, if they had lived they would have been two as worthy instruments for the church of God, as have been raised up in this age. Her majesty sighed and said no more. [22] Afterwards riding to the park, and past the place where they were executed, she demanded of the Earl of Cumberland, who was present when they suffered, 'what was their end'?' He answered, 'A very godly end, and prayed for your majesty and the State.' Again, demanding of the archbishop, on his conscience, what he thought of them, he answered, 'He thought they were the servants of God, but dangerous to the State.' 'Alas!' said she, 'shall we put the servants of God to death?' 'And this,' adds Bradford, 'was the true cause why no more were put to death in these days.'" [23]

[1] Constitutional History of Eng., pp. 115, 122, Harper's ed.
[2] Burnett, pp. 831, 837.
[3] Ibid.
[4] Ibid.
[5] Hallam, pp. 105, 107, 188-9. Act of Supremacy, and Notes.
[6] Burnett, p. 829.
[7] Hallam, 107, 110. Strype, in years, 1559, 1560. In London alone, of 98 ministers, 38 refused to conform, though some were in time restored. Burnett, 831, 838.
[8] Ibid.
[9] Hallam, 108, 110. As a striking illustration of the spirit of the Queen's proceedings, we have the following in another particular: "In several of the dioceses, the clergy, encouraged by their bishops, were accustomed to hold religious meetings, in which were discussions and expositions of particular texts of Scripture. These meetings were public; a moderator, appointed by the bishop, presided, and closed the exercises by a summary of the discussion and his decision. These exercises were called prophesyings: that is, *explaining* or interpreting the *Scriptures*. It was contended that setting forth the meaning of Scripture, and the grounds of their faith, in this manner, both instructed and edified the people as yet but poorly taught therein, and also supplied, to some extent, the great deficiencies in learning among many of the pastors themselves. To these meetings and exercises the Queen was decidedly opposed; and she directed Archbishop Parker to put them down.

"Parkhurst, Bishop of Norwich, as one, was unwilling to comply. A letter also from several of the Privy Council, as Sir Thomas Smith, Sir Walter Mildmay, Bishop Sandys, and others, advised him not to hinder them, so long as nothing contrary to the church was taught in them. Parker hearing of this advice, contrary to the Queen's and his instructions, instituted such inquiries after the authors of the advice as resulted, at the time, in the discontinuance of the prophesyings. But the succeeding archbishop, Grimdal, "bore the whole brunt of the Queen's displeasure, rather than obey her in this matter, conceiving that, under suitable rules, the abuses to which they were liable might be avoided. But the Queen would hear of no middle course, and insisted that the prophecyings should be stopped, and that fewer licenses for preaching should be given" (no parish minister being then allowed to preach discourses, except the homilies, without such license). (Burn's Eccl. Law, iii. 268.) "Archbishop Grindal steadily refusing to comply, was for about five years sequestered from the exercise of his jurisdiction, until, by a kind of submission, he was restored a little before his death; the Queen herself issuing circulars to the bishops, commanding obedience in putting an end to the prophesyings." Strype's Lives of Parker and Grindal; also as condensed in Hallam, 119, 120; Harp, ed.

[10] Burnet, 830, 840; Hallam, 121, 124, 136; Bacon on the Controversies of the Church of England; Strype's Annals, iii. pt. i. 260, 270, and Appendix, iii. pt. ii. 268.

[11] The germ of this court seems to have been a commission granted by the (Roman Catholic) Mary to certain bishops and others to inquire, and to punish, &c." "The primary model was the Inquisition," do. 122, note; see Strype's Documentary Annals, ii. 217, 218; also in relation to the illegality of the oath ex officio, and to penalties not according to law.

[12] The following is an extract: — "Ministers of the Word, by what malice we know not, are marshalled with the worst malefactors; presented, indicted, arraigned, and condemned for matters, as we presume, of very slender moment. Some for leaving the holidays unbidden, some for singing the psalm *Nunc Dimittis* in the morning, some for turning the questions in baptism concerning faith from the infants to the godfathers, which is but you for thou, some for leaving out the cross in baptism, some for leaving out the ring in marriage. Whereupon the law, neither the lawmaker, in our judgments, had ever regard, but meant indeed to bridle the enemy. Yet now (a most pitiful thing to see), the back of this law turned to the adversary, and the edge, with all the sharpness, laid upon the sound and true-hearted subject.

"We grant order to be the rule of the Spirit of God. We desire one uniformity in all the duties of the church, the same being agreeable to the *proportion of faith*. But if these weak ceremonies (and their like) be so indifferent as their use, or not use, may be left to the discretion of the ministers, we think it, in duty (and under your favorable correction we speak it), very hard to have them go under so hard handling, to the utter discredit of the whole ministry and profession of truth. And, which is more, we, that be magistrates, and under her majesty, have, as we think, equivalency of voice, and know that law and justice is one, and may not be avoided, do forbear to speak what we know, lest, by our severing in opinion, law should be rent, and justice cut in twain; and so the minds of the people, which are so easily distracted, carried hither and thither, to the moving of further inconvenience; and so, by our silence, ministry and magistracy brought into open contempt."

[13] Harleian Miscellany, vii. 58; Strype, Ann., iii. pt. i. 262. "Unjust, indeed, would it be to censure the archbishop for interfering to protect the discipline of his own church, had but the means adopted for that purpose been consonant to equity."

[14] Strype's Whitgift, 157, 163, 166; Hallam, 125; Fuller, book 9, p. 174.

[15] Ecclesiastical Polity, preface, chap. 3.

[16] Constitutional History, 113, *et seq.*

[17] Ibid. Some few of the extreme opposition had separated themselves and become organized privately in separate societies, notwithstanding the stringent application of the law.

[18] Similar was the intolerance under Presbyterian sway in the Revolution; also, under the Independents in the time of Cromwell; and we must add, in the Massachusetts colony in New England, though not, perhaps, in the same degree.

[19] The Emperor Maximilian and Henry IV. of France.

[20] Luke, ix. 52, 56; Acts, v. 35, 38, 39; Romans, xiv. 4.

[21] Copping and Thacker were called Anabaptists, and indicted and sentenced to be executed, for denying the Queen's ecclesiastical supremacy, and for distributing the condemned books of the noted Robert Brown. — Strype's Annals, iii. 186; also. Fuller and Stowe.

Penry, in the same manner, for alleged seditious writings. Of Dennis, we have not the particulars. Barrow and Greenwood were executed under the law of the 23d of the Queen, and for spreading seditious writings. As to the mode of procedure, Hallam remarks, "an oppressive and sanguinary law was made, and a construction put upon it contrary to all common sense."

[22] The same Dr. Reynolds whom King James afterwards combated at the Hampton Court, and who was subsequently one of the authorized translators of the Bible into English.

[23] Bradford, in Young, 432.

Chapter Eleven – 1603-1607

I am told thou callest thyself a king.
Know, if thou art one, that the poor have rights:
And power, in all its pride, is less than justice.

Hill's Merope.

James of Scotland, coming to the English throne without Elizabeth's capacity for government, with perhaps the strangest mixture on record of sense and of silliness, of much acquired knowledge, and low pedantic meannesses, of high pretensions to religion, with sad want of it — bred a Presbyterian, yet discarding that, and arrogating to himself the highest church as well as state prerogatives; — James, manifesting such characteristics, soon disappointed all expectations — of the court party most agreeably, of the opposite party, most sadly.

Among the very first acts of his government, was the committal of that "great error of throwing away one of the best opportunities for healing the wounds of the English church." Instead of attempting to heal, he aggravated them. On his coming into the kingdom a petition was presented to him from 825 clergymen — a petition couched in terms of devoted loyalty, asking for redress of some certain abuses, and for certain ceremonial reforms, none of them inconsistent with the principles of the establishment, and nearly the same as, but for one proxy, would have passed in the convocation of 1562.

And the aggravating act was (what Hallam has pronounced, "the most enormous outrage on the civil rights of these men") the committal to prison of ten of those who presented the petition. [1]

Also at the famous Hampton Court conference, held professedly to debate the points in question, whatever might be the merits of the case, we are constrained to acknowledge the "indecent and partial behavior of the King," even as related by Barlow; but more aggravating, as stated by Harrington, an eye witness. [2] We see the vainglorying of the man, and the rashness and want of wisdom in the sovereign — rashness in adding insult to rejection, provoking an opposition founded in the deepest, strongest, most enduring elements of man's nature. Stop the current, dam up the waters of the flowing stream, give them no vent; they accumulate until they reach a height, and attain a weight and power, that will sooner or later break forth and overbear all opposition. What might have been used to fertilize and beautify will in its fury and power, spread desolation indiscriminately over all that shall lie in its way. Streams of thought, accumulating currents of mind, coming from sources permanent and deep, long pent up, and arbitrarily forced back to revolve and react, and gather strength, at length acquire a might no power on earth can control.

A weak King, with state and church courtiers, makes the attempt: of his own sovereign will, taking counsel only of such as are interested to flatter him, he takes upon himself to dictate to Parliament. By proclamations with courts subservient to his will to give them the force of law, he presses the strictest conformity in matters of religious observances upon men conscientiously differing. As a *partisan,* he stigmatizes as *Puritans* all that body in the church who concurred not in his imperious views, and the non-conforming as "novelists," as "scarcely to be endured," "a sect insufferable in any well governed commonwealth;" and not to be tolerated in the kingdom. [3] Subsequent history relates the results.

About this time another element made its appearance in the controversy. Able men and statesmen, in and out of Parliament, saw their constitutional rights, their chartered liberties, trespassed upon, violated, even the existence of them denied. Those who would assert those rights, and defend those liberties, were stigmatized as *political Puritans.* Hence this new element soon coalesced from sympathy with the other; and a union of Church Puritans and State Puritans, followed. [4]

Ere long these elements were strengthened from another source. Not only some lower courts, but the Star Chamber and High Commission especially (as we have before noticed) had long been subservient to the sovereign's will in giving decisions and enforcing penalties against the non-conformists. But a chief justice of the Common Pleas was at length found on the bench, with sufficient weight of character, depth of legal knowledge, and, what is more, with an uprightness of purpose, and stern determination to vindicate the law, and the rights of the subject. This was none other than Chief Justice Coke. By his decisions it was shown and maintained, that the Court of High Commission, in enforcing those penalties, was in many particulars acting by usurped authority.

Mighty was the struggle; but constitutional right and law were, in part at least, and for a little time, triumphant. The sovereign concurred. The force of his proclamations, issued without authority of Parliament, was weakened. [5]

It was about the commencement of this last train of circumstances, in this long, sad controversy, and under the pressure of the measures renewedly enforced by deprivations, fines, imprisonments, and confiscations, that William Brewster left the Established Church.

For "many years" had he been engaged actively, yet orderly (and while holding office under Government), in furthering the cause of religion in the church, in procuring worthy ministers for the destitute, and in doing good according to his power; living the while in high esteem among the best in that portion of the land. With an observant eye had he beheld all that was passing. He had probably sympathies for those who wished for further reform, but it was not, as Bradford informs us, until the enforcement of conformity, by the King, in the aggravating manner mentioned, through Brancroft as primate, and by the very bishop of the diocese in which he lived, not until this, that he began to "look into the *unlawfulness*" of the course pursued, and to call in question the authority of courts and canons. [6] It was not until the suspension, deprivation, and silencing of some of those very ministers with whom he had associated, on whose ministry he had attended, from whom he had heard with profit the preached word, and whom he esteemed and loved, as good, yet persecuted ministers of Christ — it was not until all this, and till no prospect of a final change for the better could be seen, [7] that he left the national church. When, withdrawing quietly, yet decidedly, he entered into connection with that separate organization, of which the aged and confessedly pious, but lately deprived Clifton was the first pastor — of which Robinson also became the minister, and he himself, in time, and in another land, the ruling elder.

Such appear to have been the facts — such the circumstances of the case presented. [8]

[1] Hallam, pp. 173, 174; also Bacon's Tracts, vol. i. p. 387, as to the desired reforms.
[2] Do. and in Fuller, ii. p. 78, &c., and Antiquae Nugae, part i. p. 181.
[3] See his Proclamations at this period; Fuller, iii. 189, 192; Pictorial Hist. of Eng., iii. 15. Strype's Documentary Annals, ii. 60, and note.
[4] Rapin, ii, 424, 440.
[5] Life of Chief Justice Coke, by Lord Mansfield; more particularly in Johnson's Life of Sir Edward Coke, i. 206-236, and ii. 102, 139. Coke's Institutes, pt. iv. page 324, opposed to acts of Bancroft; Reports, pt. xii., vii. pp. 19, 41.

Strype's Doc. Annals, pt. ii. 601, 618. It may here be added, that in all this, the English nation, and we ourselves, owe to Chief Justice Coke a debt of gratitude due to no other. In opposition to all the exercises of an arbitrary power by King, Council, and High Commission, especially in "cases Ecclesiastical," did he most manfully vindicate the prerogatives of the Court of Common Pleas, and the principles of the common law. Most firmly did he withstand the arts, persuasions, proffered favors, and menaces of the highest and most powerful, until at length King James declared his will to "reform the High Commission in divers points, and reduce it to certain spiritual causes."

To the liberties of the people it was matter of vital concern. Thus checked in its illegal proceedings, this court became gradually more and more unpopular, until by the act of 16th of Charles I. it was finally abolished. The second section of the act declared it to be a "court by which the King's subjects sustained great and insufferable wrongs and oppressions." The attempt afterwards by James II. to revive it, proved one of the causes that hurled him from his throne.

Annexed are some specimens of Coke's Maxims.

"No proclamation can be offeree against an act of Parliament."

"If a proclamation is issued contrary to law, the law is to be obeyed, and not the proclamation."

"No subject, though ever so powerful or subtle, ever confronted or jostled with the law of England, but the same, in the end, infallibly broke his neck."

"The High Commission cannot, by force of the act of 1st Elizabeth, send a pursuivant to arrest any person subject to their jurisdiction, but ought to proceed by citation." — Reports, pt. xii. pp. 19, 41.

For one instance of Coke's acts in point, see Bradford in Young, 447.

[6] Bradford, 410.

[7] Walsingham had died in 1589, Burleigh in 1598, and Whitgift in 1604, and the extreme court party were now in full power.

[8] It is but justice to state here, what could not so properly appear in the text, that much more than was asked for in the Milenary petition was in after times provided for by law; in the various acts of toleration, charitable allowances were extensively made for differences of opinion in matters of religious worship.

And justice to the cause of truth demands this still further statement, in respect to the Protestant Episcopal Church in the United States of America: that far more than was at first objected to in England was here set aside, or left discretionary. Moreover, in its organization, a lay representation was provided for, equal to that of its clerical representation, in all its legislative assemblies and conventions. Thus constituted, it has been found, on comparison, to bear the nearest resemblance practicable to the organization of the general and state governments. And in respect to both of these branches of the Christian church, we may add here the views of a distinguished antiquarian, and minister of the congregational order, Thomas Robins, D. D., of New England, for many years Librarian of the Connecticut Historical Society, Hartford. In his "Historical View of the First Planters of New England," on referring to the "causes which induced certain Puritans to separate from the Church of England," and to the arbitrary measures of the English hierarchy of that day, he says: "No reflection is intended on the present Church of England, which was very different from that which it sustained supports to the revolution. It now deserves great veneration for its noble exertions in the cause of evangelical truth, and as an immovable barrier to infidelity. Still less will it be thought, by the candid reader,' that any unfriendly designs are entertained towards the Episcopal Church in this country, which never had any share in those prelatical usurpations." — Preface of, &c., p. v.

Hallam, in closing a chapter on the Constitutional View of the Controversy, remarks: "I am very sensible that such freedom as I have used, cannot be pleasing to such as have sworn allegiance to either the Anglican or the Puritan party; and that even candid and liberal minds may be inclined to suspect that I have not sufficiently admitted *the excesses of one side to furnish an excuse for those of the other.* Such readers I would gladly refer to Lord Bacon's 'Advertisement touching the Controversies of the Church of England,' written in the time of Elizabeth, in that tone of dispassionate philosophy, which the precepts of Burleigh had sown in his deep and fertile mind, and taught him to apply." Hallam's Con. Hist., p. 136; Bacon, ii. 375, 382, 387, &c., or pp. 411, 414, 417, 418, &c., Amer. ed.

Chapter Twelve – 1606-1608

There's no impossibility to him
Who stands prepared to conquer every hazard:
The fearful are the failing.   — Mrs. Hale.

There is a turning point in a man's life of far higher moment to him than any other; a point from which is marked his character for better or for worse ever after. Temporarily, with Brewster, had he remained in England, that turning point might have been at the fall of Davison; but now had he arrived at *another,* which casts *that* far into the shade. This was his connection with the separate religious organization just noticed. And this it was, however little suspected then, that led to results which were to distinguish the man to all ensuing time.

It was about the year 1606, evidently, when this organization or connection took place; and when Brewster was in about his 47th year. Bradford's various statements brought together, specify the time too plainly to be any longer mistaken.

First, "after they were joined together in communion, he [Brewster] was a special stay and help to them. They ordinarily met at his house on the Lord's day (which was a manor of the bishops); and with great love he entertained them;" Morton adds, "and continued so to do whilst they could stay in England." [1] This covers the whole time from their own separate organization until their arrangement to leave the country.

In another place, Bradford, speaking of this separate organization, and the trials they soon had to endure, specifies the *length of time* mentioned. "So after they had continued together about a year, seeing that they could no longer continue in that condition, they resolved to get over into Holland, which was in the year 1607 and 1608. [2] Prince adds: "This fall [1607] they began to fly over to Holland." Here we have, then, the date of their first attempt at removal, and the intervening year between that removal and their separate organization; leaving the year 1606, as that wherein their organization was completed, and when Brewster became connected with them. If there was, as appears, another earlier organization, it was that perhaps with which Mr. Smith, already alluded to, was chiefly connected.

Strikingly confirmatory of the above are the coincident historical facts — as the extremes of enforcement of rigid conformity at the time, and of prosecutions for non-conformity; — likewise, Bradford's computation of "above 36 years in which Brewster bore his part in weal and woe with this people," carrying ns back to the very year 1606; also the facts brought to light by Hunter, the resignation or removal of Brewster as "Post of Scrooby," on the last of September, 1607; the season of his departure thence, thus allowing for an intervening year; also the fine imposed on "Brewster, Brownist, or Separatist," the '22d of the next "April, 1608," for non-appearance at Southwell, and unpaid — for he had removed. [3] Finally Robinson's coming thither from Norwich, and his connection with this people about the same year, 1606; all these help to confirm the conclusions drawn. [4]

The time thus defined, and the intermediate year brought prominently to view, so also is the *place* where this church or congregation "ordinarily assembled on the Lord's day," viz., Brewster's house, still called the Bishop's Manor. Here now meeting for worship in its stately manorial hall, or in some one of its spacious apartments, the venerable Clifton, whose ministry had long before been blessed to many of them, appears to have officiated as their first pastor, assisted by Robinson as their teacher or minister. [5] Here also were called forth the marked liberality and affectionate attentions of Brewster, not only in furnishing a place of worship, but "in providing for them when they came together, himself bearing the great charge," and running the risk of consequences.

Soon, however, were they made to feel the consequences of separation. Soon were the strictest interpretations of the law, with the far more stringent proclamations and ecclesiastical instructions for minutest inquiry, put in force. [6] Accordingly, says one of their number, "some were taken and clapt into prison, others had their houses beset, and watched night and day, they barely escaping, while the most part were fain to fly and leave all — habitations, friends, and means of living." James' words were to be verified in their case: "I will make them conform, or I will harry them out of the kingdom, or else do worse;" words big with meaning, and to be attended with final consequences, of which neither he nor they could then have formed any conceptions.

In these trials, Brewster was a further "special stay and help to them." In these were his sympathies awakened, new acts of kindness called forth, and the closest bonds of union cemented. While thus harassed, and seeing no hope of anything better, by joint consent they resolved to go into the Low Countries. There, they heard, was freedom of religion for. all; thither had others gone from London and other parts for the same cause. But to go from country, homes, friends, livings, all that was familiar and dear, to go under the declared opprobrium of violators of law, and into a country known to them only by hearsay (Brewster excepted), into a country dear of living, subject to the miseries of war, of strange language, and as strange modes of life, was sorely trying, and thought by many to be an "adventure almost desperate." [7] Not the least discouraging was the fact that "they were not acquainted with the trades nor traffic by which that country subsisted," having been accustomed "only to a plain country life and the trade of husbandry." [8]

Yet, though troubled, they were not dismayed. Would they escape from persecution, and enjoy their worship in their own chosen way, they must go. There was but the one alternative. They had views of church organization, ceremonies, and discipline, which the King and bishops by him promoted would not tolerate. They determined to flee. Whatever may be thought of their faults, their minds were guided by a strong, definite, fixed purpose, conscientiously entertained, and equal to any sacrifice it might require. [9] Equally strong was their faith in an Almighty arm to guide and protect, and in the Divine mercy finally to bless them.

But resolved, and prepared to go, they encountered another trial. The ports were shut against them. They could go only in private ways, at great risk of seizure, and at extraordinary rates of passage, attended otherwise with heavy expense. Still nothing could deter them. And now followed their various efforts for removal.

Brewster, with a large company, having chartered for their sole use a ship at Boston, in Lincolnshire, the nearest port for their purpose, repaired thither at the time appointed; but neither the captain nor ship were there to receive them. After long delay, and increased expense, the captain appeared, and in the night, took them and their goods on board.

When on board, he betrayed them to the search officers, with whom he had made agreement for the purpose. Taken by these officials, and placed in open boats, they were searched; their goods ransacked, and their persons rifled for money, even to their innermost garments, and the women beyond the bounds of modesty. Most probably the wife and children of Brewster were of the number.

Plundered of their money, books, and to a large extent of their goods, they were taken back into the town, and made a spectacle of wonder to the multitudes who came flocking on all sides to see them. In this plight were they presented before the magistrates; when messengers with information thereof were dispatched to the Lords of the Council.

The magistrates treated them very courteously, and showed them every favor in their power, but could not release them without orders from the Council Board, and must therefore commit them to prison. A month were they there detained. After which, most of the company being dismissed, and sent, whence they came, Brewster and six others held in durance, were bound over to the Court of Assize.

"He was the chief person of the company, and suffered the greatest loss." The books mentioned, are supposed to have been mostly his. He was "one of the seven kept longest in prison" — "suffering most." Thus passed the first winter of their attempted removal. [10]

The next spring (1608) a portion of the same company, with others, attempted again to pass into Holland. Arranging matters more cautiously than before, and meeting with a Dutchman at Hull, with his ship from Zealand, they informed him of their condition, and with him made an agreement; hoping to find him more faithful than they had their own countryman.

Assured of this, at a certain day they agreed to meet him on a large common on the border of the Humber, between Grimsby and Hull. Against the appointed time, were the women and children of the company forwarded with their goods, in a small hired barque, while the men were to meet them by land. The barque arriving before the ship, and the sea being rough, the sickened women induced the boatmen to put into a creek, where at low water they were left aground. In the morning came the ship. The master, finding the barque to be grounded till return of tide, but seeing the men walking upon the shore, and ready, sent for them, meanwhile, by boat. Having received on board as many as could first come by the boat, while preparing to send for the remainder, he spied a large body of men, horse and foot, armed, and in close pursuit. Uttering his country's oath, the captain quickly weighed anchor, hoisted sail, and put to sea.

Trying indeed was now the condition of those on shore.

The men on board, in deep distress at being taken from their wives and children, now left to the mercy of their pursuers, could but shed manly tears, while at the same time, they found themselves for the most part destitute, penniless, and without change of raiment. But vain wore all regrets and longings to be back. There was no remedy.

Not long, however, had they to brood over what had passed. Their own perilous condition soon claimed all attention. A fearful storm followed. Seven days they saw neither sun, moon, nor stars. Driven by the tempest near to the coast of Norway, even the mariners themselves were often in despair. Once, with cries and shrieks, they gave up all for lost, the ship sinking as if foundered and past recovery. "But when man's help and hope failed," says the narrator, apparently present, [11] "then the Lord's power and mercy appeared in their recovery." Greatly to the encouragement of the mariners, the ship rose again. "And did modesty permit," says he, "I might declare with what fervent prayers some cried unto the Lord in their distress; especially when the briny waters were running into their mouths and ears, and the mariners were crying out, 'We sink! we sink!' When they, without distraction, but with great faith, cried, 'Yet, Lord, thou canst save; yet, Lord, thou canst save.'"

The ship soon recovered; the violence of the storm began to abate; and greatly were their afflicted minds comforted. In the end, some fourteen days from their departure, were they brought to their desired haven, where the people came flocking, and wondering at their deliverance, so long, furious, and destructive had the tempest been. [12]

But we return to those so abruptly left by the shore of the Humber. Such of the men as were left, and would be exposed to the greatest danger from their pursuers, eluded their grasp by escape; while those who best could, remained to assist the destitute and helpless.

Pitiable was the condition of the poor women and children; some weeping, and crying that husbands, fathers, and protectors, were taken from them, and to what trials those were exposed they knew not, nor what was now to become of themselves and their little ones; others were in tears from sympathy, and on seeing the young and defenceless hanging upon them, quaking with fear and cold, while the troop were upon them and apprehending them.

Whether Brewster was in *this* company, we cannot discover; yet it seems probable, since "he was the first in all adventures, and forwardest in any." [13]

This helpless company, thus apprehended, were next taken from place to place, hurried from one justice to another, until at length the officers were in a dilemma, not knowing what to do with them. To imprison so many women and innocent children for no other cause in respect to a large portion of them, than that they would go with their husbands or parents, appeared not only unreasonable, but all men would cry out against it. To send them to their homes was as difficult; for, as they alleged truly, they had none, having sold all in order to their removal. In the end, having passed from one constable to another, after great trouble, glad were the officers to be rid of them on any terms; and thus was forced a way for their final release.

As a consequence of these exposures and trials, not only in the country, but at Boston, Grimsby, Hull, and other places of note, their case and cause became widely known. On many minds deep and lasting was the impression, especially as connected with their patient endurance and irreproachable lives. Some of them, indeed, shrunk disheartened from their conflicts; but others came forth with fresh courage, greatly animating the remainder. [14]

Such, and other trials like these, did Brewster and this people endure. Amidst such they commenced their movements, in all of which his agency was conspicuous; through such did they resolutely pass, notwithstanding all opposition, until at length, some at one time and place, and some at another, they arrived in Holland; there meeting again together as in a secure retreat, according to their desires, and to their no small rejoicing.

[1] Bradford, pp. 411, 412; Morton, in Young, 465.
[2] Bradford, pp. 10, 11; and Prince, p. 23, 1st ed.
[3] Dean, afterwards Bishop Hall, writing to Mr. Robinson, and others, after they had arrived in Amsterdam, says: "We hear of your separation, and mourn." He

calls it "The late separation at Amsterdam:" again, "A late separation, not the first." Bp. Hall's work, vii. 171, 175, 385. And Mr. Robinson answered, "The separation we have made...is indeed late and new." Ans. to Bp. Hall's Epist.

[4] Bradford, p. 410. Those 36 years and about one month, taken from April, 1643 (old style), that is, 1642 and one month, leave the year 1606; the time given in the previous statement. Hunter's Founders of N. Plymouth, 68, 72, and Mass. Hist. Col., i. 4th series, pp. 75, 117. See also Strype's Annals, and Rapin, as to the pressure of conformity at this particular period.

[5] Bradford, p. 10, and in Young, 453, and in Hunter, pp. 42-45. ed. From the Plymouth Church Records, the intimations are clear that Mr. Clyfton was considered to be their first Pastor; as Prince also intimates, errata, p. 254, 1st ed.

[6] See specimens of the questions to which answers were demanded in Strype and in Calamy.

[7] Bradford, 10.

[8] Ibid., 11. This last is decisive as to the trade or calling of this people as altogether agricultural; any other must have been learned afterwards.

[9] Bradford, 9-11.

[10] Bradford, pp. 11, 12, and 412.

[11] Bradford, the future governor, then about 18 years of age.

[12] Ibid., pp. 13, 14, Also, Morton in Young, 465.

[13] Bradford, 14, and Morton in Young, 465.
It should be borne in mind that we have reason to trust Morton, on points omitted in Bradford's history, for he had writings by Bradford not now extant, and says, expressly respecting Brewster: "I could say much of mine own knowledge; but shall content myself with the hon. testimony of Mr. Wm. Bradford." Mem., p. 132, old ed.

[14] Bradford, pp. 14, 15.

Chapter Thirteen - 1608

"Hope without an object cannot live." — Coleridge.

Brewster with his pastor, and the emigrant company, arrived at Amsterdam, in Holland, in the summer of 1608. They were "the last to come over," having tarried "longest in England, to help the weakest over before them." [1]

And now they began to realize the fact, that they were indeed strangers in a strange land, with a people of strange speech, manners, dress, diet — a people proverbially patient, of untiring industry and most rigid economy, 'saving all gains in all manner of ways.' A country they found, densely populated, differing externally, in habits and modes of labor, from all to which they had been accustomed in the rural life of their English inland homes. Situations in business they also found preoccupied, and in them much rivalry. Unfavorable, therefore, were their prospects of immediate employment, or of obtaining a comfortable living.

But their purpose was fixed, patiently to accommodate themselves to their new circumstances, and to surmount all difficulties. They beheld a city risen from an insignificant village, built upon piles over a salt marsh, around a dam across the mouth of the river Amstel (and hence its name Amsterdam, from the *dam* of the *Amstel*), and now by unexampled industry grown into a mighty mart renowned for its increasing commerce, accumulated wealth, and stately buildings. They beheld its harbor enlivened, and wharves lined with ships from every known clime; and on its scores of canals in place of streets, water craft floating without number, of every form and for every needed purpose. Hither had fled from the blood-stained streets and blackened ruins of Antwerp, large numbers of the Protestant population of that captured and plundered city, bringing with them their arts, manufactures, and skill in trade.

Hither had come not a few like themselves, to find a safe retreat from persecution, from France, Germany, and even from England. Thus had Amsterdam become in Holland, what Antwerp had been in Flanders, the grand emporium of Europe. [2]

But while they saw all this, other things demanded their immediate attention. They were to provide at once for the necessities of themselves and families, and to arrange their church order and worship, to enjoy which in peace they had come to Holland.

But in this latter chief purpose, they met with an unexpected hindrance. Mr. Smith and his company, of whom we have already spoken, had arrived here some time before them. And years before his arrival, had another, older separate congregation, come from London, and been here settled. With this older separate company Smith and his people "were already involved in contention," which "no means that Robinson and Brewster could use would allay." Besides, in that older church itself were the flames of contention likely to break out, which afterwards lamentably came to pass. "Which things Robinson and Brewster foreseeing, prudently resolved to remove thence, before they became involved in them." [3]

Scarcely, therefore, had they been here an entire year, when, to escape from contention, and live in peace among themselves, they sought another place of abode. Thus soon breaking up all local plans and arrangements already made, and gathering all again together, they removed to Leyden, another city next in size to Amsterdam, about 38 miles distant.

This removal, and the reasons given, were characteristic of the men acting from principle and desire of peace, though they knew it would be to the prejudice of their worldly interests then, and, to appearance, in future, as the event proved. [4]

Here, also, is shown the fact that, with *neither* of those separately organized bodies (though sympathizing with them in most things), with neither of them did this company under Clifton, now under Robinson and Brewster, become united. [5] Nor did they approve, it appears, of the rigid notions of some of those Separatists in respect to modes of dress, as well as in respect to the mode of baptism, and to some particulars in church government, which caused those contentions. [6]

It was early in the summer of 1609 when this emigrant company, with perhaps a few exceptions, came to Leyden. Here, again, they saw an ancient city, situated in the midst of the district of Rhineland, a district presenting a, vast level expanse of the richest meadows in the world, adorned with seventy villages, with their towers and spires rising to view out of tufted groves, and the whole specked with interminable flocks and herds, a view extending until lost in the bluish haze beyond the cities of Delft and the Hague.

Of the city itself, built on thirty islands formed by river and canals, and connected by numerous bridges, there is a partial view in the annexed print. In the foreground are seen, on the right, the main street, through the centre, the New Rhine, with its slow moving current, bearing on its surface various water craft, the other, or Old Rhine, being concealed from sight. Of the many churches, St. Peter's, on the extreme right, and St. Pancras on the left, lift their huge masses above all inferior buildings — (St. Peter's dating back into the 12th century, and where the pastor, Robinson, was to be at length buried). On every side are ranges of buildings, high and low, public and private, with picturesque old gables in true Dutch style, of red brick, fantastically inlaid with stone-work, in some of which were doubtless, for a time, the abodes of the pilgrims. Other fine streets met the eye, with shady walks and noble edifices; and skirting the whole were walls, towers, and armed battlements, while beyond was spread out the level sea of verdure, with countless windmills, and densely populated burghs and hamlets.

"A beautiful city," says the historian, "a fair beautiful city, of a sweet situation." [7]

View of Leyden, Holland

Hither, also, as well as to Amsterdam, adding greatly to its active population, had fled large numbers of Protestants, artisans, manufacturers, merchants, and men of science from fallen Antwerp.

But the chief glory of Leyden was its university. Founded soon after the siege and almost superhuman defence of 1574, now drawing numerous students from its own and the surrounding states, already, with its eminent professors and other advantages, was it in the enjoyment of a high and justly earned reputation throughout the learned world. [8] Here, also, must have come up vividly to the mind of Brewster, historic recollections of the embassy to this vicinity, with which he was connected some twenty-three years before.

Still, though our emigrant band, to use their own words, saw around them "goodly cities, strongly armed" and "abounding in all kinds of wealth," not long could those goodly sights detain their thoughts from their own reduced condition.

Many were their discouragements here also, greater even externally than when they were in Amsterdam, By extra expenditures and detentions in England, loss of goods, imprisonment, high rates of passage, and this last removal, had their means been sadly diminished, nay, well-nigh exhausted. Lonely strangers were they still in a strange land, and still unacquainted, for the most part, with the trades and modes of procuring subsistence. Looking around, stern poverty rose up before them as a strong man armed, whom they could not escape, with whom they must contend. And with him, in faith and patience, did they most resolutely contend. Betaking themselves at once to such trades and employments as best they could, at length, "with hard, and long-continued labor," and with sore "conflicts and misgivings in some," did they succeed in obtaining a competency.

In these trials and conflicts, how was it with Brewster himself, who had shared most largely in their losses, made the greatest sacrifices, been most forward in every enterprise, spent most liberally for the general good; whose wisdom in council, discretion in action, and public experience, had won their entire confidence, their affectionate regard; nay, without whom, probably, they could never have made this formidable movement.

On coming to Leyden, and on the full organization of their church or congregation in their own chosen way, "Mr. Robinson was duly recognized as sole pastor, and Mr. William Brewster chosen as their ruling elder." [9] The aged Clifton, their first pastor, whose course of life was now almost run, had concluded to remain in Amsterdam. [10] Thus chosen to be their ruling elder, Brewster was henceforth designated by the terms, "The Elder," "Elder Brewster," and "Elder William Brewster." Nor was the name or position by any means nominal, in respect to him or them. While it imposed upon him duties, in their view sacred and important, as their lay ruler, and in certain contingencies as their instructor, it bound him voluntarily to them, and they to him, in ties deemed by them among the strongest and dearest. [11]

But how was it as to his temporal affairs? In this respect, whatever may have been his portion of wealth, whether greater or smaller while in England, by expenditures for himself and others, already noticed, we find that, by this time, his condition could be no more favorable than that of his brethren. Briefly, says one who knew, "after he came into Holland, having spent the most of his means," and "having a great charge, and many children, he suffered much hardship." [12]

This "great charge," in addition to his own family (of at least seven, with himself), seems to imply numerous dependents, or domestics, apparently a portion of his household while in England, and still here dependent upon him.

But what rendered his own condition peculiar, and his present hardships the greater, was the manner of his early training, with the refinements to which he had been accustomed, unfitting him for these "laborious employments," in which others, more hardy, could readily engage. Yet amidst it all, while using every means of alleviation within his reach, he presented (what must have had a most salutary influence upon his companions in trial) "an example of cheerful contentment with his lot." [13]

But at length, in the good providence of God, and in time of greatest need, was opened to him the way of relief.

Already have we noticed, in his early education, his knowledge of the Latin. And now, the increased intercourse, commercially and politically, between Holland and England, caused a desire and demand among the students of the university, and others of influence, for a knowledge of the English.

To Elder Brewster, peculiarly qualified, was thus presented the opportunity to meet this demand. Both he and they being masters of the Latin, it was at once a ready medium of communication to this end; and to him they resorted, as other studies would permit. To facilitate their progress, he prepared rules, or a grammar, after the Latin manner, by which their acquisition of the English became rapid and highly satisfactory. We can easily imagine how, and with what interest, he became thus engaged with gentlemen of the university; as the record states, "Danes and Germans, some of families of high distinction," they in studious attendance upon his instructions; and all resulting in a manner equally beneficial to the instructor and the instructed. [14] It was in a way suited to his early training, tastes, and studies. Here also must his early experience and intercourse in diplomatic life have added greatly to the interest in his course of instruction.

How soon after his removal to Leyden this course was commenced, we are unable to discover. Nor are we informed as to many other particulars of his life, during the several current years between 1610 and 1617. A general view, however, we have, from incidental statements. In them all he is presented before us as exemplary in his duties to his family, ready to improve all opportunities of doing good, but especially active, in connection with his pastor, in promoting the edification and increase, and, as ruling elder, in preserving, by mild yet firm discipline, the unity and peace of their congregation.

By these means, from their small beginnings increasing by accessions from England and other sources, their number, in time, amounted to about three hundred communicating members. [15]

[1] Bradford, p. 16.

[2] Bradford, 11 and 16, and Malte Brun, iii, 1000, 1103, &c.

[3] Bradford, 16 and 17.

[4] "Valuing peace (says Bradford) and spiritual comfort above all earthly riches."

[5] Bradford, 16, 17; Prince's Annals, 26, 27. These facts are here stated thus particularly, since they have been inaccurately stated in the Memoirs of Robinson, prefixed to his works, and in Mass. Hist. Coll., 4th series, i. 123. See further in Chap. XXVII. of this work.

[6] Bradford, in Young, 445-6-7, and 450.

[7] Bradford, 17; Bartlett's Pilgrim Fathers, 75, 79, &c.

[8] Malte Brun, article Leyden, and Notes; Bradford, 17, and Brandt. Ibid. It is said that the yet youthful Bradford, in this necessity learned the trade of silk dyeing. While this appears to have been the fact in respect to him, a statement usually connected with it, in respect to Brewster, is not so, and will be corrected in its proper place.

[9] Bradford, p. 17.

[10] Bradford, p. 17. Clifton came into Holland, Aug. 1608; and though connected with this congregation or church, concluded to pass his few declining years at Amsterdam, where he died, 20th May, 1616, and his wife, 3d Sept., 1613. Hunter, 44.

[11] For a particular account of this office in their church organization, see their own statements in Chaps. XVII. and XXVII.

[12] Bradford's Hist., 412.

[13] Bradford's Hist., 412.

[14] Brad., 412.

[15] Bradford, p. 17, and Winslow, in Young, 455, 456.

Chapter Fourteen – 1609-1618

To give religion her unbridled scope,
Nor judge by statute a believer's hope. — Cowper.

And how was it as to the state of religion and religious toleration in Holland at this period?

How matters stood politically during the embassy of Mr. Davison, when William Brewster attended him thither nearly thirty years before, we then had occasion to notice. Then came into view the fearful struggle with Spain. That struggle was continued. During its continuance many of the Protestant inhabitants were massacred; fair districts were overrun; yet, with the partial aid of England, the United Provinces had asserted their independence, and obtained a twelve years' truce. "With their independence, they had established, to a great extent, civil and religious liberty.

Here was now an external, though not an entire internal, toleration of all who professed the Christian name. Here were Roman Catholics who had helped to assert their liberties, and were quietly partaking of the accompanying privileges. Here were Lutherans, though the Dutch felt a strong antipathy to them, stronger even than had been felt towards them in England. Here were French Protestants and English, of different names; Anabaptists, and many others, with their peculiarities. Here was now our Pilgrim company at Leyden; also another English church or congregation, that came to Leyden the same year. All who came thither and lived peaceably under the protection afforded, and aided in the support of the State, were tolerated. Indeed, such indiscriminate toleration was made, at the time, the subject of reproach and ridicule, a theme of poetic sarcasm, particularly as to Amsterdam. [1]

In all this, the government acted not merely from regard to the Protestant cause, but also on grounds of political policy, and with shrewd calculations of commercial interest. [2] Hence, notwithstanding the desolations of war, and the limited extent and power of the States compared with Spain, great multitudes continually flocked hither, many in aid of the Protestant faith, some to escape from imprisonments and persecutions at home, and not a few for barter and commerce. From these accessions were the ranks of their armies filled, their losses supplied; even in time of war, agriculture and the arts flourished, and the Dutch were extending their commerce, and discoveries, and colonies, with persevering energy, to the distant regions of the earth.

But, along with their civil liberties and general external toleration in respect to religion, the States had their internally established Protestant Church, the legally established Church of the Netherlands, constituted under the Presbyterian form. Accordingly, its church edifices were provided, and pastors chiefly supported, by the State or by law. Congregations of foreigners also, on application, were usually provided for in like manner. Chaplains of the Church of England for English troops and garrisons, as well as English congregations, were thus accommodated or aided.

Our emigrant company, however, appear not to have been thus favored, certain influences preventing. No church edifice was opened to them, no aid provided for their pastor's support.

A church establishment there was then in Holland, as in other countries at this period, not a *peacefully established* religion, indeed, for "to speak of such in the confusion of those times, would be to speak of settled estates in an earthquake." In this state church had the "Netherlands' Confession of Faith and Catechism" been adopted, as scriptural, perhaps, as could then have been received or composed. "Its articles had been drawn originally by their most moderate and judicious divines, with a scope in the main like the English, equally removed from the extremes of latitudinarianism on either side." On those "high mysterious points commonly called Calvinistic" (in which sense they had been adopted), differences of opinion were both allowed and entertained. And it has been remarked that "it was from that intrinsic liberty of speech and of thought, which was in fact never fairly or legally withheld from the Belgic churches, that such discrepancies of judgment arose." And from the long line of facts we are bold to say, that "such will ever arise, on the same subjects, among different members of the same establishment, as long as the laws and sentiments of that establishment shall be in a healthy state; as long as they shall rest upon a true scriptural base." [3] And here is ever the field, and here the call, for the continual exercise of Christian charity towards all the pious members of the body — charity "the bond of perfectness," without which all zeal — all else, is as nothing. It is the voice of history; it is the voice of God.

To come to the point before us, our emigrant company found the established church of the Netherlands now in the midst of a most agitating controversy. It was a controversy that had agitated and shaken, and continued to convulse, large portions of the Romish church, between the rival organizations of Louvain, Douay, and the Jansenists on the one side, and the order of the Jesuits on the other; a controversy upon the deep points of predestination and grace. [4]

This controversy had become rife in the University of Leyden, and was beginning to prevail throughout the States. Arminius, from whom, among Protestants, the system took its name in contrast with that of Calvin, had been in this university a distinguished divinity professor. As a coincidence that may be remembered, he was born, as appears, in the same year as William Brewster, and in the same in which the celebrated Melancthon died. And the year that our company came to Leyden, Arminius died. [5]

In this Arminian controversy, our pilgrim company could not but become deeply interested; in it their pastor became personally engaged. With Episcopius, the successor and eloquent advocate of the views of Arminius, Mr. Robinson came into direct contact, and engaged in full discussion.

"Great," says Bradford, "were the troubles raised, greatly molesting the whole State, and Leyden in particular, where was the chief university." Frequent and warm were the disputations in the various schools; and such was the excitement, that while the two professors, Episcopius and Poliander, were themselves teaching daily in the university, the one for, and the other against the views of Arminius, few of the disciples of the one would listen to the teachings of the other.

Taking opportunity constantly to hear the readings of both, being well grounded in the controversy, and seeing the force of all the arguments, the pastor of the emigrant company, himself quick of apprehension and ready of speech, was desired by Poliander and the chief ministers of the city, to take part in the discussion. Loth as a stranger to do this, yet importuned, when Episcopius, the Arminian professor, put forth his theses, and his full strength to discuss and defend them, their pastor yielded; and, adds the perhaps too partial historian, "on several public occasions he so succeeded, and had the victory, that many praised God for the conquest for truth." [6]

This procured their pastor much honor from those learned men and others interested. And it is intimated that, were it not for giving offence to the King of England, they would have shown him and his people other public favors.

But the controversy ended not here. Many and earnest were the attempts, by private conference and by authority of local assemblies, to reconcile the differences: yet all to little purpose. The call was for a National Synod. And a national synod was finally assembled — the far-famed Synod of Dort. Delegates were invited to it from all Protestant churches of Europe, the Lutherans excepted.

The followers of Arminius summoned to this synod appeared as members. But, to their disappointment, full and free discussion of the points at issue was not permitted. The majority assumed the attitude of judges, and, without free discussion, passed sentence of condemnation. And it was a condemnation not only of the *tenets* of their differing brethren (of which, had full discussion been first allowed, they as an organized body had a right to judge), but a sentence of condemnation also upon the *persons* holding those tenets: men learned, conscientious, sincere (whether right or wrong), men against whose mild deportment and piety no accusation could stand.

Under the sentence thus passed, the principal favorers of the tenets of Arminius must suffer. At the Hague, within four days of the close of the principal sessions of the synod, that distinguished statesman and advocate, the mild and guileless Barnevelt, the very *beau ideal* of historical portraiture, for integrity to his conscience, and to his country, was brought to the scaffold and beheaded. [7]

The learned Grotius, one of the ablest Christian scholars of the day, and the well known Hogenbeets, were also sentenced to imprisonment for life. Ministers of churches, professors in their universities, were deprived of their places, and banished the country, with no time allowed even to arrange their affairs, or take leave of their families.

To this synod King James had sent a chosen delegation; another specimen of his strange acts, showing how he could "insult the laws of God and the realm" in sending forth and enforcing upon the nation "his Book of Sunday Sports," at one time, and use all his power to put down everything Presbyterian, as well as to exterminate everything Puritan in the church of the realm at another time, and yet almost at the same period, send a delegation to a Presbyterian synod in another land, with instructions to sustain it in its original form and creed against all innovations.

The delegation itself would do honor to any cause: Bishops Carlton and Hall, with Doctors Davenant and Ward, heads of colleges at Cambridge, whose influence and mild counsels in private were on the side of unity and peace. [8] Another proof, that *personal* and *political* ends, not Christian principle or church preference, were the controlling motives with the King.

James could persecute, *not for doctrines,* but for *differences of opinion as to ceremonies;* the synod of Dort could condemn and persecute equally good men, *not for ceremonies,* but for *deviations in opinion from the received Genevan points of faith.* It was the remaining barbarous custom of the times. Toleration in these respects, even in Holland, was yet unknown.

It has been more than insinuated that the pastor of our separate company took side with the persecutors, and favored the persecuting acts of the synod. [9] But of this there is no evidence; and without evidence the supposition is altogether gratuitous.

That Mr. Robinson contended earnestly for the Genevan system — conscientiously believing it to be the truth, is matter of historic fact, as we have already seen. But that he, or Elder Brewster, had any agency in or favored the condemning sentence upon the *persons* of the defenders of the views of Arminius, we have reason to think from the writings of the one, and the whole discreet and benevolent life of the other, was not the fact.

To say that they held views generally termed Calvinistic, is to say not only what was the fact in regard to them, but also in regard to the great body of the Church of England from which they had separated. Of this latter fact every reader of the Church of England's history is aware, and that the views thus termed had been there held generally from the beginning of the Reformation to the time of which we are now speaking. In such views this people had doubtless been educated while in that church. Doctrinally, on this point, there was then little difference between them. [10] This, however, in no way necessarily connected them with the extreme action of the synod.

Nor was the persecuting spirit of the synod universally prevalent in Holland. Not long before had the magistrates of Leyden, when called upon to coerce by force of law those who differed from the majority on points of religious faith, answered: "The design of the States undoubtedly is, that none should be persecuted on account of their religion."

In good sound terms, they answered further: "We do not find that we have any authority to proceed against, and punish by law, those who have not behaved otherwise than well in their civil and burgher-like capacities."

"There are no better means to root out heresy than temper and moderation; for we have often seen that certain books were little minded at first, but afterwards, when condemned as heretical, they came into repute and credit."

"Force will not make Christians, but only fill the world with vile hypocrites under the name of Christians." [11]

Such, we believe, from every recorded act of his life, to have been the matured mind of Brewster.

Discussions, in which he must have been engaged, are one thing; disputes even are another thing; to persecute those who differ from us, is still more emphatically another. This latter is the work of the enemy of God and man. History gives the evidence. Discussion, frank, candid, free, for the eliciting of truth, is the source of good, often of incalculable good; dispute, the source of incalculable evil.

[1] "A common harbor of all" opinions, of all heresies," says one; "a cage of unclean birds;" "all strange religions flock thither," says another; "the great mingle mangle of religion," says a third. Hence that sarcasm — "Amsterdam, Turk, Christian, Jew, Staple of all sects, and mint of schism, grew." Note in Young, 23, 24.

[2] Leicester Correspondence.

[3] Review of Bp. Hall and Arminius, Christ. Obs., vol. xxvii. 547.

[4] Dupin. Eccle. Hist. 17th Century. Book i. and Book iii. chap, ii.-ix.

[5] Born in 1560, he was trained first by a pious mother, next by a Protestant minister from the Roman Church, next six years at the Leyden University, then for his promising talents and piety was adopted by the Burgomasters of Amsterdam, and by them sent to Geneva. One year he was at Basle, again three years at Geneva, under the distinguished Beza from whose Calvinistic sentiments he seems not then to have expressed the slightest dissent. Then travelling to Rome, and returning to the city of his adoption, he was made pastor of one of its principal churches. Here laboring successfully for years, and called upon to answer the writings of some brethren at Delft who dissented from the high Calvinistic ground, he undertook the task, and the result was, through painful agitations and struggles, a gradual relinquishment of those distinguishing views, and the adoption of others for which he became famous, and for which he suffered. In the midst of much censure from some, loss of favor from others, yet for his learning and piety highly esteemed by many, he was, in 1602, elected to the high divinity chair at Leyden. Here candidly and learnedly he advocated his views, while the other learned divinity professor, equally devoted and sincere, advocated the opposite. And the deeply agitating controversy extended not only through the university, but through the State. The very year of the arrival of our emigrant band in Leyden, (1609) Arminius closed his labors, his sorrows, and his life. See references under note 7.

[6] Bradford, p. 20, &c.

[7] Beheaded May, 1619. See particulars in Brandt's Hist., vol. iii. 301, 303, and 307, and Strictures in Christian Observer, London, vol. xxvii. pp. 346, 349.

[8] See Bishop Hall, as well as Mr. Hale on the Synod of Dort; also Brandt, iii. 5, 32, 112, 283, 3.

[9] Mass. Hist. Collection, vol. xxix. p. 59.

[10] Even James declared this in people in their articles, see Chap, his Proclamation; so did this xxvii. *seq.*

[11] Brandt, vol. i. 384.

We have in possession sermons, with marginal notices, of evident approval, written, we believe, in the Elder's own hand; showing him to have entertained like tolerant views. See also the Seven Articles, Chap, xxvii.

Chapter Fifteen – 1615-1618

But mightiest of the mighty means,
On which the arm of progress leans,
_____ is the press. — Dr. Bowring.

Going back to the time when we left Elder Brewster instructing students of the university, Danes and Germans, in the English language, we are to notice him next engaged in another responsible undertaking.

Writers have said, and it has often served to give point to oratorical phrase, that, in their great extremity, the future governor, Bradford, learned *the trade* of silk-dyeing, and Elder Brewster, the *trade* of printing. [1] However true the statement may have been in respect to Bradford, it was not strictly true in respect to the Elder. First is the fact that Bradford was scarcely twenty years old, while the Elder was now over fifty, probably fifty-five. But attention to the language of the historian corrects the error. Along with his engagements in the way of instruction, it is added, "He also had means to set up printing by the help of some friends, and so had employment enough, by reason of many books which would not be allowed to be printed in England." [2]

To *set up printing,* by means furnished by friends, and on account of *many* books that might be printed, designates, in modern phrase, a publisher, including in some cases the duties of editor. And this corresponds with the facts; though in setting up an establishment of this nature, some knowledge of the typographic art might probably have been acquired.

And it is matter of interest to know something of the works which he published. Being, as might be expected, of a religious character, portions of them had reference to the main controversies of the day; yet were they for the most part eminently *practical.* Some of them were in Latin, others in English, two of them large and expensive works.

First, was a Commentary, in Latin, on the Proverbs of Solomon, by Cartwright, with a preface by Polyander, 1513 pages quarto, published by him at Leyden, Choralis Street (or place), A. D. 1617. A practical work much esteemed at the time; a second edition of which was published in Amsterdam, in 1638. [3] (Below are the original titles of the Latin works.)

2d. "Confutation of the Remists' Translation, Glosses, &c., of the New Testament," by Cartwright, 1618, in folio. When this large and learned work was published by the Elder, no complete work of the kind had appeared in English to meet the urgent demand. It was printed in the beautifully clear, fair type of the Leyden press of that period, resembling in this respect the far-famed Elgiver editions of the Classics, which have never been excelled. On the broad margin are pointed out successively the portions of Scripture read for the lessons on Sundays and other special days, in the Church of England service, commencing with the Sundays in Advent, Christmas, and thus proceeding in order throughout the year. [4] In this work, as well as in the following treatises, the publisher's name was omitted.

3d. A smaller treatise in Latin "Concerning the true and genuine Religion of our Lord and Saviour Jesus Christ;" of which, the evidence is clear that he was the publisher. [5]

4th. A treatise in both Latin and English, called "The People's Plea for the Exercise of Prophesying," by Mr. Robinson, his pastor. It sets forth, as its title suggests, in a moderate and guarded manner, yet fully and decidedly the arguments for that exercise, and which this people maintained while in Holland, and long afterwards. [6]

5th. "Ames' Reply to Grevinchovius," on the Arminian controversy, in Latin. [7]

Such were the principal works published by Elder Brewster, at Leyden, in the year 1617 and 1618. We omit the notice of others, of which we have not full evidence. It was a class of works which had at the time no small influence, nay whose influence has been continued through successive writers, and will continue indefinitely, as a wave of the ocean, once raised, ceases not its motion, but moves onward, combining with others, until it shall reach earth's utmost limits, to end we know not when or where.

That more works were not published by him, was owing to causes as widely diverse as the jealousy of James, and his arbitrary efforts to control the press even in Holland, on the one hand, and the first germs of thought with maturing plans for planting a new colony on the far off shores of the New World, on the other.

At the Hague, near to Leyden, resided at this time Sir Dudley Carleton, ambassador from England. Discovering that books, not allowed to be published in England, were issued from the press, and circulated at Leyden, and that some of them were apparently provided for the English market, he informed his majesty of the fact.

James, keenly alive to everything of the kind, directed the ambassador to use all influence to have the printing of such books prohibited; and not only this, but to have the persons engaged therein sought for and committed to prison. To this, the then Prince of Orange, with some of the chief rulers, unwilling to displease the King, and as a personal matter, assented; though at the expense of their national independence. [8]

The character of some of the works published by Brewster, led the ambassador to suspect that others, still more obnoxious to his master, had been published by him. Accordingly he reported as such to his court, among those we have already noticed, two others [9] on grounds of suspicion. But in respect to neither of them was there proof presented. Of the one most obnoxious, we have direct incidental proof to the contrary. [10]

But William Brewster must be sought for; his publishing house closed, and he if found committed to prison. On the 22d July (1619) the ambassador reported: "A William Brewster, a Brownist, hath been for some years an inhabitant and printer at Leyden, but is now within three weeks removed from thence, and gone back to dwell in London, where he may be found out and examined." Again, August 20th: "I have made good inquiry after William Brewster, at Leyden, and am well assured that he is not returned thither; neither is it likely he will, having removed from thence both his family and goods."

And again, September 12: "In my last I advertised your honor that Brewster was taken at Leyden; which proved an error, in that the schout who was employed by the magistrates for his apprehension, being a dull drunken fellow, took one man for another." [11]

Among the facts here reported, are some particulars, which were more than Sir Dudley knew. And well it is that, even in these apparently small matters, we have other accurate history to correct the errors. Elder Brewster had indeed gone to London; and there had been, not three weeks merely as above, but for some five months. [12] And he was there, not on account of the ambassador's movements in respect to him, but for other purposes than Sir Dudley appears to have known or suspected.

But who were the *friends* that furnished the means for this printing establishment? And what were the consequences to them? The ambassador's letters give the answer in respect to the chief of them. "Thomas Brewer (says he), a professed Brownist, [13] a gentleman of a good house, both of land and living, a man of means, and who bore the charge, is apprehended, and being a university man, is made fast in the university prison." "The printing house, which was not an open shop, was also searched; the types, books, and papers were seized and searched as well as sealed." After undergoing inquisitorial scrutiny, and all without criminating proof. Brewer himself was "remanded into England."

Here, however, the officers of the University took their stand, claiming the exercise of their chartered rights. And the ambassador, unable to prevail as he wished on account of the popular opposition, yielded to a compromise. Brewer, in prison, harassed, importuned, and not knowing how long this might be continued, at length consented to go "of his own accord" to England to be examined in the matter, and to go, not as a prisoner, but as a freeman, in charge of some confidential person, and not to be ill used in body or goods, nor placed in any common prison, but suffered to return in due time, and not at his own charge. [14] The ambassador concurring, and giving pledge accordingly, and promising particular favor if all was done as desired, Brewer departed for England, and was favorably received and finally discharged, much to the satisfaction of the officers of the University, though, it would seem, not to the full content of Sir Dudley. [15] Such was the treatment of Brewster's friend. Had Brewster been found at Leyden, the facts show what treatment he would have received from the same source.

It was only one of the thousand attempts to control, by arbitrary force, the freedom of the press. That great principle, or axiom, had not yet been conceived, or, if conceived, had not been acted upon, that truth, in man's present state — all contested truth — *must* come into full, free, open, unrestricted conflict with error, and that this conflict must be gone through in order that truth may be felt to be truth, and that it may not only have, but *be seen* to have, the victory. Any forced checks upon such full, free, candid discussion, only *delay* the victory of truth; all arbitrary restraints upon *press* or *speech* but retard its final triumph. Every historic instance proclaims this fact.

The only check which the case justly admits is as to *manner* and *temper;* and that check should be firm and effective. It is unlicensed manner, and uncontrolled temper, not free discussion, that cause the mischief. Truth has nothing to fear. Is error at times mighty? It is might "stolen from *seeming truth.*" Truth itself is mightier; partaking of the nature, it has also the power and pledged support of Him who is almighty.

[1] Mather's Magnalia, Belknap, and others.
[2] Bradford, pp. 412, 413.
[3] "Commentarii Succincti et Delucidi in Proverbia Salamonis. Authore Thoma Cartwrightio, S. S. Theologiae in Academià Canta brigiensi quondam Professore. Quibus adhibata est Praefatio clarissimi viri Johannis Poliandri, S. Theologiae Professoris Leidensis, Lugduni Batavorum. Apud Gulielmum Brewsterum in vico Chorali, 1617, 8vo.," pp. 1513. A copy of this work, and of this edition, was deposited, in 1828, with Dr. Kendall, Pastor at Plymouth, Mass. Another copy of the Amsterdam edition of 1638 is in the Pilgrim Hall, of the same place.
[4] The old church historian. Fuller, says: "Now came forth the Remish (Roman) translation of the New Testament. Secretary Walsingham solicited Mr. Thomas Cartwright to undertake the refuting of this Translation." To aid in the matter," he sent him an hundred pounds out of his own purse. Whitgift, learning what Cartwright was writing, prohibited his further proceeding therein. Many commended his care not to intrust the defence of the *doctrine* of England to a pen so disaffected to the *discipline* thereof. Others blamed his jealousy to deprive the Church of so learned pains of him whose judgment would so solidly, and affections so zealously, confute the public adversary. Distasteful passages might be expunged, whilst it was a pity so good fruit should be blasted in the bud for some bad leaves. Thus disheartened, Cartwright desisted; but afterwards, encouraged by a noble lord and others, he resumed and perfected the work as far as the 15th chapter of the Revelations." And, adds Fuller, "many years lay this worthy work neglected, and the copy mouse-eaten, whence the printer excused some defects in his edition, which, though late, came forth in the year 1618; a book which, notwithstanding the aforesaid defects, is so complete that the Remists durst never return the least answer thereto."
Fuller's Church History, vol. iii. pp. 68-70. Such was the work which Elder Brewster rescued and published this year at Leyden. A copy of this same edition (1618), by the Elder, without name, is in the Pilgrim Society Hall, Plymouth, New England. See also Strype's Whitgift, pp. 482, 484, and Sir Dudley Carleton's Letters, pp. 380, 390.
[5] "De vera et genua Jesu Christi Domini et Salvatoris nostri Religione," "1618, Sine Locum," says the Bodleian Catalogue, vol. iii. 254. The publishing of this, "Brewster doth avow," says Sir Dudley Carleton. Letters, p. 380. A copy of this, as well as of other works printed by him, appears to have been in the Elder's library at his decease,
[6] An original copy of this work is in the hands of Dr. Shurtleff, Boston, date 1618, name of place and publisher not given; but the date and evidences, internal and external, leave little or no doubt of its being from the Elder's press.
[7] "Amissii in Grevinchovium," by William Ames, at Leyden. We are not certain which of two kindred works of this noted writer is here meant. But from the title and dates and place of publication mentioned in the Bodleian Catalogue, we con-

clude it must have been that of 1617, or 1618. See said Catalogue, art. Ames, and Sir Dudley Carleton's Letters in respect to the writings of Ames.

[8] Sir Dudley Carleton's Letters to Secretary Naunton, July 22, and Sept. 12 and 18, 1619.

[9] De Regimine Ecclesise Scoticanae Brevis Relatio. To this treatise there was a reply by Archbishop Spotiswood. Of its publication by Brewster, we have said there was only suspicion. Sir Dudley does not even speak confidently.

[10] Of this most offensive treatise, "The Perth Assembly," Winslow, who was then present and one of the chief men of the company, and who would have known whether or not the suspicion had any foundation, states incidentally that it was published by a certain minister from Scotland. Winslow's Brief Narration, in Young, p. 395. Sir Dudley's Letters, July 22, Sept. 12 and 18, 1619.

[11] Sir Dudley's Letters to Secretary Naunton, 380, 386, 389.

[12] Bradford, p. 30; and in Young,   pp. 57, 68, 71. In a note, Dr. Young says Cushman and Brewster were sent (by the Leyden emigrants as their agents to England) in February, 1619, and returned late in the same year, p. 59. His remark at bottom of p. 468 differs, indeed, from this, as to the Elder's return, but without evidence.

[13] Letters, pp. 389, 393,395, 398, &c. We cannot but notice how often, by way of stigma, Sir Dudley uses the reproachful term Brownist, showing how little he knew really of the faith and principles of these men, much less of their aims, and what might be the final results.

[14] Do., Letters, pp. 395, 398.

[15] Do., pp. 406, 423, 482, &c. He went in the care of Sir William Zouch.

Chapter Sixteen – 1617-1619

The world was all before them, where to choose
Their place of rest, and Providence their guide.   — Milton.

We have said that Elder Brewster was in England, and for a very important purpose. It was a purpose which, if carried into successful execution, would change his own entire temporal condition, and that of the people with whom he was connected.

Early in the year 1617, we trace the beginnings of thought in his own and his pastor's mind, which, at length, grew into a conviction, that Holland was not suited to their habits, and could not meet their desires, as a permanent home. *Nine* years of trial and experience had they already passed through, and eight of them in Leyden. In this time, some of their number had been re- moved by death, others were becoming advanced in years. The "twelve years' truce" between the States and Spain would, before long, come to a close, [1] when the long bloody war might again be resumed, and they might be involved in its calamities. "Taught by experience (say they), our prudent governors (their pastor and ruling elder), with some of the sagest members, began deeply to apprehend, and wisely to foresee, the dangers, and to think of a timely remedy." [2]

In the "agitation of thought, and after much discourse" (at first in private conference), the inclination for removal became strong; "not (says one of them) out of any newfangledness, or other such like giddy humor, by which men are oftentimes transported to their great hurt and danger, but for sundry weighty and solid reasons."

"First, the hardness of their present place and country, to them so great, that few would come to continue with them; while, could a place of better and easier living be found, such discouragements would be removed."

"Second, though in general their people bore all difficulties cheerfully and resolutely in their best strength, old age was coming on some; great and continued labors and trials were hastening it before its time on others." It was, therefore, apparent that in the then state of things there was danger of ere long being "scattered, or of sinking under their burdens."

"Third, over them was the task-master Necessity, forcing them to become task-masters not only to servants, but, in a measure, to their children, wounding the heart of many a father and mother, and producing sad consequences. Children of best dispositions and gracious inclinations, who were learning to bear the yoke in their youth, and willing to share in their parents' labors, were yet, at times, so oppressed with labor, that, though with minds free and willing, their bodies became bowed under the weight and early disfigured, the vigor of nature being exhausted in the very bud." But what was to them of all sorrows the heaviest to be borne, "many of their children, by the surrounding temptations, and the great licentiousness of the youth of the country, and their evil example, were drawn away, grew headstrong, leaving their parents, some becoming soldiers, others sailing on far-distant voyages, others taking to worse courses, to their parents' grief, their souls' danger, and the dishonor of God, all foreboding a degenerate and corrupt posterity." [3]

To these reasons were added "their great desire to live under the protection of England, and to retain the language and the name of Englishmen;" likewise "their inability here to give their children such an education as they had themselves received;" also "their grief at the profanation of the Sabbath in Holland." [4]

But the last, not least, of the reasons was (and the Christian's heart warms at the noble sentiment), "A great hope and inward zeal they had of laying some good foundation, or, at least, to make some way thereunto, for propagating and advancing the Gospel of the kingdom of Christ in those remote parts of the world; yea, though they should be but *stepping-stones* unto others for the performing of so great a work." [5]

Such were their principal reasons for removing from Holland. The deep feeling and discussions on the subject by the pastor and elder, and other chief members, had been confidentially and discreetly kept from the public until some wise and feasible course could be resolved upon. On the subject being made known and generally discussed, many and various were the opinions, many the doubts and fears. [6] Some, for well-weighed reasons, and with hopes of the future, though distant, advocated at once the founding of a new settlement by themselves in some newly discovered portion of the earth, beyond the seas; and they labored to arouse and encourage others accordingly.

Others raised objections, and sought to divert attention from the project, alleging "it was a great design, subject to inconceivable dangers, to the casualties and hardships of the sea, unendurable by their aged and feeble men and women, the liability to famine, destitution and want, to sickness from change of climate and diet and only water to drink. And should all this be overcome, there was still the exposure to the barbarous and treacherous savages, who, unreliable as friends, and merciless as enemies, were not content to kill, but must cruelly torment, roast, and eat the flesh of their victims, with other practices too horrible to be contemplated."

It was objected further, that for such a voyage and its bare necessaries, larger sums would be required than the sale of all their possessions could procure. And yet supplies must also be provided for the future as well as for the present. Added to these, were the ill success and lamentable miseries that had lately befallen others on the American coast. And, had they not already been taught a lesson of caution by bitter experience in coming into Holland, the hardships here endured, even in this civilized, enlightened, and rich, though stranger land, in securing a comfortable living? What then must be the trials when away, few and solitary, in a far-off wilderness? [7]

To all of which objections it was answered: "All great and honorable actions are accompanied with great difficulties, difficulties to be met and conquered with corresponding courage. Granting the dangers to be great, they were not desperate; and the difficulties to be many, they were not invincible; many of them *probable* only, not *certain*. Some things feared might never befall them; others by providence, care, and good use of means, might in a great measure be prevented; all of them by fortitude, patience, and divine help, could be borne, or overcome."

"True, such attempts were not to be made but upon good grounds and urgent reasons, not rashly or lightly, or from curiosity or hope of gain, as with many." Besides, their condition was not ordinary; their ends were good and honorable; their calling lawful and urgent; therefore they might look for God's blessing upon their undertaking. Should they lose their lives therein, yet could they have comfort; their endeavors were upright. They now lived here but as men in exile, in poor condition. The twelve years' truce having nearly expired, as great miseries might here befall them, amid the preparations for war, and its always uncertain events; while the Spaniard might prove as cruel as the savages of America; and the famine and pestilence as sore here with less liberty in providing a remedy.

Such, and other like things being alleged and answered, the "major part determined to put the design into execution; and by the best means in their power."

But to what country should they go? First, every movement in the matter was begun and ended in prayer. Too deep were the interests involved, and the consequences were too lasting, for Christians to do otherwise. Next by mutually and openly conferring together, and casting their thoughts abroad over the world, they examined the advantages and disadvantages of the many places suggested.

Some, and they not the meanest of the company, were earnest for Guiana, a country lately discovered or explored by Sir Walter Raleigh, and by him described in glowing colors, as a country most to be desired, lying between the Amazon and the Orinoco, in South America. Its rich plains with finest grass, its goodly groves, its beautiful hills and vales, and flowing streams, its flocks of gentle deer, the sweet music of its birds issuing from every tree, its gentle eastern gales, its very stones rich with the promise of mineral stores — all constituted "a region which (says Sir Walter) I am resolved cannot be equalled, for health, air, riches, pleasure, by any region either east or west." [8] It was the very El Dorado of the Spaniards; and here had the English, as well as the Dutch, their claims.

Others of the company were in favor of some part of Virginia, where English settlements had already been commenced. [9]

Respecting Guiana it was answered, that though the country was unquestionably fruitful and pleasant, and might more easily than any other yield maintenance and riches, yet the heats of a tropical climate, and exposures to diseases there prevalent, were ill suited to English constitutions. And even were they there, and well established, the jealous Spaniard would not suffer them to remain long in peace, and might destroy them in their weak estate, as he had the French in Florida. [10]

Respecting Virginia, the answer was, that the Church of England was there exclusively established, and there they might be in danger of troubles or persecutions, with less opportunity of defence than in England itself. Thus there were objections and difficulties on every side.

But at length they arrived at this conclusion — To apply to the Virginia Company, of London, for a grant to plant themselves separately under its general government, and petition his majesty for a grant of liberty or "freedom of religion." To this course were they encouraged by prospects of favor and aid from persons high in rank and influence, among whom were Sir Edwin Sandys, Elder Brewster's faithful and highly esteemed friend, and Sir Robert Naunton, the principal Secretary of State. [11]

Accordingly, in the autumn of 1617, were two messengers sent to London, to make application to the Virginia Company. These found the Virginia Company desirous to arrange with them, and willing to grant a patent with as ample privileges, and to further their enterprise as far, as was in their power.

Some chief men of the company believed their suit to his majesty for liberty in religion, confirmed by the King's broad seal, could also be obtained. This latter application, however, though supported by the Secretary of State and others, of high influence with the King and the archbishop, failed of success, though they prevailed so far as to be assured "that his majesty would connive at them, and not molest them, provided they carried themselves peaceably." [12]

This being all that they could then obtain, the agents returned to Leyden, and reported the whole state of the matter, with their difficulties, and the efforts of their worthy friends in their behalf; also the advice of those friends to go forward in their enterprise.

It was the month of November; and on the messengers' return to Leyden, Sir Edwin Sandys sent, and probably by them to their pastor, and the Elder, the following truly Christian and encouraging letter; expressive of his warm continued friendship for Brewster with his pastor, and of his deep interest and readiness to aid in their proposed undertaking. The letter with the annexed answer, throws much light upon this important period of Brewster's and this people's history.

To Mr. John Robinson and Mr. William Brewster.

After my hearty salutations.

The agents of your congregation, Robert Cushman, and John Carver, have been in communication with divers select gentlemen of his majesty's council for Virginia; and by the writing of seven articles, [13] subscribed with your names, have given them that good degree of satisfaction, which hath carried them on with a resolution to set forward your desire in the best sort that may be for your own and the public good; divers particulars whereof we leave to their faithful report, having carried themselves here with that good discretion as is both to their own, and their credit from whom they came. And whereas, being to treat for a multitude of people, they have requested further time to confer with them that are to be interested in this action, about the several particulars, which in the prosecution thereof, will fall out considerable, it hath been very willingly assented unto; and so they do now return unto you. If therefore it may please God so to direct your desires, as that on your parts there fall out no just impediments, I trust by the same direction it shall likewise appear that on our parts all forwardness to set you forward — shall be found in the best sort which with reason may be expected. And so I betake you with this design (which I hope verily is the work of God) to the gracious protection and blessing of the Highest.

Your loving friend,
Edwin Sandys.

London, Nov. 12th, 1617.

To Sir Edwin, the pastor and elder returned the following answer.

Right Worshipful,

Our humble duties remembered, in our own, our messengers, and our church's name, with all thankful acknowledgment of your singular love, expressing itself as otherwise, so more especially in your great care and earnest endeavor of our good in this weighty business about Virginia; which the less able we are to requite, we shall think ourselves the more bound to commend in our prayers unto God for recompense; whom as for the present you rightly behold in our endeavors, so shall we not be wanting on our parts (the same God assisting us) to return all answerable fruit and respect unto the labor of your love bestowed upon us.

We have, with the best speed and consideration withal that we could, set down our requests in writing, subscribed, as you willed, with the hands of the greatest part of our congregation; and have sent the same unto the Council by our agent, a deacon of our church, John Carver; unto whom we have also requested a gentleman of our company to adjoin himself; to the care and discretion of which two we do refer the prosecuting of the business. Now, we persuade ourselves, right worshipful, that we need not to provoke your godly and loving mind to any further or more tender care of us; since you have pleased so far to interest us in yourself, that, under God, above all persons and things in the world, we rely upon you, expecting the care of your love, the counsel of your wisdom, and the help and countenance of your authority.

Notwithstanding, for your encouragement in the work so far as probabilities may lead, we will not forbear to mention these instances of inducement:

1st. We verily believe and trust the Lord is with us; unto whom and whose service we have given ourselves in many trials, and that he will graciously prosper our endeavors according to the simplicity of our hearts therein.

2d. We are well weaned from the delicate milk of our mother country, and inured to the difficulties of a strange and hard land, which yet, in great part, we have by patience overcome.

3d. The people are, for the body of them, industrious and frugal, we think we may safely say, as any company of people in the world.

4th. We are knit together as a body in a more strict and sacred bond and covenant of the Lord, of the violation whereof we make great conscience, and by virtue whereof we do hold ourselves strictly tied to all care of each other's good, and of the whole, by every one, and so mutually.

5th, and lastly. It is not with us as with other men, whom small things can discourage, or small discontentments cause to wish themselves at home again. We know our entertainment in England and Holland.

We shall much prejudice both our arts and means by removal; if we should be driven to return, we should not hope to recover our present helps and comforts, neither indeed look ever to attain the like in any other place during our lives, which are now drawing towards their periods.

These motives we have been bold to tender unto you, which you in your wisdom may also impart to any other our worshipful friends of the Council with you, of all whose godly disposition and loving towards our despised persons, we are most glad, and shall not fail by all good means to continue and increase the same.

We shall not be further troublesome, but do, with the renewed remembrance of our humble duties to your worship, and (so far as in modesty we may be bold) to any other of our well-willers of the Council with you, we take our leaves, committing your persons and counsels to the guidance and protection of the Almighty.

Your much bounden in all duty.

JOHN ROBINSON.
WILLIAM BREWSTER.

Leyden, *the* 15th *of December*, 1617.

[1] This truce was signed April 9th, 1609, to end at the close of that month, in 1621.

[2] Bradford, p. 22, and Winslow in Young, pp. 381-2.

[3] Bradford, pp. 22-24.

[4] Winslow's Brief Narrative, in Young, pp. 381-2. Of the profanation of the Sabbath, the English divines took notice, and the Assembly, at the Synod of Dort. Even Sir Dudley Carleton reported: "It falls out in these towns of Holland that Sunday, which is elsewhere the day of rest, proved always the day of labor; for they never knew yet how to observe the Sabbath." — Letters to Secretary Naunton, p. 380.

[5] Bradford, p. 24. These were the reasons, as given by them selves, for removing from Holland. That they were the true reasons and all-sufficient, can never be doubted by any who have examined the original authorities in the case. Douglas, Chalmers, in his Annals of Virginia, Robertson, of Scotland, and others, not having the original sources of information, misled all who copied their statements. Even Chief Justice Marshall was, at first, in his Life of Washington, led into error by those writers; but after he had obtained the facts, as his impartial mind ever would do, he corrected the error. See his History of the American Colonies, p. 78; also Dr. Young's Summary, note, p. 48, of his Chrons. of the Pilgrims.

[6] Ibid., p. 25, and Winslow, p. 382.

[7] Such as the attempted settlement at Sagadahock, under the patronage of Chief Justice Popham; and other sad failures after great sufferings and losses.

[8] Bradford, p. 27; Raleigh's Works, vol. viii. Guiana.

[9] The first permanent settlement at Jamestown, was in 1607, about the time of the removal of our Leyden Company from England to Holland.

[10] Bradford, p. 28. The massacre was that of French Huguenots in E. Florida, in 1650. On the choice and comparative advantages of a Northern or a Southern and Tropical location, 'the discussion of which we have just noticed,' the author remembers a spirited debate, at a complimentary dinner in Florida at the residence of the Judge of the Western District. It was observed by a distinguished officer of the American army: "I think we owe no great thanks to our forefathers, for settling in the cold bleak region, and on the hard soil of the North; when they could have chosen for themselves the rich soil, the easy living, the choice fruits, and the greater wealth of the Tropical climates." It was answered by way of in-

quiry: "In what consists the best good, truest eminence — the highest glory of a people? Is it in the ease, the pleasure, the luxury, the rapidly acquired wealth, just mentioned? These are usually followed by enervation of mind and body, as experience has proved. Is it not rather in the fruits and rewards of industrious — if you please, of necessitous exertions? exertion calling into vigorous exercise every faculty of mind and body; taxing the energies in all the ways of culture, of invention, of scientific discoveries; resulting in the noblest productions of each? Is it not under such circumstances, that true patriotism, the higher virtues, and the spirit of the Christian religion are more fully developed?" "It may be so," was the answer.

[11] Bradford, 29, and notes, Other names may be added, as Sir John Wolston-holme, Sir Fulke Greville, the chancellor, after wards Lord Brooke.

[12] Bradford, p. 29. Winslow relates that when Sir Robert Naunton was urging with James the request of the Leyden Company, "to live under his government and protection, and to enjoy liberty of conscience in America," adding that "they could not live so comfortably under any other government," and that their endeavor would be the advancement of his majesty's dominions, and the enlargement of the Gospel by all due means; "his majesty said, this was a good and honest motion, and asked what profits might arise therefrom in the region intended." To which it was answered — fishing. To which he replied, with his usual asseveration." So God have my soul, 'tis an honest trade; 'twas the apostle's own calling." — Winslow, in Young, pp. 382, 383.

[13] See these seven articles, Chap, xxvii. They were lately recovered from oblivion by Mr. Bancroft, from the state paper office, England.

Chapter Seventeen – 1619-1620

Men judge actions always by events:
But when we manage by a just foresight,
Success is prudence, and possession right.   — Higgons.

The letter of Sir Edwin Sandys to the pastor and elder at Leyden having been answered, the bearers of that answer to London were empowered to use all suitable means to procure the desired charter, with defined religious privileges. [1]

But the affairs of the Virginia Company in London were becoming daily more and more complicated, and the conflicting movements of its honorable Council involved in discouraging difficulties. [2]

At the same time, his majesty's Privy Council commenced action on the subject of the Leyden people. Certain of its honorable members, who had received some unfavorable impressions respecting them, "desired of them further explanations," especially on three particular points.

Mr. Robinson and Brewster, "grieved that such unjust insinuations had been made against them," yet "glad of the opportunity of clearing themselves in the matter," immediately furnished a statement of their principles and views as desired.

Their statement was in two forms or "declarations," accompanied by the *following letter,* addressed to Sir John Wolstenholme, a friend of their proposed enterprise, and one of the principal members of the Virginia Council:

Right Worshipful:
With due acknowledgments of our thankfulness for your singular care and pains in the business of Virginia, for our, and we hope the common good, we do remember our humble duties unto you, and have sent, as is desired, a further explanation of our judgments in the three points specified by some of his majesty's honorable Privy Council. And although it be grievous unto us that such unjust insinuations are made against us, yet we are most glad of the occasion of making our just purgation unto the so honorable personages. The declarations we have sent inclosed; the one more brief and general, which we think the fitter to be presented, the other something more large, and in which we express some small accidental differences, which, if it seem good unto you and other of our worshipful friends, you may send instead of the former. Our prayer unto God is that your worship may see the fruit of your worthy endeavors, which on our parts we shall not fail to further by all good means in us. And so praying that you would please, with the convenientest speed that may be, to give us knowledge of the success of the business with his majesty's Privy Council, and accordingly what your further pleasure is, either for our direction or furtherance in the same, so we rest.

Your worships in all duty,

JOHN ROBINSON.
WILLIAM BREWSTER. [3]

Leyden, *Jan.* 27.
Ano. 1617, Old Style. [4]

THE FIRST BRIEF STATEMENT

Touching the ecclesiastical ministry, namely, of pastors for teaching, ciders for ruling, and deacons for distributing the church's contribution, as also for the two Sacraments, baptism, and the Lord's Supper, we do wholly and in all points agree with the French Reformed Churches, according to their public confession of faith.

The oath of supremacy we shall willingly take if it be required of us, and that convenient satisfaction be not given by our taking the oath of allegiance. [5]

JOHN ROBINSON.
WILLIAM BREWSTER.

THE SECOND WAS AS FOLLOWS:—

Touching the ecclesiastical ministry, &c., as in the former, we agree in all things with the French Reformed Churches, according to their public confession of faith; though some small differences are to be found in our practices, not at all in the substance of the things, but only in some accidental circumstances.

1. As first, their ministers do pray with their heads covered, ours uncovered.

2. We choose none for Governing Elders but such as are able to teach; which ability they do not require.

3. Their elders and deacons are annual, or, at most, for two or three years; ours perpetual.

4. Our elders do administer their office in admonitions and excommunications for public scandals publicly and before the congregation; theirs more privately, and in their consistories.

5. We do administer baptism only to such infants as whereof the one parent, at the least, is of some church, which some of their churches do not observe, though in it our practice accords with their public confession, and the judgment of the most learned amongst them. Other differences, worthy mentioning, we know none in these points.

Then about the oath, as in the former.

(Subscribed)   JOHN R(OBINSON.)

W(ILLIAM) B(REWSTER.) [6]

On the reception of these communications in England, and while the agents and friends of the Leyden people were taking every opportunity to forward their application, untoward occurrences in the Virginia Council baffled all their efforts. "So disturbed had the company and council become by factions and dissensions among themselves" that nothing else could receive attention. In this state of things, long and sadly were the hopes of this people delayed. Messengers passed and repassed for furthering their purpose, but all to little effect. To their great discouragement, affairs were at a stand. [7]

In the mean time, Sir Edwin Sandys was "chosen treasurer and governor" of the company. [8]

Amidst these great discouragements, and the sad contests in the Virginia Company, the Leyden people delegated their ruling elder to unite with Mr. Cushman in their pending, and now to them most important negotiation. Hence the cause of his absence from Leyden, when Sir Dudley Carleton sought for him, and his continued absence from February until late in the autumn of 1619, perhaps longer. [9]

In his abilities, discretion, and integrity, they had the fullest confidence. In experience in public life, and in knowledge of men and things, he had among them no equal. While the mutual friendship between the Elder and Sir Edwin, and the deep interest of the latter in the success of their contemplated purpose, rendered this appointment most opportune.

During this summer, then, and amidst the continued conflicts and delays mentioned, the Elder was in London with his powerful friends and the other agent, furthering their application for a patent, and awaiting the issue. While there, he appears to have written letters full and explicit, respecting the whole matter. Our knowledge of them now, however, comes from the communication of the other messenger. "I doubt not but Mr. Brewster hath written to Mr. Robinson. But I think myself bound also to do something, lest I be thought to neglect you." Again, "Mr. Brewster is not well at this time; whether he will come back to you, or go into the north, I yet know not." Finally, "Having summarily pointed at things which Mr. Brewster (I think) hath more largely written of to Mr. Robinson, I leave you to the Lord's protection." "London, May 8, Ano. 1619." [10]

At length, they succeeded in obtaining the long desired patent. It was granted under the seal of the Old Virginia Company of London, "not in any of their own names, but, by the advice of some friends, in the name of Mr. John Wincob (a gentleman in the service of the Countess of Lincoln), who intended to go with them." [11]

On obtaining the patent, with the previous assurance of the King's connivance as to religious liberty, the Elder and his associate appear to have returned very soon to Leyden. [12] Along with the patent, came propositions from such merchants and friends in London, as would either go themselves, or adventure with them, and on whom they might depend for means and shipping. At the same time, the people were requested to prepare for their departure with all speed.

On receipt of these, a solemn assembly was called, for the purpose of humbly seeking God's gracious guidance. No important step would they take in the matter without thus publicly asking Divine direction. Their pastor addressed them in a manner suited to their condition, bringing before them considerations calculated to strengthen them against their fears, and to encourage them in their resolutions.

The question was next taken, who should go first, and who should remain; those to go to offer themselves freely. It being the minor part that offered themselves, as they only could at first be ready, they desired their ruling elder, Brewster, to go with them officially, as their spiritual guide; to which assent was given, he having himself resolved, with them, to enter upon this great work. [13] It was also covenanted that the minor part, on going, should be an absolute church of themselves, as well as those who remained, the difference in number not being great; also, that if any of those remaining should come to them, or if any of themselves should return, "they should be reputed as members" still with either. And the promise of those remaining to those going was, "The Lord giving them life, means, and opportunity, they would come also as soon as they could." [14]

About this period, certain merchants and others, in Holland, "made them large offers to induce them to go into Zealand," "or to go under them to Hudson's River," whither they would freely transport them, and furnish every family with cattle and other conveniences. [15]

But an agent arriving from London at this time, a Mr. Weston, in behalf of himself and certain merchant adventurers, persuaded them, after much intercourse, to set aside all other proposals, as he, and those adventurers and friends, would provide the shipping, money, and whatever was needful, for their removal. Accordingly, at his suggestion, articles of agreement were drawn up for the purpose, and approved by both parties, and a messenger was dispatched with them to London, with instructions to receive the money, arrange for shipping, and all else for the voyage. Those who were to go prepared with all speed, selling their estates, and putting their money into a common stock, under the direction of appointed managers. Stringent, indeed, were the conditions of the agreement finally required by the London agent; yet harder were two modifications afterwards admitted by their own agent to suit the "merchant adventurers," though without authority from the company at Leyden. [16]

Now, however, a new trouble arose. A new company was formed in England, with a grant from the King, of the northern part of what had been under the Virginia grant, and this, with other tracts, was henceforth to be named New England. In consequence, some were now for uniting with this new company, while some in England, that were to go with them, declined; other merchants and friends, that had offered to adventure means, withdrew, presenting excuses,, some because they would not go to Guiana, others because they would go to Virginia, while others would do nothing if they went not to Virginia. [17]

"In the midst of these distractions, they of Leyden who had put off their estates, and laid out their money, were brought into great straits, greatly fearing the issue to which things might come." [18]

Yet the great cause of discontent was the altering of the conditions of the agreement, at Leyden, by their agent in London, to meet the demands of the merchant adventurers. That the reader may have a view of them as thus altered, they are presented below. [19]

The oppressive modifications were that all their houses and improved lands, even home lots and gardens, were to belong to the company of adventurers and planters, to be divided, as all other property, at the end of seven years; and that, instead of having two days in a week for their own private employment, for the comfort of themselves and families, the whole six days should be devoted wholly to the common service.

To such conditions were the Elder and his company constrained to submit, in order to their transportation, and this for a settlement in the far off wilds of the new hemisphere.

The month of June had arrived, and yet additional trials, of faith and patience, must be endured. Between the differences of those who received the funds and made outlays for provisions, and the long delays by Mr. Weston in providing shipping, precious time was lost, and piteous was the case of many who had embarked their little all in the enterprise. [20]

At length, after hindrances and trials more numerous than have been mentioned, [21] preparations were concluded, and notice accordingly sent to Leyden.

A small ship, the Speedwell, of about sixty tons burden, was purchased, and fitted in Holland; while the Mayflower, of one hundred and eighty tons, was hired in London. All being ready at Leyden, they passed another day in deep devotion, their pastor addressing them from the words of the Prophet, "I proclaimed a fast, that we might humble ourselves before our God, and seek of him a right way for us, and for our children, and for all our substance," [22] words aptly suited to the occasion; and on which "he dwelt most impressively and profitably, a good portion of the day."

Says Winslow, who was present, "among other wholesome instructions and exhortations, he used these or like expressions. * * Being now ere long to part asunder, and the Lord knowing whether ever he should live to see our faces again, he charged us before God and his blessed angels, to follow him no further than he followed Christ: and if God should reveal anything to us by any other instrument of his, to be as ready to receive it as ever we were to receive any truth by his ministry; for he was very confident the Lord had more truth and light yet to break forth out of his Holy Word.

"He took occasion also miserably to bewail the state and condition of the reformed churches, who were come to a period in religion, and would go no further than the instruments of their reformation. As, for example, the Lutherans — they could not be drawn to go beyond, what Luther saw: for whatever part of God's will he had further imparted, and revealed to Calvin, they will rather die than embrace it. And so also, the Calvinists, they stick where he left them; a misery much to be lamented; for though they were precious lights in their times, yet God had not revealed his whole will to them; and were they now living, they would be as ready and willing to embrace further light, as that they had received.

"He also put us in mind of our church covenant, at least that part of it whereby we promise and covenant with God, and one with another, to receive whatsoever light or truth shall be made known to us from His written word; but withal exhorted us to take heed what we received for truth, and well to examine and compare it, and weigh it, with other Scriptures of truth, before we receive it. For, saith he, it is not possible, the Christian world should come so lately out of such thick anti-christian darkness, and that full perfection of knowledge should break forth at once.

"Another thing he commended to us, that we should use all means to avoid and shake off the name of Brownist, being a mere nickname and brand, to make religion and the professors of it, odious to the Christian world. 'And to that end,' said he, 'I should be glad if some godly minister would go over with you before my coming; for there will be no difference between the unconformable ministers and you, when they come to the practice of the ordinances out of the kingdom.' So (he) advised us by all means to endeavor to close with the godly part of the kingdom of England, and rather to study union than division; to wit, how near we might possibly without sin close with them, than in the least measure to effect division or separation from them. And be not loth to take another pastor or teacher, for that flock that hath two shepherds is not endangered but secured by it."

Such were the expanded views and teachings of the pastor of this Leyden Company, Such were doubtless the views of Brewster. And to show that they partook not of the spirit of the "rigid Separatists," Winslow testifies on another occasion: "If any joining us formerly, and with the manifestation of their faith, and profession, held forth separation from the Church of England, I have divers times heard either Mr. Robinson, our pastor, or Mr. Brewster, our elder, stop them forthwith, showing them that we required no such things at their hands; but only to hold faith in Christ Jesus, holiness in the fear of God, and submission to every ordinance and appointment of God; leaving the Church of England to themselves and to the Lord, before whom they should stand or fall, and to whom we ought to pray to reform what was amiss amongst them." [23]

[1] Bradford, 31, 36. Those who bore this answer constituted the 2d agency.
[2] Ibid., 36, 37.
[3] Bradford's History, 33, 34.
[4] 1618, New Style.
[5] See p. 34, and Hallam, on these oaths; Constitutional History, p. 73, note, Harper's ed.
[6] Bradford, 34, 35.
[7] The occasion of this great trouble in the Virginia Company, (says Cushman, one of the Leyden agents), was this: "Sir Thomas Smith, who had all along been the governor and treasurer of the company, and held, at the time, other high offices, repining under his burthens and troubles, and wishing the company to ease him of this office, the company took the occasion to choose Sir Edwin Sandys in his stead. The votes were, for Sir Edwin, 60, for Sir John Wolstenholme, 16, Alderman Johnston, 24. Sir Thomas, finding that he had lost some portion of his honors, became angry, and raised a faction to contest the election. In the heat of this contest they were neither ready nor fit to engage in business." "What will be the issue," adds Cushman, "is yet uncertain. It is most likely Sir Edwin will carry the day; and if so, things will go well in Virginia; otherwise, they will go ill enough." Letter in Bradford, p. 37; note in Young, 68, 69. Chalmers' Annals of Virginia.
[8] Sir Edwin was elected April 28, 1619.
[9] See Bradford, pp. 30, 36, 38, 43, Notes. Young's Notes, pp. 57, 59.
[10] Cushman's Letter in Bradford, pp. 36-38.
[11] "But he never went." (Bradford, p. 41.) This countess was a lady eminent for piety and intelligence, and a friend to the cause. Two of her daughters, Susan and Arabella, married two of the subsequent principal colonists of Massachusetts. Lady Arabella died in 1630, about six weeks after her arrival, deeply lamented. A supposed reason why the patent was not taken in the name of the Leyden people

is, that they were not now within the English realm. This patent, in the end, after the emigrants failed to reach their intended location in North Virginia, near the mouth of the Hudson River, ceased to be of any further use. Young's Notes, pp. 74, 75.

[12] Winslow says expressly: "Our agents returning, we sought the Lord by a public and solemn fast;" these agents were now Brewster and Cushman, as just mentioned. In Bradford, the same is immediately afterwards implied. On deciding who were to remove, and who were to remain, "the greater number required the pastor to stay." "The other desired the Elder, Mr. Brewster, to go with them, which was also condescended unto." Again, says Winslow, "The minor part, with Mr. Brewster, resolved to enter upon this great work." (In Young, p. 384.) Dr. Young concludes (note on page 59): "Cushman and Brewster — sent in Feb., 1619 — returned late in the same year," and he admitted to the author, that Wier was right in his representation of the Elder in his admirable embarkation scene.

[13] Bradford, and Winslow's statements combined; see p. 42 of Bradford and Winslow in Young, p. 384, quoted preceding note 12.

[14] Bradford, 42; Winslow adds, "If the Lord frown upon our proceedings, then those that went were to return, and the brethren that remained were to assist and be helpful to them; but if God should be pleased to favor them that went, then they also should endeavor to help over such as were poor and ancient and willing to come." In Young, 383.

[15] Bradford, pp. 42, 43, and note; also 48, and particularly Winslow in Young, 385, and Broadhead's History of New York, 123, &c.

[16] Bradford, 43, 45.

[17] Ibid., 44, 45.

[18] Bradford, p. 45.

[19] "Ano. 1620. The adventurers and planters do agree that every person that goeth, being aged sixteen years and upward, be rated at ten pounds, and ten pounds to be rated a single share.

"That he that goeth in person, and furnisheth himself out with ten pounds, either in money or other provisions, be accounted as having twenty pounds in stock, and in the division shall receive a double share.

"The persons transported, and the adventurers, shall continue their joint stock and partnership together the space of seven years (except some unexpected impediment do cause the whole company to agree otherwise); during which time, all profits and benefits that are gotten by trade, traffic, trucking, working, fishing, or any other means, of any person or persons, shall remain still in the common stock until the division.

"That, at their coming there, they choose out such a number of fit persons as may furnish their ships and boats for fishing upon the sea; employing the rest in their several faculties upon the land, as building houses, tilling and planting the ground, and making such commodities as shall be most useful for the colony.

"That, at the end of the seven years, the capital and profits, viz., the houses, lands, goods, and chattels, be equally divided betwixt the adventurers and planters; which done, every man shall be free from other of them of any debt or detriment concerning this adventure.

"Whosoever cometh to the Colony hereafter, or putteth any into the stock, shall, at the end of the seven years, be allowed proportionably to the time of his so doing.

"He that shall carry his wife, children, or servants, shall be allowed for every person now aged sixteen years and upward, a single share in the division; or, if he provide them necessaries, a double share; or if they be between ten and sixteen years old, then two of them to be reckoned for a person, both in transportation and division.

"That such children that now go, and are under the age of ten years, have no other share in the division but fifty acres of unmanured land.

"That such persons as die before the seven years be expired, their executors to have their parts or share at the division, proportionably to the time of their life in the colony.

"That all such persons as are of this colony are to have their meat, drink, apparel, and all provisions, out of the common stock and goods of the said colony," Bradford, 45, 46.

[20] Bradford, pp. 48, 58.
[21] Ibid., 62.
[22] Bradford, p. 59.
[23] Winslow's Brief Narrative, in Young, 396, 399, and 400.

Chapter Eighteen - 1620

"A slow developed strength awaits
Completion in a painful school;
Phantoms of other forms of rule,
New majesties of mighty states."
        — Tennyson.

All things being ready, and the time having arrived for these voyagers to the New World to depart, those that were to remain, prepared a feast for those that were to go. It was at their "pastor's house, which was large," and where probably they had usually assembled for worship. "Earnest were the prayers for each other, and mutual the pledges." Tears flowed indeed; but they refreshed themselves with appropriate psalms, making melody in their hearts, as well as with the voice; "many of the congregation being very expert in music." "Indeed (said Winslow), it was the sweetest melody that ever mine ears heard!" [1] True was all this to the instincts of nature, under the guidance of grace. When deeply oppressed, the soul finds relief in devotion, and refreshment in melody, fitting melody, plaintive at first, to touch soothingly the cords of the sorrowing heart, then gradually merging into the animating, and then into the invigorating and soul-inspiring. Thus refreshed and strengthened to put in execution their great resolve, the departing company left Leyden for the haven of Delft, their place of embarkation; — left that "goodly and pleasant city," where for eleven years they had had their resting place, bidding adieu to loved countenances, sundering strong ties of attachment cemented by trials, and recollections of joys and sorrows past. No wonder, under the circumstances, that a deep feeling of loneliness came over them, as of "pilgrims" without country or home.

Pilgrims indeed they were; not in the classical sense, derived from heathen use, nor from the periods of the Church's sad declensions, nor as used in the romances of the crusades, nor in the sense of the devotees of the prophet of Mecca; but in the primary sense, as well as in the divinely inspired use — "Strangers and sojourners," "strangers and pilgrims on the earth." This was the inspired language to which their minds reverted when they declared that "they knew they were pilgrims here, and in the sorrow of departing lifted their eyes towards heaven as their dearest country, and quieted their spirits." [2]

On the 21st of July, 1620, they were on their way to Delft, and thence to the Haven of Delft, their brethren from Leyden accompanying them. [3] Arriving at Delft Haven, again their brethren prepared for them a social feast. "Little sleep was there to most of them that night." Friendly entertainment. Christian discourse, and expressions of deep affection in parting, "held their eyes waking." "Never," says Winslow, "I persuade myself, never people on earth lived more lovingly together, and parted more sweetly than we, the Church of Leyden." "Often seeking, not rashly. but deliberately, the mind of God in prayer, and finding His gracious presence with us, and His blessing upon us." [4]

Delft Haven

The morning of the 22d dawned upon them favorably. After prayer by their pastor, and many tears, they repaired to their little ship, lying at the

97

quay ready to receive them, accompanied not only by their brethren from Leyden, but by some even from Amsterdam, who had come to take leave of them (and to many it was a final leave). Going on board amidst sighs and sobs, their grief became too deep for utterance.

"Loath to separate, yet the wind being fair, and the tide admonishing, their pastor falls down upon his knees, and they all with him, while he, with watery cheeks, commends them most fervently to the Lord and his blessing." Then, with mutual embraces and short leave-takings, they part. With sails set, the ship recedes from the quay, while three volleys from the small arms and three pieces of ordnance announce their departure. [5]

The last silent tokens, as long as their eyes could discern them, were the lifting up of hands to each other, even as their hearts were for each to the Most High, while they passed out upon the broad Meuse, and were borne away to the sea. On shore, the pastor and the remainder of his saddened flock returned to Leyden, while the Dutch strangers, that stood on the quay as spectators, had not been able to refrain from "tears" at the view of that parting.

In all this, what must have been the emotions of their elder? Deeply must he have felt the responsibility of his position, while, as their spiritual leader and instructor, though a layman, he was now committed with them, and they with him, to the uncertainties of the voyage, and to the greater uncertainties and trials of a settlement beyond the seas, in a savage land.

Scarcely, however, could he have had time to collect his thoughts of the past, and of the memorable present, and to glance dimly at the future, when the Speedwell, with the pilgrim band, approached and passed the Briel. There, doubtless, he must have called to mind the time when, in younger years, he was with the ambassador while receiving possession of that town and its fortresses, and also when leaving the country for England and the court, himself buoyant with youthful hope, bearing the golden chain in token of faithful service, and with brightest prospects of advancement to higher positions.

What had he since passed through? What changes had been his? What strange contrasts in life? What unlooked-for occurrences? What, even in the past twelve years, in the land he was now leaving, ending with the last painful scene, this very day, at the Haven of Delft"?

But the Speedwell speeds rapidly on her course. Ere long, with "a prosperous wind," after a short passage, they are on the coast of England, and in the port of Southampton.

[1] Winslow in Young, p. 384.
[2] Bradford, p. 59. Objections have been made on classical grounds, to the use of the term *pilgrims*, and to its application to this people, but to little purpose.

The term is not Greek, or Roman, but of German or Belgic origin, from pelgrim (or Teutonic) pilgram. Its first and general meaning is, a traveller, a wanderer, also one who travels on a religious account, and one who, on that account, is a sojourner in another land. In accordance with this primary definition, is its use in our translation of the Old and New Testament; a sojourner and wanderer in another land; or, a sojourner on the earth in reference to a heavenly home. Accordingly, the terms, "strangers and sojourners," "strangers and pilgrims," are considered to be nearly synonymous, especially in Gen. xxii. 4; Ps. xxxix. 19; 1st Peter, ii. 11; Heb. xi. 13-16. In this sense it is used in that generally adopted hymn

—

"Guide me, O thou great Jehovah!
Pilgrim through this barren land."

In this sense only is it used in Bunyan's inimitable allegory. Such, also, is the use of the term pilgrimage. "Few and evil have been the days of the years of my pilgrimage."

Shakspeare used it with still greater license: "In prison thou hast spent a pilgrimage," and Dryden, "Painting is a long pilgrimage." The terms are extensively used indeed in a classical sense, as of journeying to some shrine for purposes of penance and devotion; as in heathen, Mohammedan, and corruptly Christian usage; but not such is its primitive, biblical, or Protestant application.

[3] The mode by which they were conveyed doubtless was by the "Trackchuit" (canal boat), the canal passing from Leyden directly through Delft to Delft Haven; this being then, and for ages since, the almost only mode of travelling in that country under like circumstances.

[4] In Young, pp. 88, 380.

[5] Bradford and Winslow. Of the "Embarkation of the Pilgrims" (the interesting scene of which has just been described), at superior historical painting, by Professor Wier, in the rotunda of our National Capitol at Washington, presents a most graphic and striking view. From it is the faithfully executed engraving for our frontispiece; which see.

The painter seized the moment when, on the deck of the Speedwell, just ready to depart, all were kneeling in prayer. True to history in minutest particulars, true to nature, and to the customs and costumes of the times, as well as true to the higher attainments of the art, this historical painting stands before us in this country for unrivalled.

The figure with outstretched hands and devout look, nearest the foreground of the central group, is Mr. Robinson, their pastor, earnestly commending them to the grace and blessing of the Almighty. He remained in Holland.

Their ruling elder, William Brewster, in like earnest devotion, is near the centre of this group, with open Bible in his hands, and a look of deep emotion, firm purpose, and holy trust.

Between these two is Mr. Carver, afterwards governor.

On the right and left of Carver are the youthful Bradford, subsequently governor, and his wife.

On the right of the elder are Mrs. Brewster and child, in feeble health.

Further to his right, in the foreground, and kneeling side by side, are Mr. and Mrs. White.

Prominent in the middle ground, on the elder's extreme right, are Mr. and Mrs. Winslow, she in bridal attire; and right and left of them, two lads under their care.

Back of the elder are Mr. Fuller, the physician, and his wife, to be separated for a season.

On the left of the pastor are Mrs. Carver, child, and boy.

Farthest on his left, and prominent in the foreground, is the brave Miles Standish, in military garb, with his beautiful wife Rose.

In the back ground, to the right of these, is seen the Captain of the Speedwell, giving orders to a seaman, while children, domestics, spectators, &c., in the distance, with various implements on the deck, fill up the scene.

But the painting must be studied to realize its truthfulness and excellence. As far as practicable, however, in so small a space, clear ideas of it may be gathered from the engraving for the frontispiece.

It should also be added here, that in England a painting has been executed on the subject of the "Departure of the Pilgrims." Of its merits, compared with that of our own countryman, we are unable to speak. Being, as we understand, a national work, it is undoubtedly worthy of the subject, and of the people who have called for its execution, and given it a location in their National Museum.

Chapter Nineteen – 1620

Perseverance is a Roman virtue,
And plucks success
E'en from the spear-proof crest of rugged danger. — Havard.

Arrived at Southampton, an ancient seaport on the southern coast of England, the Leyden Company met their companions and others with the larger ship, the Mayflower, from London. Joyful was their meeting, and mutual were the congratulations. Seven days had these friends been awaiting their arrival. [1]

Here were they again in England, the land of their birth, after twelve years of voluntary exile, for their distinctive views, in a land of strangers. Yet they had little time for reflection upon scenes and events and associations of early life: now was the time for stern resolve and action. [2] They were to leave again immediately as exiles for life, beyond the vast and yet seldom frequented ocean.

Proceeding with the necessary arrangements for the voyage, they authorized the needed outlays, and prepared to depart. In the meantime there arrived from Mr. Robinson, in Leyden, a most affectionate and earnest parting letter, which was read to the company, to the profit of many, and acceptance of all. And now on distributing the whole company on board the two ships, they chose for each a manager with assistants, to order the people and provisions, and all else of a like nature that might be for the best good of the whole. [3]

About the 5th of August, some thirteen days after their embarkation at Delft Haven, the pilgrim company, numbering, with the additions from London, about one hundred and twenty, set sail from Southampton. But further disappointments awaited them. Scarcely were they at sea, when the master of the Speedwell declared his ship to be so leaky, that he dare not proceed. [4] Both masters, on consultation, resolved to put into the harbor of Dartmouth, an old town of note on the southern coast of England. Here a week longer was passed during the Speedwell's repairs, an unexpected loss of time, as well as expenditure of means; after which both vessels again put to sea.

Nor was this all. After having proceeded over "a hundred leagues off the Land's End," the master of the Speedwell again complained of her leakage, and declared that he must return or sink. Upon this, both vessels put back into the harbor of Plymouth, another port on the southwestern coast of England; which, for beauty of situation, strength, wealth, and historic incident, had no rival in that part of the kingdom. Judging the Speedwell to be unseaworthy, they there dismissed her. Those who "were willing," and some who "were weakest," though it was grievous and discouraging, went back to London, in all about twenty, Mr. Cushman and family being of the number. The others joined those in the Mayflower, arranging themselves and provisions as they could. [5]

September the 6th, after kind treatment from friends at that place, and another sad parting, the now entire Mayflower company set sail again. [6]

Henceforth, few things are known of what took place on board during their long and dreary voyage. The few facts recorded, however, furnish some interesting insight into their condition and trials on the deep.

One hundred passengers, added to the ship's captain and men, with provisions for all, and the implements and effects for settling a colony, all compacted together in one small ship, of but 180 tons, can give no very favorable idea of internal convenience or comfort. Yet, with a fair wind, they proceeded prosperously at first, until about half way over the sea, though the usual sea sickness was to them no stranger. Then commenced "cross winds and fierce storms." Encountering these, the ship labored, and her upper works became leaky. A main beam amidships was bent and cracked. The mariners manifested fears of the ability of the ship and much distraction and difference of opinion. Though willing to do what they could, they were yet loath to hazard their lives to any extremity. Perceiving this, the chief of the pilgrim company consulted with the officers of the ship as to the danger, and whether to return or to proceed. All opinions and reports being examined, and the captain being in favor of further exertions, various expedients were used to lessen the danger. By a huge iron screw, brought by some passengers from Holland, the wrenched main beam was brought into its place. With this and other appliances, they so strengthened and tightened their laboring bark, that, committing themselves to the will of God, they resolved to proceed. Yet often afterwards, in fierce storms and winds, and high running seas, was their frail weakened vessel unable to bear sail, and forced to lie by for days together. [7]

And how, during all this time, was their elder chiefly occupied? Doubtless, as we would expect, as their counsellor, their instructor, and spiritual guide; with whom, and by whose resolve to go with them, they had undertaken this arduous enterprise. Doubtless he led their daily devotions, as winds and sea, and other circumstances would permit, and spoke to them from portions of the Word of truth aptly suited to each new occurrence, and in way and manner best calculated to instruct, to cheer, and to edify. [8]

Among the incidents of the voyage, was one that appears to have left on the minds of both navigators and passengers a strong impression. A certain stout, able-bodied, yet haughty and profane young seaman, was constantly treating these people with contempt, and in their sickness daily "cursing and execrating them," not hesitating to tell them he hoped to help cast half of them overboard before they came to their journey's end, and "to make merry" with what they should leave. If spoken to ever so gently respecting this treatment, "he would curse the more bitterly." This young seaman was "smitten by a grievous disease," before half of the voyage was completed, and died in great "desperation," and "was himself the first to be thrown overboard," to the "astonishment of all his fellows," who marked it as being by "the just hand of God." [9]

As another incident, a stout young man, of the passengers (John Rowland), coming above the gratings, as the ship lay to in a raging storm, was, by a sudden lurch of the ship, cast into the sea; yet, catching hold of the topsail halliards that hung overboard, running out at length, and holding to them, even though fathoms under water, he was drawn up by them to the surface, and, by boathooks and other means, was raised on board, and his life preserved. Thus rescued, in the providence of God, he lived many years a valuable member of their community. [10]

On the 6th of November, one month after leaving Plymouth and the English coast, died William Button, a youth in the family of Mr. Fuller, their physician. He was the first and only one of their own company whose mortal remains they were called upon during the passage to commit to the great deep.

One also was born during the passage at sea, a child of Mr. and Mrs. Hopkins, who thence named him "Oceanus," [11] child of the ocean. Thus was the number of the Mayflower company continued the same.

At dawn of day, on the 9th of November, land was discovered from the Mayflower's deck. It proved to be the cape, not long before named Cape Cod, from the abundance of that fish caught on its coast. Cheering indeed to the suffering passengers was the sight, after so long a confinement in their crowded and storm-worn ship.

But as it was their intention to find a place for settlement near the Hudson river, on consultation, the ship's course was directed southward, the wind and weather favoring. Sailing this course half of the day, they found themselves among the perilous shoals and breakers off the southerly portion of that cape. Apparently in much peril, and the favorable wind failing them, they resolved to turn back, and bear up again for the point of the cape, thankful to free themselves from the threatening dangers before the night should overtake them. [12]

On the 11th day of November, 1620, sixty-five days, or more than nine weeks after their last departure from the shores of England, they entered, and anchored in safety, in the Harbor of Cape Cod.

Here arrived, before all other movements, "they fell on their knees, and blessed the God of heaven," who had brought them through all their trials and perils on the deep, to their present place of safety. [13]

Truly, with interest no less deep than when, at their embarkation, Robinson committed them to the guidance and keeping of the Most High, Brewster, their elder, now bowed with them —

"At prayer, at prayer," upon the Mayflower's deck.
$\qquad$ "Holy man!
Heart on thy lips, and Bible in thy hand,
Pour forth, as far as feeble speech can do,
The intense emotion of the ocean-toss'd
And care-worn group that thus encircles thee." [14]

Next, being out of the jurisdiction of the Virginia grant, and their patent, which cost them so much, giving them no authority here, and expecting, even from the first, under that patent, to organize for themselves a civil government, as a colony, and to choose, for the time, their own Magistrates, [15] and now especially, seeing signs of insubordination and faction in some — not from Leyden, but of the "strangers that joined them from London," who were not well affected towards them and their purpose, they proceeded at once to accomplish this most important object. In the Cape Harbor, and before going on shore, they drew up, and signed this solemn compact: —

"In the name of God, amen.

"We, whose names are underwritten, the loyal subjects of our dread sovereign lord, King James, by the grace of God, of Great Britain, France, and Ireland, king, defender of the faith, &c., having undertaken, for the glory of God, and the advancement of the Christian faith, and honor of our King and country, a voyage to plant the first colony in the northern parts of Virginia, [16] do, by these presents, solemnly and mutually, in the presence of God and one of another, covenant and combine ourselves together into a civil body politic, for our better ordering and preservation, and furtherance of the ends aforesaid; and, by virtue hereof, to enact, constitute, and frame such just and equal laws, ordinances, acts, constitutions, and offices, from time to time, as shall be thought most meet and convenient for the general good of the colony, unto which we promise all due submission and obedience.

"In witness whereof, we have hereunder subscribed our names, at Cape Cod, the 11th of November, in the year of the reign of our sovereign lord,

King James, of England, France, and Ireland, the eighteenth, and of Scotland the fifty-fourth. Ano. Dom. 1620." [17]

Such was the compact, the "foundation of their government," drawn up and signed by this people, on board the Mayflower, before setting foot on the cape shore. Herein, for the first time, and as the first example in the world's history, were the dreams of philosophers for such a purpose realized, and made matter of fact.

"Never were any civilized people placed more completely in a state of nature than this little band of pilgrims, as they have been justly called. They had, indeed, literally, a world before them, but that world was a wilderness, and Providence was their only guide." [18]

In the instrument itself are the marks of a ready hand, of a sound practical, and even far reaching mind. All is expressed in terms full, comprehensive, complete, and 'capable of application without limit. Good authorities have pronounced it to have been the Germ of American Constitutions. [19]

And who probably was the man by whom this instrument was chiefly penned^ Who other than he who alone had seen public life, was early trained in the principles of government and diplomacy, and concerned in the forming and executing of treaties, and who had been foremost, and most confided in by this people, for his wisdom and ability, though perhaps the meekest of their whole company — who other than their ruling elder?

And the reason why he was not chosen to be their first governor, says Hutchinson, was that "He was their ruling elder, which seems to have been the bar to his being their governor; civil and ecclesiastical office in the same person being then deemed incompatible." [20] While in his place as elder they could furnish no substitute; to them as a church, his position and office were the most important. [21]

[1] Bradford, 60.

[2] Ibid. 60-1.

[3] Bradford, 62-8.

[4] Ibid., 68.

[5] Bradford, pp. 69, 70. No slight censure has been passed upon the master of the Speedwell; as afterwards, when put in proper trim, she performed service to the great profit of her owners,

[6] Bradford, p. 74. Prince, p. 80.

[7] Bradford, pp. 75, 76.

[8] Bradford, p. 413.

[9] Bradford, p. 75.

[10] Bradford, p. 76.

[11] Ibid., p. 448.

[12] Bradford, p. 77, and Winslow in Young, p. 385.

[13] Bradford, pp. 77, 78.

[14] Mrs. Sigourney.

[15] Robinson's Parting Letters, in Bradford, pp. 66 and 67. "You are to become a body politic, using among yourselves civil government." "You are, at least for the present, to have only them, for your ordinary governors, which yourselves shall make choice of for that work." And Bradford, p. 89.

[16] In Bradford, pp. 89, 90. To settle in the then northern parts of Virginia was their first purpose, yet it did not fail still to form one of the reasons for the present proceeding.

[17] See Bradford, 89, 90.

[18] Pitkin's Political and Civil History of the United States of America, i. p. 32. "About a week before, or on the 3d of Nov., 1620, King James had signed a patent for the incorporation of the adventurers to the northern Colony of Virginia, or New England." This was the great civil basis of all the subsequent patents of this portion of the country. But the Pilgrims did not hear of this until the arrival of the Fortune, a year later. In Young, pp. 80, 101.

[19] "It contained the elements of those forms of government peculiar to the New World." — Pitkin's History, i. p. 33, and others.

[20] Hutchinson's History, ii. p. 460.

[21] "The power of the Church, in effect, was superior to the civil power," — Judge Baylie's Plymouth, i. p. 227.

Chapter Twenty - 1620

"In the wilderness astray,
    In the lonely waste they roam,
Hungry, fainting by the way,
    Far from refuge, shelter, home."

It is Saturday evening, the 11th of November. The solemn compact has been drawn and signed, and a governor of the pilgrim band chosen. A party of some sixteen men, armed for defence in case of emergency, have gone on shore, the first of their company to set foot on New England's soil. These examined their locality, and the character of the nearest land. Their ship is in the little bay or harbor of the cape; they are on this strange neck of land of sickle shape. Southwesterly is the Great Cape Bay, while over the land, north and easterly, is the broad ocean. The soil they find to be black earth, and sand hills, wooded variously to the water's edge. At night they return on board, and report the not altogether favorable prospect; while they bring with them for their needed fuel, and as their first fruits of the New World, the gratefully fragrant cedar. [1]

The next day was the Sabbath, their first Sabbath on this wilderness coast. And it was the province of the Elder to lead their devotions, and present to them holy truths adapted to their new condition.

On the next Monday morning they awoke afresh to the arduous work before them.

Lately the discomforts, sickness, and hardships of a long sea voyage, in their small, crowded barque, and the often threatening dangers of the sea, had largely occupied their anxious thoughts. Yet hope, and a good purpose, had cheered them on. Now, thankful for their preservation through all these, and for their present prospects of an unmolested home, yet already they began to realize that it was to be to them a hard-earned, dear-bought home. On every side were to be seen naught but wild forests, bleak sands, or the briny deep. No defined place, no houses, not even huts, to receive them. And this was but the beginning. Dread winter was at hand; a winter in such a climate as they had never seen; though, in the providence of God, the present was comparatively mild.

But where was to be the place of settlement? Where shelter from the coming snows, wintry blasts, damps and chills'? Where protection from prowling savage beasts, and far more dreaded savage men? [2]

The shipmaster's warning voice, too, was heard, that he would ere long leave them, and that their stores of provisions could not long suffice.

And why was all this? Why had they come thus late, on the very verge of winter, upon this rock-bound, and soon to be to them, an ice-bound coast 1 Not for any want of foresight, or of wisdom of plan on their own part, but from the unfaithfulness and delays of others.

The troubles in the Virginia Council, the grievous delays of the contracting agent in furnishing the shipping, the detentions on the coast of England by the failure of the Speedwell, finally, the unexpected prevention of their going to a more southerly location, were the true causes.

Yet now they were here, with the new trials staring them in the face. And was there heard among them any desponding voice? It appears not. [3] We see but evidences to the contrary, with yet stronger resolution, increased patience, and firm trust in an Almighty arm. They were no ordinary men or women. Their ruling elder and pastor had truly said to Sir Edwin Sandys, "It is not with us as with other men, whom small things can discourage, or small discontentments cause to wish themselves at home again." "We verily believe and trust the Lord is with us, unto whom and whose service we have given ourselves, and that he will graciously prosper our endeavors according to the simplicity of our hearts therein." With such trust and heroic resolve, were their trials met, and plans of action promptly formed. From the Mayflower, as the centre of operations, they commenced their first week's labors. There was no time for delay. Their large shallop, which had been cut down, and stowed away, and greatly injured in storms, and as a lodging-place for passengers, was unshipped and hauled to land, for repairs and sailing rig - a work of many days. The men and women repaired to the shore by way of relief, and for refreshing and cleansing processes needful after such a voyage. [4]

An exploring party of sixteen men, voluntarily formed and fully armed under their energetic Capt. Standish, went forth by permission, and with much counsel and caution, to examine the wild cape and coast. For three days they explored woods, forded creeks, traversed vales, climbed sand hills, followed the trails of discovered natives, until, after many adventures, with torn armor, weary, worn, and wet, yet in safety, they returned to the ship; to the great relief and joy of the anxious company. They had found strange graves, various implements of human construction, some lately cultivated fields, and traces of natives and of other men unknown, also, one desolated station of defence, and, to their great relief from suffering, springs, and a pond of fresh water. They had found, and brought with them, some wild fruits, with small portions of concealed corn, [5] a ship's kettle, and had seen various wild fowl, the wild deer, and, at a distance, the dreaded Indian savage. They also had found another harbor, [6] but no satisfactory place for settlement.

The repairs on shore progressing, Sunday intervenes, the second in the New World; when all are again on board the Mayflower to unite in their accustomed worship, and listen to the words of truth. [7]

The second week presented an equally busy scene. Repairs were urged forward; tools put in order, timber sought out and sawed; and there was constant going to and from the shore. Much wading, however, on account "of shoal water, exposing to wet and cold, and the frequent chilling storms, laid the foundations of diseases from which many never recovered.

Sunday, November 26th, succeeded (the third in the Cape Harbor), and was doubtless improved as usual. Would that we had a sketch of the exercises and 'addresses of the Elder, on these various occasions!

On the next Monday, the second and larger exploring expedition went forth in their scarcely completed shallop, consisting of some thirty-four men, including nine of the ship's crew, with Capt. Jones in command. Proceeding down the interior coast, cross winds and rough freezing weather attended them by water; while steep hills, deep vales, numerous creeks, and lately fallen snow, were encountered by land. Thus exploring in military armor and order, by day, feeding chiefly on wild game, and lodging under the forest pines, as best they could, at night, they examined further locations, and made other discoveries. By cleaving the frozen earth with their cutlasses, they found other concealed stores of corn, but no good harbor or location for the emigrant colony.

On the third day, sending back their shallop to the ship, with some fifteen of the weakest and sick, with Capt. Jones, who was urgent to return, the remaining eighteen resolutely continued their laborious examinations amidst all the exposures. Following the Indian trails farther into the interior, and returning by other ways, they discovered open corn-fields, deserted huts, with signs of foreigners that had been on the coast, and various objects of curiosity, and also more land suitable for cultivation, but no other harbor than the shallow one of Pamet. And, having gathered additional mementos of their discoveries, they resorted to their shallop, now returned, and on the fifth day arrived again, worn and fatigued, on board the Mayflower, and there made another not very encouraging report. [8]

In none of these exploring expeditions does it appear that the Elder was engaged. It has been said, indeed, that "he was able to use his armor as well as his Bible." But probably such enterprises were deemed unsuitable to his position; they would certainly have interfered with his appropriate duties, required most wherever was the largest portion of the company.

It belongs to the history of the colony, and *not to this narrative*, to mark the minute particulars of these explorations. Yet, who felt in them all a deeper interest, or a more anxious concern as to the hazardous exposures and the final result, than their Elder"?

Among the providential incidents connected with these expeditions, was the discovery of corn; which, otherwise, could not have been obtained; and which, as seed for the next spring's planting, proved to be the means of preserving the colony from perishing by famine. This they gratefully acknowledged. And on the first opportunity, about six months after, they repaid the natives to their full satisfaction, and secured thereby their respect and confidence.

During the absence of this latter exploring party, there was born on board the Mayflower, a son of Mr. and Mrs. White, the first-born child of the colony, and they called him Peregrine, a *stranger,* or *wanderer;* and on Monday, Dec. 4tli, died Edward Thompson, a servant of Mr. White, being the first death since their arrival.

On the next day was a narrow escape from explosion. A son of the Billington family (not from Level en, but of London) mischievously found his way to the powder, in the absence of his father, there making squibs, discharging pieces, one even in his father's cabin, where was powder in cask, and scattered around with flints and iron, while the fire between decks was also within a few feet, and many people near, and yet all were mercifully preserved. [9]

The latter exploring party having made their report, a full discussion followed as to place for settlement. Different locations were advocated, particularly the one last discovered; but no one, yet seen or known, proved satisfactory to the majority, pressing, even, as were all the circumstances for a speedy decision. Accordingly, another expedition was determined upon, to explore the whole remaining circuit of Cape Cod Bay.

Another Sabbath intervened, the fourth since their ship had been moored in the Cape Harbor, and all were again on board, resting and profiting by that holy day.

By the sixth of December was the third exploring expedition ready. Organized, armed, and fitted out in their shallop, they set forth, ten of themselves and two of their own seamen, with the two master's mates, the master gunner, and three sailors, of the ship's company. [10]

With difficulty, and late in the day, did they clear from the harbor. Chilly and baffling winds, with a rough sea, caused sore sickness with some, and frozen garments upon all. Getting under the weather shore, they skirted down the coast, and discovered the bay of Wellfleet. Crossing its mouth, and drawing near to the shore, they espied Indians, who fled at their approach. Landing, after much trouble, they prepared their barricade, fire, and food, set their sentinels, and reposed for the night. The following day the bay was sounded, the adjacent land explored, with success similar to that of their previous explorations. And again, the second night, they constructed their barricade, kindled their fire, and with weary limbs betook themselves to rest. Near midnight the sentinel's cry was heard — "Arm! arm!" Aroused and standing to their arms, one or two pieces being discharged, they heard no more, and concluded that what they heard was the howl of wild beasts.

At earliest dawn, and after prayer, while preparing their morning meal, suddenly they heard again the strange though varied cry. It was the battle cry, the "hideous yell," the savage warwhoop — by them heard for the first time. Immediately was raised the alarm — "Indians! Indians!" Some seized their arms ready at hand, and discharged them, defending the barricade. Others ran for theirs to the shallop, when the foe, wheeling upon them, sent thick and fast among them the flying arrows. For their relief, the mail-clad men rushed forth, cutlass in hand, and presently those that ran for their muskets came up, discharging them in return. The Indians soon recoiled. One alone, more bold than his fellows, still launched forth his arrows from behind a tree, standing three shots from the aimed musket, till one shivered the tree's side about his ears, when, with a shriek, he fled. The foe, thus foiled, retreated, and soon was out of sight. Thus delivered from their savage assailants, and providentially preserved even from wounds, with only some coats pierced with arrows, the exploring party returned solemn thanks and praise to God for their deliverance.

They named the place "the First Encounter." [11] Then taking to their shallop, they proceeded on their expedition, coasting along the whole southern portion of the bay, but discovering no good harbor. The air in the mean time became thick with snow and rain. Being informed by the pilot of a good haven further onward, on the northwestern side, which could be reached before night, they pressed forward, the wind and storm increasing. At length, the sea running high, their rudder-hinges broke, and they were obliged, though with difficulty, to guide their disabled craft with oars. Night was coming on, and the storm still increasing, yet the pilot bid them be of good cheer — he saw the harbor. Bearing what sail they could, to enter ere it was dark, their mast gave way and broke in pieces, and their sail went overboard. All were now in peril. Still, mercifully spared, they recovered themselves, and the flood being with them, they pressed for the entrance. Entering, and bearing northward, the pilot discovered new dangers, and exclaimed, "The Lord be merciful! my eyes never saw this place before." Running towards shore, with a cove full of breakers before them, the lusty steersman "called to the rowers to about with her if they were men, else they were all cast away." This quickly done, he bade them row lustily, with good heart, for a fair sound was before them. Entering that, though dark and rainy, they bore up under the lea of a small island, where their disabled shallop rode out the night in safety.

But we pause not here. The exploring party, having moored their little barque, were now suffering from wet and cold, with no means of relief. While some feared to go on shore, lest they should fall into the hands of the Indians, others, weak, and not able to continue as they were, took to the land and kindled a fire, where, at length, their companions joined them, forced to follow by the piercing wind, changed to the cold northwest.

Here, the next morning, the sun rose upon them in brightness, and they were comforted and cheered, in contrast with the suffering and dangers of the last day and night. Finding themselves to be on an island, secure from the Indians, they dried their clothing, put in order their pieces, refreshed themselves, and rested, giving thanks to their Almighty Deliverer for his continued mercies.

And this being the last day of the week, they prepared here to keep the Sabbath.

The Sabbath came; it was the *fifth* to the pilgrim band in the New World. And while the main portion of their company was with the Elder on board the Mayflower at the Cape, this exploring party, now separated for the first time from their brethren on the Lord's day, here, among this island's forest trees, offered their prayers and praises to the same Almighty Father, Deliverer, and Guide.

---

[1] Juniperus Virginiana, or, red cedar. Brad. in Young, pp. 118, 122, 124.

[2] Bradford, pp. 78, 79.

[3] The distinction between the emigrant company, and the ship's officers and men, is to be all along borne in mind.

[4] Bradford, p. 80, and in Young, 125, 138.

[5] Maize, the first that they had ever seen.

[6] Pamet Harbor. Brad., p. 82, and in Young, 135.

[7] Bradford, p. 413.

[8] Bradford, 82-3; in Young, pp. 138, 145.

[9] Bradford, in Young, p. 143.

[10] Ibid., p. 149.

[11] Bradford, pp. 84, 87, and in Young, 158, 159.

Chapter Twenty-One – 1620-1621

"They little thought how pure a light,
    With years, should gather round that day;
How love should keep their memories bright.
    How wide a realm their sons should sway."

— Bryant.

We left the last exploring party on the little islet, afterwards named Clark's Island. On the next day, sounding the harbor into which they had entered with so much peril, and finding it fitted for shipping, they landed on the main shore of the inner bay.

It was on the 11*th of December, old style, or the* 21*st, new style* — a day since made memorable from that event in the annals of New England.

Examining the main shore, they judged it to be suitable for their settlement, the best that they could find, and which the advanced season and their

110

present necessities made them glad to accept. Returning, therefore, across the broad bay, they brought to their companions the encouraging news of their discovery.

Bay and Harbor of New Plymouth, New England

And now all were again on board of the Mayflower, in the harbor of Cape Cod. The report of this last exploring expedition was received. It brought comfort to all the pilgrim company. But sorrow had also come to the heart of at least one of those brave explorers. The wife of William Bradford, soon after his departure on this expedition, had fallen overboard, and was drowned. Two others also had been taken from the emigrant company.

Prompt to act on the information received, on the 15th of the month (old style), they weighed anchor, and the ship was under sail for their newly discovered port; but, before arriving, adverse winds forced them back.

The next day, Saturday the 16th, they sailed again, and ere night they were in their intended haven. It was just five weeks from the day of their arrival and the signing of their *compact* in the harbor of the Cape. And to them what a period of anxiety, of trial of faith, and of enduring effort, had these last five weeks been!

Now arrived, and safely moored in their new location, they saw around them a bay, hook-shaped, and larger than that at the Cape, which they had just left, and in it two fair islands, wooded and uninhabited. On the mainland, on the hills and in the vales, were seen the tall oak, the pine, the beech, walnut, with other trees of the forest to them as yet unknown; and there was also, to appearance, a kindly soil. No wonder that they, wanderers, storm-tossed, long wearied and worn, should look upon that which was before them as "a most hopeful place," "a goodly land." But night soon closed in upon them. The following day was the Sabbath, their sixth in New England, and the first in their new home; where newly awakened emotions, and thoughts of deep interest, must have been felt by each worshipper, and marked the address of their elder.

On Monday, portions of the company landed, perhaps on the same rock (the now far-famed, though diminished, Plymouth Rock), whereon the discovering party had set foot on the previous Monday. Marching along the main land, armed, and in order of defence, they discovered no Indians, or Indian habitations, but forests extending inland, and open grounds and fields near shore, where inhabitants had lived and planted corn. Searching for a place for settlement, they found no navigable stream as desired; but saw running brooks, fresh and sweet, and soil of various kinds, in some places rich, in others, clay, sand, and gravel; also, fruit trees, vines, and berries. But over all was the dreary garb of winter.

Again, the next day, as the point of location in respect to soil, navigation, and defence, was important, they searched further, some by water and some by land, in a northwesterly course, for the desired place. Coming to a beatable stream, which they entered and named after their ship's captain, Jones' River, they found on its borders a location more desirable than the one explored the day previous; but on reflection it was deemed to be too far inland and exposed to be occupied in their present weak condition. Next, at the desire of some, crossing the harbor to the island first discovered, they examined also its suitableness for their purpose. But returning on board again at night, still undecided, they resolved that on the next morning, after some further examination, the matter of location should be determined. There was no time for delay.

Accordingly, on Wednesday, the 20th, after solemnly invoking the guidance of the Most High, they repaired again to the main land; and after a brief scrutiny, determined on the place by a majority of voices. It was that first explored, and on the high ground facing the bay; "where (says one of them) are cleared lands, delicate springs, and a sweet brook running under the hillside, with fish in their season; where we may harbor our shallops and boats. On the further side is much corn ground." Near at hand "is a high hill, on which to plant our ordnance. Thence we may see into the bay, and far out at sea, and have a glimpse of the distant cape. Our greatest labor will be the bringing of wood. What people inhabit here we know not, as we have yet seen none." And this was to be New Plymouth.

On the ground, therefore, now selected, they immediately made their rendezvous, not far from their first landing-place, "leaving some twenty of their people that very night, and resolved in the morning that all should come on shore and build." [1] Each day was important. But disappointments and hindrances in the advance of winter must naturally be expected. Storms and tempests followed. Sad were the exposures during the two following days and nights, of the poorly protected ones on shore, while no little anxiety was felt by those on shipboard.

December the 23d, the storms ceasing, they commenced, and henceforward urgently carried on, as weather would permit, their toilsome work of building. All were in earnest: they came on shore; they felled trees; they hewed; they sawed; they rived; they carried; each laboring according to his skill and ability.

First was prepared their common house for rendezvous, and in which to store their goods. There was a street projected eastward from the hill towards their landing-place. On each side of this, were building plats laid off, and drawn for by lot. [2] Next were foundations laid, and the work pressed forward, each for his own dwelling. The holy Sabbath was the only day of rest; and this was often interrupted by alarms of savages, and the frequent flying to arms. Christmas came and went with no relaxation from labor, no kind cheer to greet them. Cold water only was their drink; and not till after the day's toil, and an alarm-cry of "Indians!"' was it, that even on that day, to a portion of them returning on board, did the captain distribute some beer, but none to those on shore.

Next was constructed the rude platform for their ordnance on the after-named fort, or "Burial Hill"

To lessen, as far as possible, the number of dwellings to be constructed, all were apportioned or arranged in nineteen families. It was also determined that every man should build his own habitation.

Thus urged on by their own exposed condition, and by reason of the short-ness of time that the ship could remain with them, day after day, and week after week, did they work as they could — work as for life; or worse conse-quences would follow. [3]

Besides, in this work, all must be done with their own hands — by their own bodily strength. No ox had they, no horse, no beast of burden, to relieve from the most oppressive labors. The materials must be gathered wherever they could be found, and no small portion of them from very inconvenient distances.

Such were some of the labors and hardships of this people in commencing their new settlement.

And was the "Elder," by reason of his position, freed from any of these la-bors? It appears not. As he had been "first" and "forwardest" in their adven-tures, and suffered the greatest loss while in England, and "had endured equal hardships with them in Holland," so in this wilderness, he bore his part in weal and woe with this poor people. On removing into this country, "he was in no way unwilling to take his part, and to bear his burden with the rest." [4] To the *agreement* "that every man should build his own house," no exception was made in favor of the Elder.

His own family, as it came in the Mayflower, consisted of himself, Mrs. Brewster, and two young sons. Love and Wrestling, and two boys placed with him by the name of Moore [5] (the remainder of them being still in England or Holland). With the aid of these youths, it would seem (and with such addi-tional assistance as might be obtained from some others more skilled in the work), he erected his own dwelling.

Nor should the fact be omitted that no income appears to have been re-ceived by him from the people. Literally true, in his case, were the words of an apostle, "these hands have ministered to my necessities, and to them that were with me."

Added to all this, were his constant and efficient labors on the Lord's day. Emphatically is it said of him that, in this, he did more in a few years than do many in all their lives. [6]

But sorer, sadder trials than any yet mentioned, had their Elder and his companions now to endure. From exposures to wet and cold, amid frequent storms while on the cape, and equal, if not greater exposures in their labors here, and likewise from want of suitable dwellings and healthful food, sick-ness had begun to make fearful ravages in the ranks of the pilgrim company. Commencing almost from the time of their landing, and increasing, under various forms, for nearly three months, it became general, and its effects alarmingly fatal.

In the chief extremity, "the living were scarce able to bury the dead; the well not sufficient to attend upon the sick; seven only remained in health." Of these seven, the record distinguishes, along with the brave and hardy Miles Standish, their revered Elder Brewster. "Tender-hearted and compassionate to the afflicted, as a nursing father he shrank not from the most self-denying offices." Touchingly does Bradford allude to them, "as sparing no pains night or day, but, with abundance of toil and hazard of their own health, they brought for the sick their wood, made their fires, dressed their meat, made their beds, clothed and unclothed them; in a word, did all homely and necessary offices for them, which the dainty cannot endure to hear named; and all this willingly and cheerfully, showing herein their true love unto their brethren; unto whom myself, with the others," he adds, "were mercifully beholden in our low and sick condition. Yet these were preserved without any infection."

During this period, including Mrs. Bradford, who was drowned, there died in December, six; in January, eight; in February, seventeen; in March, thirteen; and before the close of Spring, six others, among whom, to their great sorrow, were their first governor, Mr. Carver, and his wife; in all fifty, *just one-half* of the emigrant band that arrived in the Mayflower on the 11th of November. [7]

In the time of their greatest mortality, two or three died in a day. Faithful, patient, noble-hearted women, weakened by deprivations and suffering, some in the bloom of life, yielded to the fatal maladies, and often in the triumphs of faith. Ere the return of their ship to England, Bradford, Standish, Allerton, and Winslow, were left *widowers*.

And what must have been the Elder's feelings as he beheld the sufferings and sad diminishing of his little flock? What the deep workings of thought, trials of faith, and continued purpose of himself and companions, during this fearful period? Would we reach the nature and depth of those struggling thoughts, or give utterance to those feelings and purposes, we must take the preceding facts, and, pondering them deeply and with a soul tried by a like ordeal, go in mind to the place, and fix the attention upon some one of those most trying scenes through which he was called to pass. Let it be (says one), near the close of their first spring month. [8] A diminished procession of the pilgrims is seen coming from the abode and following the remains of another of their most dearly beloved and newly dead to that bank of graves where was buried what was mortal of their dear departed ones during the first year, and near the place where their feet first trod this soil. Here they pause to take the last look. The Mayflower is still riding at anchor full in view, but soon to sail to their fatherland, and leave them alone, the living and the dead, to the weal and woe of their new home. The afflicted and bereaved gather around their venerated Elder, dearer to them now than ever. They listen to his voice, subdued yet animated by firm faith and hope, whilst, in tones that reach hearts as noble as his own, he gives utterance to his struggling emotions: "Man is altogether vanity." [9] He passeth away as a shadow. His only true home is Heaven. Strangers and pilgrims indeed are we on the earth. Still the spot on which we stand, this shore, this now familiar scene, this whole land, becomes dearer daily, were it only for the precious dust which we have here committed to its bosom. Here, rather than elsewhere, would I sleep when my own hour shall come. Here would I have my body repose, with these endeared ones who have shared in our exceeding labors, and whose burdens are now unloosed forever. I would be near them in the last day, and have a part in their resurrection.

"Fearful, indeed, has been our loss. Unutterable and long has been our anguish; many our mingled agonies, tears, and prayers. Our departed ones are at rest. For some divine purpose we yet remain. It is on my mind that the darkest of our night is past; the morning is at hand. The dreary winter is departing; the balmy breath of spring is returning. The sore sickness is stayed. [10] Thankful to Almighty God should we be that our case is not worse, that so many of our number yet live, and among them some of our best and wisest.

"Cheering is the fact, that among you all, the living and the dead, not one, even when disease had seized him, and sharp anguish had made his heart as that of a little child, not one repented of the step we took, or desired, yea, could have been persuaded to go back by yonder ship to their former homes. Evident is it to me, that it is our Master's will that we stand or fall here. Our very condition was not unthought of even in Holland. And in our heaviest trials has not the Divine Presence been with us"? Did not His providential hand open for us the way through every difficulty? In that bitterest hour of embarkation, did we not see His bow in the cloud, the bright bow of promise and hope, whose arch spanned for us the broad ocean, and is over us still] Wherefore let us stand in our lot. We believe this movement to be from Him. If he prosper us, we shall be the means of planting here a Christian colony and a pure church, as we believe, in this vast wilderness, and of extending hence its precious blessings to these savage heathen.

"Blessed will it be for us, blessed for this land, for this vast continent! Nay, from generation to generation will the blessing descend. Generations to come shall look back to this hour, and these scenes of agonizing trial, this day of small things, and say, 'Here was our beginning as a people. These were our fathers. Through their trials we inherit our blessings. Their faith is our faith; their hope our hope; their God our God.' The prospect brightens before me; it ends not on earth, it enters heaven! Let us go hence, then, to work with our might, that which we have to do. No small undertaking is it, that we have in hand. The opportunity for working will soon be past, and we shall be called to our account, and, if faithful, to our reward." [11]

With subdued emotions, calmly and with firm faith, they turn from those graves; the Mayflower is sent away; and those men of stern resolve and high purpose, press onward in their incessant imperious labors.

[1] Bradford and Winslow, in Young, pp. 166, 168. Precisely when the name was given to the settlement, we cannot discover.
[2] Bradford and Winslow in Young, p. 173.
[3] Bradford and Winslow, in Young, pp. 109, 170.
[4] Bradford, 412, 413, and in Young, 465, &c.

[5] See both Appendixes, Brad., pp. 447, 451.

[6] Bradford, p. 413.

[7] Bradford, 91, and notes; also in Young and Prince. "In this month of April came Governor Carver out of the field sick. He complained greatly of his head, and lay down, and within a few hours his senses failed, so as he never spoke more till he died. Whose death was much lamented, and caused great heaviness amongst them, as there was cause. He was buried in the best manner they could, with some volleys of shot by all that bore arms.' —Brad., 101.

[8] Partly in the words of the pilgrims themselves, and partly in those of one of New England's gifted sons, at Plymouth.

[9] The Elder's own motto.

[10] Bradford, p. 99.

[11] In Young, pp. 87, 241. Do. do. do., 473-4, 268. Bradford, p. 51. In Young, Wins., &c., 272, 382, 384. The Council of the Virginia Company said, "The thing was of God." Young, 383; see also pp. 59, 60. Again in Young, 95, 47, 121, 246. "Let it not be grievous to you, that you have been instruments to break the ice for others. The honor shall be yours to the world's end." — Letter from Leyden. Brad., 145.

Chapter Twenty-Second - 1621

"Wise men ne'er sit and wail their loss,
  But cheerly seek how to redress their harm."

Shakespeare.

Under the appalling circumstances which we have just been noticing, it is matter of wonder, that with the slender means, reduced number, and enfeebled strength of the colonists, amid the cold and storms of winter, with attendance upon the sick and dying, and due offices for the dead, so much should have been accomplished.

Before the close of May, from the raw materials of earth and forest, and wild grass for thatching, gathered wherever it could be found, they had built their "common house," or "general rendezvous" for goods and lodging; a house for the sick, and two for storing provisions; and they had made such further progress, that, before the close of summer, they could look down their newly-formed street [1] upon seven private dwellings, completed and occupied, and others in the course of preparation. [2]

And having almost from the first discovered Indians peering about, causing alarm and a painful sense of insecurity, they had made provision for defence. On the hill rising abruptly westward from the head of their street, to the height of one hundred and sixty feet, they had with much labor constructed their platform, and with the aid of the Captain and his men before the Mayflower sailed, they had brought on shore and drawn up thither, their "minion," or largest piece of ordnance, and others smaller, and there mounted them, to command the harbor, and the entire range of vale and plain below.

117

It was a work, the completion of which caused such a feeling of gratitude and relief, that, notwithstanding the cloud of gloom that had hung over them, it was made the occasion of a cheering feast. [3]

Before the close of May, likewise, fields had been prepared and planted; twenty acres of Indian corn or maize, and six of barley and peas; while at the same time they were compelled by hunting and fishing, and often with poor success, to search for most of their daily food. [4]

Military order, too, had been established, and Captain Standish called to the command, with orders to drill the men, station guards, and nightly watch, and execute all else that in this department might be required.

In like manner had they in general meetings, from time to time, by a majority of votes, established such "laws and orders as they thought meet for their present condition, as a body politic" under the crown of England, and according to the compact entered into on their first arrival.

Moreover, with much labor, personal risk, and expenditure of means, had they sought after and kindly treated such native Indians as could be found, cultivating friendly relations with them, and removing, as fast as possible, their prejudices and enmities. [5]

Such is a part (it would require many pages to give a detailed view of the whole), of what this small company had accomplished within five months, amidst opposing elements, sickness, and death; an amount of bodily and mental labor in their circumstances truly wonderful. Where is there a parallel?

But their intercourse with the natives demands a more extended notice. To be the means, whereever they should go, of carrying, as far as they could, the blessings of the Christian religion, so dear to themselves, to the uncivilized heathen Indians, was one of the prominent purposes of the Elder and his people. It was a *worthy* idea, conceived and long dwelt upon before they left Holland, and of which they never lost sight. [6]

Yet how was this to be done'? How reach them amidst the prejudices, oppositions, and enmities of their savage state 1 The unprincipled and villainous conduct of certain captains and seamen on the coast in plundering and destroying some, and in carrying away captive a number of others, had fixed in the breasts of these savages, otherwise unscrupulous, enmities too deep and strong to be easily overcome. [7] This, in connection probably with their own propensities to war and revenge, had caused the attack upon the pilgrim explorers on the Cape. Coming to the present place of settlement, and finding traces indeed of natives — grounds once planted, but for some time deserted, huts going to decay, but no inhabitants, no possessors of the soil in the whole neighborhood, and having a sight even of only a few transient wanderers, or some scattered bands, ranging around them at a distance, serving only to excite alarm — our emigrant company had yet no opportunity of opening any intercourse with them. Indeed, this whole condition of things was to themselves a matter of mystery. [8]

It was not until the 16th of March that this mystery began to be solved. Assembled, on that day, to complete their military arrangements, to their surprise, a tall Indian, in his nude savage state, with bow and arrows, came boldly along the line of their houses directly to their rendezvous, calling out in broken English, "Welcome, Englishmen! welcome, Englishmen!" As boldly would he have entered their rendezvous had he not been prevented. Being the first savage with whom they had spoken, he, of course, caused no little excitement. Free of speech, and of seemly manners, to their inquiries as far as each could understand the other, he answered that "he was not of these parts," but from "the eastward, one day's sail with a great wind, but five days by land," where Englishmen came with ships to fish, with whom he was acquainted, and of whom he had learned his English." He signified to them also that he was a Sagamore, or a kind of chief there, and that his name was Samoset. He likewise informed them of the whole country in general, and of each particular portion, and of their sagamores, number of men and strength, that the place where they now were was called Patuxet, and that about four years before all the inhabitants had died of an extraordinary plague, and there was neither man, woman, nor child remaining; therefore there were none to claim, none to hinder possession by the English. [9] He also informed them that it was the people called Nausites, on the Cape, that first assaulted their exploring company; that this tribe had been incensed by the English, and slain three of Sir F. Gorge's men, and that one Capt. Hunt had carried away and sold for slaves seven of their men, and twenty from this present place. And (showing his knowledge of what was taking place around them), he informed them respecting some tools which some of the company had left in the fields on a late alarm, and which had been taken away.

Deeply interesting and important to the new settlers was all this information. It solved the mystery as to what had become of the inhabitants of this portion of country. The facts, they afterwards learned, had before been known in England.

With kindness did they receive and entertain their strange visitor, setting before him such food as they could, which they thought would be most acceptable, and of which he partook with good relish. But at night, as he was not inclined to go, who should entertain the nude Indian guest in his family, was a delicate question. At length disposed of, the next day, with presents, and promising to come again and bring others to trade with them, he departed. And Samoset, as good as his word, returned the day after, with five other tall Indian men, with painted faces, clad in skins of the deer and the wild-cat, with feathers standing up fan-like in their hair, and other like strange appendages. These also were kindly received; and partaking heartily of the food provided, gave tokens of readiness for social acquaintance, singing and dancing after their manner. Yet it being Sunday, and there being no trading on that day, they were kindly dismissed, as they best could be, with presents, and military attendance for a short distance, by way of distinction, for which they returned thanks, and departed, glad, and promising to come again. Still Samoset would tarry. [10] On the third day, those Indians not returning, Samoset was requested to go for them. On the same day appeared armed savages, in threatening attitude, on a neighboring hill, causing much alarm.

Previously, and unknown to the colonists at the time, a great assembly, or "powwow," of Indian conjurers from all the country, had been held for three days in a dark dismal swamp, in order to curse and execrate, according to their savage rites, and in their most horrid manner, the settlers of New" Plymouth.

Samoset returning, brought with him three other Indians, one of them named Tisquantum or Squanto. He, the only remaining native of the place they now occupied, had been one of those twenty taken and carried away captive by Capt. Hunt. Released, and after dwelling for a time in England, where he had learned some English, he had, not long before, by various ways, returned to this his native soil. Of more immediate and special consequence to the new colonists than they could be aware, was the visit of these two Indians (Samoset and Tisquantum) at the present time. This the train of events will soon show.

Assembled on that same day, March 22d, for their public business, the governor and company were informed, by Samoset and Tisquantum (both able to aid as interpreters), that the great Sagamore Massasoit, King of all the bordering Indians, with his brother, Quadequina, and all their train of attendants, were near at hand.

An hour after, King Massasoit appeared on the hill over against them, with a train of sixty warriors. The pilgrim company unwilling to send their governor to them, and they unwilling to come to him, Tisquantum was dispatched with a message of inquiry respecting their desire and purpose. Answer was returned that the King desired some one to be sent for a parley. The dignified and courtly Winslow was dispatched, with refreshments, and presents, and a message to King Massasoit and brother, that King James saluted Massasoit with words of love and peace, and would receive him as a friend and ally; also that the governor desired to see him, to confirm a peace with him, and to trade with him as his next neighbor.

King Massasoit, pleased with the message, though imperfectly interpreted, and receiving the presents and partaking of the refreshments with his company, retained Mr. Winslow in the custody of his brother (hostages having been previously retained by the governor for his safety), and with twenty of his men, unarmed, descended the hill, and advanced to the stream between them and the New Town. There met by Capt. Standish, with a small band of musketeers, who saluted him, and he them, they passed the stream, and were escorted to the house prepared for their reception.

Here had been placed a green rug and cushions as seats of state. Immediately the governor arrived with drum, trumpets, and musketeers. The parties saluted each other, the governor kissing the King's hand, and the King kissing him. Both being seated, and refreshments ordered, the governor, in due state ceremony, drank to him, and he heartily, in return, to the governor. Next, after partaking of some meat, and the King also giving of the same to his attendants, ^he parties treat of peace and an alliance. Simple in word and form was the treaty; the work of a few hours, the first of the kind in New England. And worthy was it of the parties concerned; and to both did it long continue a source of mutual blessing. [11]

The treaty being concluded, and the ceremony ended, the governor conducted the King back to the brook, when they embraced each other, and the King departed.

But all did not end here. Word arrived that the King's brother, Quadequina, was coming with his attendants. Accordingly, he too was received, and conducted to the place of reception, and entertained in like manner. He was a young man, well-formed, tall, of a modest and comely countenance, and manifested satisfaction with all, except the guns of the musketeers, which, at his signs of dislike, were put aside. [12] This entertainment over, he also was escorted to the brook, as the king, his brother, had been; when all retired, though two of the warriors were inclined to remain. All this time were the Indian women, who attended Massasoit and his men, in the forest not far distant, beyond the hill.

Strange to the whole pilgrim company — man, woman, and child — must this day's sight have been, and deep the excitement throughout the settlement. They had this day seen, in the most favorable light, not in war, but in peace, a savage king, attended by his no less savage warriors, himself grave of countenance, of few words, lusty, and strong, in his best years, clad in skins of the bear, fox, and deer, with head oiled and face painted. Around his neck, as the badge of kingship, was the great chain of white bone beads. Suspended from this chain, and nearly in contact with his long, smooth, black hair, and falling backwards, hung that other appendage, a bag of tobacco, from which to take for himself and offer to others a portion as friendship's token. At his breast hung his long huge knife. And not unlike him were his warriors; some clad in garments nearly as whole and in shape as when on the wild beasts from which they had been taken; others of them were almost in nature's nakedness; while all faces were painted, wholly or partially, and variously (a savage characteristic), black, white, yellow, red, in lines, crosses, or in strange figures, according to each one's fancy. All were in form erect and tall, strong of muscle and nerve, ready at call to string the bow, to sound the terrific war-whoop, and fiercely speed the arrow in battle, or swift of foot to pursue in hunting the bear, the wolf, or the deer.

Wild and uncultivated they were as their own native forests; wily, and, when aroused by passion, fierce and cruel as the savage beasts with whose fur-skins they were clad, though among them were some with better qualities, yet all in the darkness of heathenism.

Such were the native Indians whom our forefathers now met, with whom they had now to deal, whose friendship they desired to gain, whose highest good they would seek to promote, whose respect and confidence they must secure, and against whom, should unwelcome necessity compel, they must be ready to protect themselves, and those, whom of all else on earth, they held most dear.

This day had a step been taken, the wisest and best that, in their condition, could be conceived for their intended purpose. And of it, who had a more enlarged view, or in it, a deeper interest, than their elder?

[1] Now Leyden Street.

[2] Bradford and Winslow, in Young, pp. 173, 179, 230.

[3] Brad, and Winslow, in Young, 181.

[4] Brad., p. 100, and Winslow in Young, 230.

[5] See the journal in Young.

[6] Bradford, pp. 24, 90, and Cushman in Young, pp. 246, 248.

[7] Bradford, 96, and in Young, p. 186.

[8] In Young, pp. 170, 171, 179, 181.

[9] Brad, and Winslow in Young, pp. 182-186.

[10] In Young, 187, 189.

[11] Articles of this Treaty: —

1st. That neither the King, nor any of his, should injure or do hurt to any of our people.

2d. That if any of his did any hurt to any of ours, he should send the offender that we might punish him.

3d. That if anything was taken from any of ours, he should cause it to be restored, and we would do the like to his.

4th. If any did unjustly war against him, we would aid him; if any did war against us, he should aid us.

5th. He should send to his neighboring confederates to certify them of this, that they might not wrong us, but might be likewise comprised in the conditions of peace.

6th. That when their men come to us, they should leave their bows and arrows behind them. — Bradford, 94.

[12] These it was that struck terror, more than all things else, into the hearts of the otherwise invincibly fearless and brave chiefs and warriors of the savage tribes of New England.

Chapter Twenty-Three - 1621

"Then glory to the steel
 That shines in the reaper's hand;
 And thanks to God, who has blessed the sod,
 And crowns the harvest land."
                                        — Eliza Cook.

From the month of May of this their first year, to November, the prospects of the pilgrim colony became gradually more encouraging. "With the genial breezes of summer came health to the enfeebled survivors. Their Indian friend, Tisquantum, made his abode with them, and taught them how to plant and nurture the Indian corn, or maize, a grain then new to them, and with the cultivation of which they were unacquainted.

He also informed them when and where to take fish from the bay. In these ways, and with wild game, and such other products of the soil as industry could procure, the colonists were beginning to obtain a comfortable supply of food.

Other valuable services were rendered them by this Indian friend. Also Hobbamock, another Indian, became useful as an interpreter and guide, in opening an intercourse with the various neighboring nations or tribes around them.

Accordingly, first, about midsummer, an embassy was dispatched with presents to their neighbor and ally, King Massasoit, in his own country, to confirm their alliance, to promote and regulate friendly intercourse, and to learn his residence, strength, and power. [1]

Another embassy was dispatched to the Nausites, on the Cape, with whom they had their first encounter. With them it was their purpose to cultivate, if possible, a friendly intercourse, and to reward them in full for the corn discovered and taken in their time of need on their first arrival at the Cape; also, to recover a lost boy, who had strayed away from the colony, and was now with that people. [2] Both of these embassies were attended with success, though with much hardship, and the latter with imminent danger.

Scarcely had the messengers returned, however, from this last mission, when the colonists found themselves involved in a most unexpected difficulty. Information came that Massasoit, their ally, was driven from his country by the powerful Narragansetts, whose country bordered upon his; and that a conspiracy was likewise formed against him by one of his own chiefs, who was an enemy of the colonists.

Their two friends, Tisquantum and Hobbamock, on going forth to ascertain the facts of the case, were seized by the conspiring chief; and, while the latter made his escape, Tisquantum was treated with violence, scornfully taunted with being the white men's friend, and with brandished knife, threatened with immediate death. [3]

Informed of all this, the governor and company held consultation as to what was to be done. To suffer their ally to be thus overcome, and not attempt his relief — their friendly interpreter, and at times, official messenger, to be thus seized, abused, and perhaps slain, even on their account, and not attempt to rescue him, would be to confess to these savages their weakness, and the worthlessness of their friendship.

An armed expedition, under Captain Standish, was therefore at once resolved upon; and a chosen band of ten men marched forth the next morning, and reached the abode of the conspirators the next night. Immediately surrounding and taking the place by surprise, they released their friend; but the chief ones sought for were gone.

No lives were lost; only a few who attempted to escape, contrary to the warning given, received some wounds. Thus was the conspiracy broken up, while the report of the *fire-arms* filled those around them with fear. Having treated with kindness the unoffending, and warned all others against the like proceedings in future, they returned (after having been refreshed), accompanied by their friends and such of the wounded as voluntarily accepted their offer to come and be healed by their physician. [4]

Another and peaceful expedition was next sent to the people of the Massachusetts, who occupied the country north of their settlement. "From these they had heard words of threatening," but they would cultivate peace with them, and arrange terms of mutual intercourse and traffic. This expedition was also successful; as explorers, they obtained a knowledge of the Massachusetts Bay, with "better harbors," and made report of the place, wishing, says the governor, "they had been there seated; but the Lord, who assigns to all men the bounds of their habitations, had appointed it for another use." [5]

These bold and fearless movements, made generally in a trustful and confiding manner, the messengers being often in the power, and relying on the good faith and honor of those among whom they went, so won upon the noble-hearted and brave among the Indians, while their prompt action, and the terror of their guns, so wrought upon the fears of the evil-minded, that, before the close of the year, all the surrounding princes and people, following the example of Massasoit, came or sent to treat of peace and friendship. In all this their Elder appears to have been their special counsellor and adviser.

At length, autumn being far advanced, and their first summer's harvest of Indian corn being gathered in, they fitted their houses, and made their arrangements against the coming winter. And now, while some were employed in service abroad, and some in fishing, to furnish for each family a goodly supply, others again were engaged in hunting, procuring, among other game, water fowl, wild turkey, and venison. Of meal, or Indian corn, one peck a week for each person was the apportioned supply. Of other meal, or wheat, they had none; nor had they any mill for grinding; therefore their corn must be pounded or mashed by their own hands. Yet even this supply, being deemed sufficient for the present colonists, caused some of them to write home to their friends, in England, in more glowing terms than was prudent or warrantable. The effect was, that these descriptions of plenty induced subsequent emigrants to come without bringing with them their needful stores. [6]

The provision for the little colony being secured for the ensuing winter, their governor set apart a day for public thanksgiving. Accordingly, with the fruits of their labors, the thankful feast was prepared, that all might in a special manner rejoice together, under a grateful sense of these tokens of divine mercy. It was their first thanksgiving or harvest festival in the New World. [7] And we may well conjecture what were the feelings, and what the theme of the -Elder, as, assembled in their "Common House," [8] he led the devotions of these worshippers, and spoke to them words befitting the occasion.

The occasion was likewise improved, as a fit time, to interest and favorably influence the neighboring Indians. "Among other recreations," says Winslow, "we exercised our arms; many of the Indians coming amongst us, and with them came their greatest King, Massasoit, accompanied by some ninety men, whom for three days we entertained and feasted. They also went out and killed five deer, which they brought to the plantation, and bestowed on our governor, and upon the captain and others. And though it be not always so plentiful as it was at this time with us, yet, by the goodness of God, we are so far from want that we often wish our friends partakers with us." [9]

Thus are we brought to the conclusion of the first year's trials, hardships, and sufferings of the pilgrim company, with the loss of life, and the present temporary relief.

During all this, we have marked the "Elder's" position and prevailing influence; an influence unobtrusive, yet ever active, ever felt, and possessed by no other. All along, in the mind's eye, we have seen him ever present, as the leader of their public devotions, whether on shipboard or in their rudely constructed place of worship on shore, as their constant instructor in the Divine Word: "teaching publicly twice on every Sabbath." [10] We have marked, also, his position not only as ruling elder, but as counsellor, ever interested, always consulted in every affair of importance. [11] We have found him likewise ministering most patiently and affectionately at the bedside of the sick, and, with all the alleviations that Christian faithfulness could impart, sympathizing with them, and sharing in their trials. And thus closes the first year of the first English colony on the coast of New England.

[1] Massasoit's dominion extended over nearly all the country, from Cape Cod proper to Narragansett Bay, while his residence was where now stands the town of Warren, in Rhode Island.
[2] Bradford in Young, 214-18.
[3] Bradford, 103; in Young, 219.
[4] Bradford, 104, and in Young, 220, &c.
[5] Bradford, 105; in Young, 224, 229.
[6] Hilton, in Young, 250.
[7] Winslow, in Young, 231.

[8] This was the best place for assembling which they yet had been able to prepare. In it they appear to have held their public worship from the 21st of January preceding. Prince, 97; Russell's Guide to Plymouth.
[9] Young, 231, 232.
[10] Bradford, 413.
[11] "As the governor had used, in all weighty affairs, to consult with their Elder, Mr. Brewster (together with his assistants)." — Bradford, p. 172.

Chapter Twenty-Four – 1621-1622

"Much danger makes great hearts most resolute." - Marston.

On the 9th of November, just one year from the day when the pilgrim company first beheld land in the New World, a little ship was seen standing in from sea, which immediately caused no little commotion. The first notice of its approach reached the little colony from the Indians on the Cape. Was it friend or foe? The Indian informers thought it to be a Frenchman, and boding no good. In the colony were doubts and conjectures, they not expecting any one then from their fatherland. [1]

Passing the point of the Cape, the ship stood on its course for the Plymouth Bay. Towards it every eye was directed. The governor ordered the great signal gun to be fired, to call home from their work every one that was abroad. Every man, every boy even, that could handle a gun, was ready, with full purpose, if she were an enemy, to stand firm on the defence. But on drawing near, to their great relief and joy, she proved to be a friend. It was the little ship Fortune, bringing additional members to the colony; to many families, respected and endeared ones, from whom, more than a year since, they had parted. [2]

To the colony, weakened in numbers and strength, and surrounded by dangers, it was an event marked, and of deep concern. It was so in particular to the family of the Elder. To him and Mrs. Brewster came, among the passengers, their eldest son, Jonathan, and to the others an elder brother. Of the Elder's family, therefore, now present, were himself, his wife, and their three sons. From their daughters, they were still separated. How soon, or when, Lucretia, the wife of Jonathan, came with her son William, there appears to be no record.

Often are favors and mercies the occasions of additional trials. Joyful and welcome as was the reception at this time of dear friends and connections, greatly as it added to the strength of the colony, it was soon apparent that a great scarcity of food must follow. With no knowledge or expectation of the arrival this season of additional consumers, no provision had been made for additional supplies, especially for a number nearly equalling their own. On board the Fortune, no provision had been made even for her own return, much less for the wants of those whom she had brought.

They soon dispatched the ship homeward, however, laden with the avails of their hard earnings and self-denying efforts, as the best returns in their power to the merchant adventurers, for their first outlay in England. The value of their returns, in beaver, wainscotting, choice wood, and other articles, was five hundred pounds. [3]

The ship being dispatched, and their stores of provisions examined, the supply for all until the next summer's harvest of corn, eight months distant, was found to be only for six months, on half allowance, and upon this were they now placed; all taking it patiently.

Not long after the return of the Fortune, came reports to Plymouth that the Narragansetts, a nation bordering upon the bay of that name, and who could assemble five thousand warriors, were assuming a threatening attitude, and were preparing to attack them, notwithstanding the peace that people sought with them the preceding summer. From Canonicus, their chief Sachem, came, by a messenger, as significant of his purpose, a bundle of new arrows wrapt in a snake-skin. The governor, suspecting, but not knowing, its import, on consultation, returned for answer that he had heard of the Sachem's many threatenings — that himself and people wished to live in peace, but if the Sachem would not live peaceably with him, as his other neighbors did, he might do his utmost. Learning afterwards from the interpreter the significance of the suspicious token, the governor, on taking counsel, returned the snake-skin filled with powder and shot, with a corresponding message. The savage king, receiving the message, but fearing the charged skin, would neither touch nor suffer it to remain in his kingdom; but one and another posted it from place to place, until it came back to the settlement entire, as it had been sent. [4]

In this state of things it was that the yet feeble colony adopted measures, in February of this second year, to inclose with paling their whole town. Outside of this paling, encircling the top of the hill and the town underneath, were arrangements for four jetties or bulwarks, from which to defend the whole. In these were gates, to be locked at night, while watch also was kept by day.

Next was a general muster day, and the organization of their men in four companies, each under its own leader, and all under the command of their well-skilled Capt. Standish. [5]

The men, trained and drilled, were assigned their respective posts of duty, to be ready on any emergency or alarm. Special arrangement was also made in case a stealthy foe should attempt the destruction of their dwellings by fire. The elder had his armor, as the others, to be used in case of necessity. [6]

Thus, with great additional labor, was their town inclosed, including a garden for each family, and the whole put in a state of defence. And all was clone while upon short allowance. In the mean time, to keep their promise with their Massachusetts Indian neighbors of coming to trade with them, and to secure, even though it might be but a small supply of food, they sent out, amidst much danger, another expedition thither, which had the effect of securing, for the time, the body of that people in their favor.

By the last of May, their stores of food were cone, even on their half allowance. Adding to their difficulties, a boat from a fishing ship, bound eastward, appeared passing before the town, causing alarm and fear that it was from the French in league with the Indians. It brought, however, not enemies; yet seven additional men for the colony, but no food even for their own sustenance.

By this boat came the startling news of the terrible massacre by the Indians of near four hundred of the English in the Colony of Virginia. This, of course, added to the alarm of the Plymouth Colonists in their present extremity, their stores of provisions being consumed, and famine staring them in the face. "Without bread, with abated strength, the flesh of some swollen, all were in fearful apprehension." Yet how often in man's extremity is God's opportunity! In the letter by this same boat that brought the seven additional destitute men, and in which was the information respecting the Virginia massacre, were kind expressions of the interest of the writer, though a stranger, in the welfare of the Plymouth Colony.

Influenced by these kind expressions, immediately was Mr. Winslow dispatched with the colony boat, and with a message of thanks to the kind stranger, informing him of their extreme condition, and the desire to purchase provisions. Readily and kindly did the Captain [Huddleston] part with such as his ship could spare, and asked of others at the fishing station to do the same. The boat returned, bringing such relief, as, with great care, availed them until the ripening of their growing corn, though but one-fourth of a pound of bread a day for each. "Without this relief (in Winslow's words), some had starved." "And had we not been in a place where divers sorts of shell-fish are, that may be taken with the hand, we must have perished, unless God had raised some unknown or extraordinary means for our preservation." [7]

The month of June of this year appears to have been the season of the colony's greatest extremity. The threatenings of famine, at other times, were remarkably relieved, in the good providence of God, before such long endurance. At such a time it was, when they had no bread, no vegetables but a few groundnuts, no meat, and only such shellfish and herring as could be caught by hand, that Elder Brewster lived months together, even with no drink but water. Yet in calmest submission to his lot, he would thank God that they were enabled to "suck of the abundance of the seas, and of treasures hid in the sand." [8]

It was in this extremity of weakness, and while affected by news of the awful massacre in Virginia, that the evil-disposed Indians around New Plymouth began to throw out their insulting speeches; intimating how easy it would be now to cut them off. Even King Massasoit appeared less friendly to them than formerly. Too critical, indeed, was the state of things now, not to cause the deepest concern.

Therefore, they resolved to erect on the hill, without delay, a strong timber fort, whereon their ordnance should be still more advantageously mounted, and from which a few men would be able to defend the whole settlement from assault, while the rest of the company might be more safely employed in their daily labors. [9] This, amid all their deprivations and labors, was the great work of the second year, begun with eagerness and general approbation, and with the hope that being once finished, and with a continual guard, it would utterly discourage the savages from again attempting to rise against them. It was strong and comely, with a flat roof and battlements, with guard and watch rooms. Yet what added greatly to the interest in its construction, was, its ground story fitted for their place of public worship. Here for years their elder led their devotions, and in the words of their governor, "taught both powerfully and profitably," to the great contentment of the hearers and their comfortable edification. "Yea, many were brought to God by his ministry; he doing more in their behalf in a year, than many do in all their lives." [10]

Here, again, we are to mark another trial, followed by what was esteemed by them, in their sad destitution, another merciful providence. Near the first of July, came into their harbor, two ships with men, sent by Mr. Thomas Weston, their former agent, to found another colony near by them, on Massachusetts Bay. From these were landed some sixty men, stout and strong, but with many sick. They were hospitably received, and the sick provided for by the best means in their power; out of respect to their condition and to Mr. Weston.

While some of them were variously employed with their ships, the most of them remained for months, and became not only burdensome, from their rude, disorderly behavior, but from their wasteful and stealthy depredations upon the ripening corn, which, with great labor and care, the poorly provided Plymouth people were raising for their own supply.

After the departure of these ungrateful visitors, from these and other causes, a scanty harvest ensued; and, notwithstanding all their diligence, gloomy was the prospect before them as to the coming winter and spring. Famine, it appeared, must again ensue. To uncertainties they dare not trust. No market was there within their reach, to which they could apply, except to the Indians; and for this they had no articles of trade.

But now came in a ship (one Master Jones, commander), sent to explore the coast, and having on board stores of knives and beads for this purpose. Of him they most gladly purchased, though at the dear rate of over two-fold per cent. Therefore, now were they fitted again to trade for beavers, and some supply of corn to relieve present and future necessities. [11]

[1] Brad, in Prince, 114. Though not at the time open enemies, the French were looked upon as secret foes, especially in the New World.
[2] Bradford, pp. 105-6.
[3] On her way homewards, how ever, this second emigrant ship to the colony, and the first to take returns of freight to their creditors, was taken by the French, and carried into France, despoiled of all that was worth taking; but the vessel and those on board (among whom was Mr. Cushman) were allowed to return to England, where they arrived on the 17th of February. — In Bradford, 118, 122.
[4] Bradford, 111.
[5] The origin of the New England militia system.
[6] In the inventory of his estate were the items of his armor specified, and in the division of his estate, they were assigned to his son Jonathan, as his eldest born. — Plymouth Records.
[7] Winslow, in Young, 293-4; Bradford, 124-5.
[8] Belknap's Memoir of Brewster. Deuteronomy, xxxiii. 19.
[9] Brad, and Winslow, in Young, 295.
[10] Bradford, 413.
[11] Bradford, 127.
In this ship was a gentleman passenger, Mr. John Poory, who had been secretary in Virginia, and was now on his return to England. Having received favors from the Elder and governor, after his return he gratefully acknowledged the same,

thus: "To your self and Mr. Brewster, I must acknowledge myself many ways in-debted, whose books I would have you think very well bestowed on him, who esteemeth them such jewels, &c." * * "God have you all in his keeping.

Your unfeigned and firm friend, J. POORY."   August 28th, 1622.

In one of the ensuing expeditions, in November, to purchase corn on the cape, Tisquantum fell sick of the Indian fever, at Manamoick (now Chatham), where he died; desiring the governor to pray for him, that he might go to the Englishman's God in heaven; bequeathing various of his things to sundry of his English friends as remembrances of his love. Greatly was his loss felt. — Brad., 128.

Chapter Twenty-Five - 1623

Timely advised, the coming evil shun. — Prior.

This third year of the Pilgrims in New England was full of stirring inci-dents; and their condition was one of continued though varied trials. A mo-ment's glance shows it to have been such as to cause the most anxious thoughts and concern of the whole body; and of no one more than of their Elder. New dangers now surrounded them. Firm as was their trust in the di-vine mercy and care, equally firm was their conviction that their progress, if not their very existence, depended, humanly speaking, upon their own *most strenuous exertions* to procure subsistence; also to keep up and extend a friendly influence and intercourse among their Indian neighbors, and to guard against the combinations of such savage foes as wished for their de-struction.

In these circumstances, while there was caution, their course was still open, bold, and confiding, so open and confiding as to attract the attention, and even wonder, of the natives. [1] With this were united kindness, up-rightness in dealing, and hospitable entertainment; in short, a striving to manifest before them the principles of their religion. [2]

In this manner already had they won, as we have seen, and were winning, the friendship of not a few, the respect and confidence of more, while others had been kept in check from combining to exterminate them.

But much of the influence of their upright course, kind and hospitable treatment, was now sadly counteracted by the base conduct of some of their own countrymen, men of another plantation lately commenced, called the "Weston Plantation." By these were their trials and dangers greatly increased.

These men had been sent out by Mr. Weston to plant another English colo-ny. They came (as we have seen) to Plymouth the preceding summer, and proved themselves to be mostly unprincipled, indolent, and ungovernable men. On settling in the Massachusetts country, bordering upon the remaining Indian settlements of that name, their conduct had almost immediately pro-voked a quarrel with their Indian neighbors. The disaffection soon became so great between the two, that plunders were committed on both sides, and blood was shed. A league, not yet known to the English, was now formed by warriors of the various tribes for the extermination of the Weston people. Among the chiefs thus leagued, as afterwards discovered, was a noted insulting savage named Wituwamat, who boasted of his valor, and derided the weakness of the English. He had before imbrued his hands in the blood both of the English and French. Captain Standish, while abroad at Manomet for food, barely escaped being assassinated at his instigation. [3]

This secret league or plot to exterminate the Weston people, and finally the Plymouth Colony, was disclosed by an incident of no little interest.

King Massasoit, the ally of the English, had fallen sick and was likely to die. The governor, hearing of it, dispatched Mr. Winslow, with a companion and Hobbamock, an interpreter, to visit him, and, if it might be, administer to his comfort. [4] On this friendly but self-denying errand, the messengers went, through forests and unfriendly settlements, and arrived late the second night at Massasoit's dwelling. "They found him extremely low, his sight gone, his teeth set, having for two days taken nothing." In his house were men assembled performing charms or incantations, with fiendish noises; "enough (says one messenger), to sicken those that were well, and not likely to ease him that was sick; while the women were chafing him to keep heat in him." Made to understand that Winslow had come, Massasoit put forth his hand as Winslow approached, uttering "*Keën Winsnow?*" (Art thou Winslow'?) Being answered yes, "Oh, Winsnow," he uttered again in his native speech, "I shall never see thee again." It being made known to him that the governor, hearing of his sickness, had sent messengers to him with some things which, if he would take, might do him good, he signified his desire to receive them. Such "confectionary" as they had brought was prepared and introduced between his teeth, and some dissolved, which he was made to swallow. As he called for drink, more of the same was administered. Little by little he began to revive, which gave encouragement. For two days nothing but hard meat, which he could not receive, had been offered him. Ere long his sight began to come to him. Mr. Winslow continued to administer to his relief as far as his medical knowledge would permit, adapting his efforts to the neglected condition and necessities of the patient. And he had the satisfaction of seeing, as well as those present, his efforts crowned with success. As the sick man's appetite returned, he called for food, and requested Mr. Winslow to prepare him some English pottage. The request being complied with, though with much difficulty for want of materials with which to prepare it, he drank of the savory dish, and with increasing benefit. Benefited himself, he desired Mr. Winslow to go among his sick people, and do the same for them; and this was done, notwithstanding the self-denying and forbidding nature of the office, owing to the neglected and filthy condition of the sufferers. At the end of two days and nights, the royal patient was so far restored, that, amid warm expressions of thankfulness from Massasoit and his people, the messengers took their leave, while many, gathering together on report of the case from far and near, manifested their wonder at seeing with their own eyes the reality of the king's unexpected recovery.

Most opportune was this visit of duty and kindness. Before the messengers' arrival, one sachem had chidingly said to him that "he might now see how hollow-hearted the English were. If they were indeed such friends as they pretended, they would have visited Massasoit in his sickness." "With these and other arguments had such ones tried to turn him from them. But now, upon his recovery, Massasoit answered, "Now I see the English are my friends, and love me; while I live I will never forget this kindness they have shown me." But there were other words spoken of deepest concern to the people of Plymouth.

Ere Mr. Winslow had left, Massasoit had called to him the faithful interpreter Hobbamock, and, in presence of only a few of his council, had disclosed to him the secret plot, and charged him to make it known to Mr. Winslow on his way homeward; which was, that six of the surrounding tribes, led on by those of the Massachusetts, had leagued together to cut off the Weston people, and, lest those of Plymouth should avenge it, to cut them off also; and further, that he himself had been urged since his sickness to join with them, but would not. "And he advised his friends at Plymouth, by all means, as they valued their own lives and the lives of their countrymen, to have the instigators of the plot dispatched at once. Then the plot would cease; otherwise, it would be too late." [5]

Important was this information, and marked the Providence thus manifested while, and only while, they were in the course of their plain duty. Had not this mission been undertaken, this plain duty performed, this plot would not have thus been made known to them. Therefore, it stands out among others a marked case, teaching a striking lesson.

The messengers, returning, reported the success of their mission, but especially the fearful disclosure by Massasoit. From the Weston people came also messages, confessing their wretched condition and danger. [6] Another sachem, brother of the Massachusetts chief, signified the same. [7]

It was the 23d of March, the yearly court day, when the governor communicated the startling intelligence to the whole company, and asked their advice. "A troublesome and grievous business it was," says Winslow; "but especially, for that we knew no other means to deliver our countrymen, and preserve ourselves, but by returning their malicious and cruel purposes upon their own heads, and causing them to fall into the same pit they had digged for others: though it grieved us much to shed the blood of those whose good we ever intended and aimed at, as a principle, in all our proceedings. But they must come to a conclusion, however sudden it might seem; the fear being that the exterminating work would be commenced before they could inform the Weston people of their danger. [8]

The court publicly resolved that a "matter of such weight be committed to the governor, with a certain select council, to do as they should conclude to be best." Already had the governor and council plead most earnestly with the Weston settlers not in any extremity to deal unjustly or provokingly with the Indians around them; "it being," said they, "against the law of God and nature." "It would cross the worthy ends and proceedings of the King's majesty and council for this place - the peaceably enlarging of his dominions, and the propagation of the knowledge of God, and the glad tidings of salvation, which we and they were bound to seek, and were not to use such means as would breed a distaste in the savages against our persons and possessions." [9]

But the extremity had come, and the people of Plymouth must act, or all must suffer. Order was given to Captain Standish to take men and go, not in a manner to excite suspicion, but first to the Weston people, and inform them of the plot, and examine, "so as to judge of the certainty of it;" "but forbear, if possible, until he could make sure of the bloody Wituwamat." [10]

Arriving at the Weston settlement, and informing them of the purposes of his coming, seeing likewise their deplorable condition, the conspirators often coming and going, the captain scrutinized appearances, heard the taunts of the savages who came, awaited the arrival of the two bitterest conspirators, Wituwamat and Pecksuot, and skilfully prepared for the encounter. Those two, now coming and daring the captain to do what he could, tauntingly insulted him from day to day. He bore all patiently until a favorable moment, when he and his men seized, and after a severe struggle slew these chief conspirators. [11]

Fearfully responsible was the whole proceeding; especially so was the concluding act. Self-preservation, and the extremity of the case, were the reasons assigned. As to the results, the plot was broken up, the colonists relieved, and the death of these chief movers m the conspiracy put a stop to further proceedings among those who had leagued together in this project of extermination.

The Weston people likewise abandoned their plantation, the most of them resolving to seek their way home, with such food as the captain could spare, while some few accompanied him and his men to Plymouth. "Thus ended this plantation in one year: all able-bodied men, who boasted of their strength, and what they would bring to pass, in comparison with the people at Plymouth, who had many women, children, and weak ones with them." [12]

What Elder Brewster felt and judged respecting this first shedding of the blood of the native savages, even under the necessities of the case, and to prevent a probable general massacre, we cannot now discover. But their pastor in Holland, on hearing of it (and it is a testimony of the workings of a benevolent Christian heart), wrote to them, "He hoped the Lord had sent the captain among them for good, if they used him right; but doubted whether there was not wanting that tenderness of the life of man, made after the image of God, which was meet;" and concludes thus: "O how happy a thing had it been that you had converted some before you had killed any." [13]

From this tragic affair, we turn to more peaceful, though still bitterly trying scenes. Having all along been disappointed in their expectations of obtaining food from England, the colonists bad been taught, by sad experience, the necessity of a more extensive cultivation and enriching of their own soil; a soil which had proved to be not the most fertile.

Actual experience had also taught them that the practice of cultivating their fields in common, and gathering the produce into a common store for distribution, was not the wisest. It was therefore ordered that, all being ranged in families, each family should have its enlarged allotment of land, and plant, and trust for food to its own exertions; while at the harvest, each should bring a specified portion to the public store for the maintenance of their chief officers and men engaged in fishing, and for other necessities. This latter arrangement was required in connection with their gains in trade and other ways, to secure means for making returns to the "merchant adventurers" in London.

The plan now adopted met with encouraging success. Greater industry, especially in the case of some that had been burdensome, was soon manifested. Even women and children entered the fields to share in the labors. Wherefore more was planted than in the former way, and their future prospects became brighter.

As the third summer advanced, however, notwithstanding their increased industry in planting, in hopes of large supplies, sore disappointment awaited them again. They were to meet trial in another form. Even these people must be taught still more practically the meaning of that declaration — "I will be inquired of by you, saith the Lord." *So they* viewed and improved the occurrence. Says Bradford, "By the time our corn is planted, our food is spent, not knowing at night where to have a bit in the morning, and have neither bread nor corn for three or four months together; yet bear our wants with cheerfulness, and rest on Providence."

"Having but one boat left, we divide our men into several companies, each take their turn to go out and fish, and return not till they get some, though they be five or six days out; knowing there is nothing at home, and to return empty would be a great discouragement. When they stay long, or get but little, the rest go a digging *shell-fish*, and thus we live the summer, only sending one or two to range the woods for deer; they now and then get one, which we divide among the company; in winter, we are helped with *fowl* and *ground-nuts*." [14]

Having in weakness and want completed their first planting, they awaited the kindly showers upon the fields to "bring forth the blade, then the ear, and then the full corn in the ear;" but the needed rain came not; "their grounds became parched," their young corn withered. Day by day, even from May to July, the parching heat increased; the "heavens became as brass over their heads, and the earth as ashes under their feet." At length nearly all hope was at an end, and threatened famine was before them.

In their own language, "Now our hopes were overthrown, and we discouraged, and our joy turned into mourning." "To add to this, a supply that was sent unto us, many months since, having two repulses before, was a third time in company with another ship, three hundred leagues at sea, and now, in three months' time, is no further heard of; only the signs of a wreck were seen on the coast, which could not be judged to be any other than the same, seemingly thus to deprive us at once of all future hopes. The most courageous were now discouraged; because God, who hitherto had been our only shield and supporter, now seemed in his anger to arm himself against us. And who can withstand the fierceness of His wrath?" [15]

Hobbamock, their friend and interpreter, living among them, said, "I am much troubled for the English, for I am afraid they will lose all their corn by the drought, and so they will be starved." [16]

"These and like considerations," continues Winslow, "moved not only every good man privately to enter into examination of his own estate between God and his conscience to humiliation before him, but also to humble ourselves together before the Lord by fasting and prayer." [17]

It was about the middle of July. A day of fasting was set apart by public authority. It was no new observance with them, but was the first for the like occasion. It was founded on the "hope that the same God who had stirred them up thereunto would be moved thereby in mercy to look down upon them, and grant the request of their dejected spirits, if their continuance there might consist with his glory and their good."

Assembled thus for humiliation and prayer, how especially and with what long pleading earnestness the Elder poured forth the soul's confessions and entreaties for mercy, and spoke to the hearts of his people from the Word of Truth, we need scarcely be reminded.

Peculiarly striking (says one of them) was his manner of *laying open the heart and conscience before God in confessions of sin, and begging the mercies of God in Christ for pardon.* [18]

"But, O! (exclaims Winslow) the mercy of our God, who was as ready to hear as we to pray." The morning was clear, and it so continued; the heat unabated; not a cloud or sign of rain to be seen; the drought as likely to continue as ever; yet the exercises on this special occasion, as of life and death, being continued eight or more hours ere their close, the clouds gathered, the heavens were overcast, and before the next morning passed, gentle showers were distilling upon the earth, and so it continued some fourteen days, with seasonable weather intervening. "It were hard to say whether our withered corn or drooping affections were most quickened and revived; such were the bounty and goodness of our God." So revived and recovered were the fruits and corn, as still to give promise of a joyful harvest. Even by the Indians it was viewed as a matter of remark and astonishment. Being in the town, and asking the reason of the day's solemnity, as it was but three days from Sunday, and when informed, seeing what had followed, they confessed the goodness of the Christians' God compared with the answers to their own incantations. Hobbamock, who had before expressed his fears for the English, after the relief came, expressed himself in this manner: "Now I see Englishman's God is a good God, for he hath heard you and sent you rain, and without storms, tempest, or thunder beating down your corn. Surely your God is a good God."

Still further, this people's experience had indeed verified the proverbial saying, that trials and afflictions come not single; and now, they could say their acknowledged mercies came not alone. In this their extremity. Captain Standish arrived from an expedition among the Indians with such supply as would relieve their famishing state until the newly revived corn should ripen.

Fears also had been entertained that certain persons in England, among whom was one Mr. Pierce, for private ends, had succeeded in obtaining new grants of powers, and a new patent for New Plymouth, by which the patentee would hold the lands in perpetuity, and the colonists now settled on them would become only tenants, and be deprived of the liberties, rights, and privileges which had cost them so dear. [19] But now, information reached them that, in ways most remarkable, and which they deemed truly providential, every such attempt had been frustrated, every project brought to naught.

For "these many signs of God's favor and acceptation," to use their own words again, especially for that great one of relief from threatened famine, another day was now set apart for special acknowledgment, a day of thanksgiving by public authority, considering that it would be great ingratitude to be content to pass over with only private thanksgiving that which by private prayer only had not been obtained.

And with what grateful hearts this next day of thanksgiving was kept, we need no other evidence than the circumstances of the case, and the character of the worshippers and of the leader of their worship; "a day," concludes Winslow, "wherein we returned glory, honor, and praise, with all thankfulness, to our good God, who dealt so graciously with us; whose name, for these and all other mercies, be blessed and praised evermore. Amen." [20]

But along with all these incidents of struggle and relief, there was still to the Elder, as well as to many of the company, another remaining cause of anxious concern. They had heard from time to time of the fitting out of one or more ships from England with other members of their families, and others of their company, left in Holland and England; and they had heard of the changes and delays of their sailing. And now for three months nothing further had been heard of them, except by a Captain West, [21] lately arrived, who informed them of his meeting those ships at sea, and of the storm that followed, and their probable shipwreck. Fourteen days, from the arrival of Captain West, did the Elder and his family, with others, pass between hope and fear; when, to their great relief, the ship Ann arrived (and soon after, the little James), bringing to the colony 60 passengers, and to the Elder his two daughters, Patience and Fear. [22] The joyous welcome that followed from the warm-hearted, affectionate father and the tender and now feeble mother, taking to their hearts and homes in this new world their only, long looked-for, almost despaired of daughters, after three years' separation, and now come to them across the perilous ocean, in health, in the freshness of young womanhood, can all be better imagined than described.

But with what deep concern must these loving daughters have beheld the traces of care, exposure, and famishing want in the faded complexions and emaciated forms of their dearest ones, the cause of which was too plain in the poor and scant fare set before them. "The best dish we could present them," says Bradford, speaking of the whole, "is a *lobster* or *piece of fish,* without *bread,* or anything else but *a cup* of fair *spring water.*"

"When these passengers see our poor and low condition, they are much dismayed, and full of sadness." "Only our old friends rejoice to see us, and that it is no worse, and now hope we shall enjoy better days together." [23]

Of Elder Brewster personally he says: "He bore his burden with the rest, living many times without bread or corn, months together; having many times nothing but fish, and often wanting that also."

But the autumn harvest, revived by the gentle showers, and ripened by the favorable weather that followed, came in plentifully at last, to the great joy of all hearts.

By the same ship also came a letter, signed by thirteen of their yet absent friends, in which they write: "*Let it not be grievous to you that you have been instruments to break the ice for others who come after with less difficulty; the honor shall be yours to the world's end.*" "The same God who hath so marvel-lously preserved you from seas, foes, and famine, will still preserve you, and make you honorable amongst men, and glorious in bliss at the last day." [24]

[1] Winslow, in Young, 325.

[2] All the lands occupied by the first settlers, or possessed by this colony, were amicably conveyed to them by the Indians, according to the forms of law. — Russell, keeper of the Plymouth Records.

[3] Winslow, 310.

[4] Winslow's Narrative, in Young, 313, &c.

[5] Winslow, in Young, 320-324.

[6] Winslow, in Young, 328; Bradford, 130.

[7] Ibid., 330.

[8] Ibid., 331, and Bradford. 131, 132.

[9] Winslow, in Young, 328, 329.

[10] Ibid., 332.

[11] Ibid., 337, 339.

[12] Bradford, 132.

[13] See his Letter in Bradford, 164-5, in which is much that partakes of the same spirit.

[14] Prince, 135. Bradford, 134-7.

[15] Winslow, in Young, 348, 349.

[16] Bradford, 141, 142, note.

[17] Winslow, in Young, 349.

[18] Bradford, p. 414.

[19] Bradford, 138-9.

[20] Winslow, in Young, 351.

[21] Winslow, do., 348; Bradford, 141.

[22] Winslow, in Young, 351-353; and Bradford, 142-3, and notes.

[23] Bradford, 145, 146.

[24] Bradford, 145.

Chapter Twenty-Six - 1624

"That is the best history which is collected out of letters." — Bakonius.

In the spring of 1624, arrived the last known letter (of the 20th of December previous), from their pastor in Holland, addressed to Elder Wm. Brewster at Plymouth, New England. Its first and last portions related to the Elder and members of his family *individually*, while an important portion had respect to him, and the Plymouth congregation *officially*. And these portions, being all that relate to our purpose, are as follows: —

To elder Brewster.

"Loving and dear Friend and Brother:
That which I most desired of God in regard of you, namely, the continuance of your life and health, and the safe coming of those sent unto you — that I most gladly hear of, and praise God for the same. And I hope Mistress Brewster's weak and decayed state of body will have some repairing by the coming of her daughters; [1] and the provisions in this and former ships I hear are made for you, which makes us with the more patience bear our languishing state, and the deferring of our desired transportation, which I call desired rather than hoped for, whatsoever you are borne in hand by any others. For, first, there is no hope at all that I know, or can conceive of, of any new stock to be raised for that end; so that all must depend upon returns from you, in which are so many uncertainties as that nothing with any certainty can thence be concluded." * * * * "Now, touching the question propounded by you, I judge it not lawful for you, being a ruling elder (as Romans xii. 7, 8, and 1 Timothy v. 17, opposed to the elders that teach and exhort, and labor in the word and doctrine, to which sacraments are annexed), to administer them, nor convenient, if it were lawful. Whether any learned man will come unto you or not, I know not; if any do, you must Consilium capere in arena — (Take counsel in the time of action). ******" Be you most heartily saluted, and your wife with you, both from me and mine. Your God and ours, and the God of all his, bring us together, if it be his will, and keep us in the mean while, and always to his glory, and make us serviceable to his majesty, and faithful to the end. Amen.

Your very loving brother

JOHN ROBINSON. [2]

"Leyden, December 20th, 1623."

Here we have a further insight into some of the circumstances of the Elders family at the time, and a testimony of the high and affectionate regard in which he himself was held.

And the official decision was one of no small concern to the Plymouth congregation. To the question which the Elder had propounded to Mr. Robinson (for his own satisfaction, or that of others), whether it were lawful or expedient for him as ruling elder to administer the Christian sacraments, Mr. Robinson answered, he *judged it not lawful, nor convenient if it were lawful.*

We leave the statement as it stands, as a recorded fact without discussion, without any added opinion, without gloss or disguise, a witness of their pastor's judgment in the case. [3]

Connected with this judgment of the pastor in Holland, stands the other fact that the Elder acted in accordance with it; declining to do the duties of the pastoral office in respect to the sacraments, however plausible the arguments for doing so, or urgent the circumstances might seem to be. He had not been ordained to that office: he would not assume it. And as to his declining the pastoral office, writers have suggested his extreme modesty as the cause. [4] Yet in this, also, he doubtless acted conscientiously. The whole course of his life shows that he was not the man to do otherwise.

The pastor, indeed, hoped that himself, or some other one, would ere long come to supply the deficiency. When it was objected against them, by some in England, that they had not the Sacraments, they answered: "The more is our grief that our pastor is kept from us, by whom we might enjoy them; for we used to have the Lord's supper every Sabbath, and baptism as often as there was occasion of children to baptize." [5]

With the facts before us in relation to the parts of the pastoral office which Elder Brewster *did not* perform, according to their order of church government, we next notice more specifically than we have yet done, the official duties which he did perform, and likewise *how* he performed them, and the *results*. Here we have the words of both pastor and elder, defining their views of the duties of the office: —

1st. As to "ruling or governing." "Our elders do administer their office in admonitions and excommunications, for public scandals, publicly, and before the congregation." [6] In relation to Elder Brewster, says Bradford, "For the government of the church, which was most proper to his office, he was careful to preserve good order in the same, and to preserve purity, both in the doctrine and communion, and to suppress any error or contention that might begin to rise up amongst them." And as to the results of his labors in this particular, it is added, "God gave good success to his endeavors, and he saw the fruit of his labors herein all his days."

2d. As to "teaching." "We choose none for governing elders but such as are able to teach." Accordingly, says Bradford, of *their* elder, "when the church had no other minister, he taught twice every Sabbath, and that both powerfully and profitably, to the great contentment of the hearers, and their comfortable edification." As to method, "he was very plain and distinct in what he taught; by which means he became the more profitable to his hearers." In manner, "he was easy of speech, of grave and deliberate utterance, effective in arousing the affections." "In prayer, both public and private, he was singularly gifted in laying open the heart and conscience before God, in the humble confession of sin, begging the mercies of God, in Christ, for pardon. He was not long and tedious, but divided his prayers, except upon solemn and special occasions, as on days of fasting and humiliation." And as the fruits of these labors, it is added: "Many were brought to God by his ministry; he did more in this behalf in a year than many do in all their lives." [7]

From this statement of his position and labors, and their results, we here pass over various incidents, however interesting, concerning the colony in *general,* and proceed to those which, henceforth, more than others, concerned the Elder and his church in *particular.*

Mr. Winslow having been in England near the close of the last year, and returning in the spring, brought with him, by the urgent request of a portion of the "merchant adventurers," a minister named Lyford. Apparently he was intended by them to supply the place of Mr. Robinson. His subsequent course, however, proved him to be of no more credit to those who sent, than benefit to those who received him.

Complaisant, humble, shedding many tears, and blessing God that he had been brought to see their faces, he was received by them and entertained to the best of their ability. Admitted at his desire into their church, he blessed God for the opportunity and freedom of enjoying the ordinances in purity among them. A larger allowance was made him for maintenance than to any other of the colony. And as the governor had been accustomed to consult in weighty matters with Elder Brewster, in council, with the assistants, he now called Mr. Lyford to the same. Not long after, however, it was discovered that their confidence in him was misplaced. He privately formed a party, without notifying either the Elder or governor, withdrew and held separate public meetings, and wrote letters to certain ones in England against the colony. Yet upon being accused of this last, he denied it; but being confronted by his own letters, was confounded. When tried and convicted, he confessed all; and in the end he was sentenced to expulsion, though with leave to remain six months. On this being done, he declared that his sentence was far less than he deserved, and that what he had written against them was false.

A like confession he also made before their church; and such were the appearances of his sincerity and repentance, that he was restored to his place of teacher as before. But after a while, he again relapsed, and again wrote to England, affirming the truth of what he had before written, which caused the "adventurers" yet further trouble.

He was invited the next season, as minister, to a new plantation at Nantasket. In the mean time Mr. Winslow, being again in England, the "adventurers" there took the matter in hand; when on Lyford's former misbehavior in Ireland being disclosed, for which he had been forced to leave that kingdom, it was resolved by the Moderators, to whom the case was committed for decision, that his conduct at New Plymouth was sufficient cause for his rejection, and that this further disclosure rendered him unmeet longer to do the duties of the ministry. We may well imagine how sore a trial all this must have been to the Elder, who doubtless presided in all their church meetings on the subject, and must have witnessed and passed through the excitement caused by it in his New Plymouth congregation. Greatly must he have feared its effects likewise among those friendly or unfriendly to their principles of church order in England. [8]

What might have been the result in the Plymouth colony had the company in England sent over an enlightened and worthy minister, imbued with the spirit of his Divine Master, and truly sympathizing with this people in their trials, yet conscientiously attached to the Church of England, while he disapproved of the oppressive acts of the court, and of the course of all who sustained those acts, we are not called upon to decide, or even to conjecture. Our business is with what did, and not with what might have taken place.

Of Elder Brewster's public labors during this period, even while in connection with the other minister, we have ample testimony in the following record: "Our revered Elder labored diligently in dispensing the word of God unto us before he (Lyford) came; and since hath taken equal pains with himself in preaching the same; and be it spoken without ostentation, he is not inferior to Mr. Lyford (and some of his superiors), [9] either in gifts or learning, though he would never be persuaded to take higher office upon him." [10]

At the election of officers this spring (1624) the governor desired the people to elect another than himself, as the opportunity to do this was the object of a yearly election. If it were an honor or benefit to be elected, it was meet that others should be partakers; if a burden, others should help to bear it. But they elected the same governor with five assistants in place of one, and gave the governor a *double vote!* [11]

This spring, also, Mr. Winslow brought over with him from England *four neat kine,* "the first in the land," [12] a fact which brings vividly to mind the sore deprivation hitherto endured in this particular, and of the now anticipated luxury of milk, cream, and butter.

At this time, the people requested of the governor land for continued possession, and not by *lot yearly,* as before; and hence was granted one acre to each person, and as near the town as practicable, for safer and easier defence. [13]

The acre granted to the Elder, as well as those to some others, might probably be yet recognized by the necessary search. No more land was granted until the expiration of the seven years, or rather until the closing of the term of the original contract with the adventurers in London.

As to the amount or extent of the "fisheries" on the coast of New England this year, the report presents the number of fifty ships from England. [14] Few of them, however, visited New Plymouth.

On the 5th of August of this year, was an occurrence in the family of the Elder, an event of no small interest in every family wherever it takes place. It was the marriage of his daughter, Patience Brewster, with Mr. Thomas Prince. Thus were they "bride and bridegroom, pilgrims for life, henceforward to travel together." Mr. Prince came to the colony more than four years previously, in the ship Fortune, had brought a respectable patrimony, and was now in his 24th year. He was frequently elected assistant to the governor, and afterwards governor. [15] It was the ninth marriage in the colony. At the close of this year, there were in the colony about 180 persons, 32 dwelling-houses, and a well-built fort of wood, lime, and stone, on "Fort Hill" (now Burial Hill), with a fair "watch tower," as well as the commodious room for public worship. The town had been surrounded by palisades, about half a mile in compass; and they had just returned a ship of 180 tons, with a valuable cargo, to the "adventurers" in London.

The settlement was healthful, not one of their company having died since the close of the first year, notwithstanding their extreme suffering and want. All of which success no one could have viewed with more interest than he who, from the first, had been a chief promoter of the undertaking.

[1] Daughters Patience and Fear Brewster, as stated in the preceding chapter.

[2] See the whole letter in Bradford, 165-7.

[3] Could facts be always stated in historic writing just as they were, history would take the place, and have the authority, which belongs to it. Facts would thus stand forth unperverted as so many faithful, truthful witnesses, ever ready to be used for the eliciting or establishing of truth. Immensely would this course lessen the fields of angry controversy.

[4] See Morton, Hubbard, Belknap, &c.

[5] Bradford, 161, and Plymouth Church Records.

[6] Bradford, 35.

[7] Bradford, 413, and 414, and 34, 35. As to his official costume, he appears to have worn a gown and bands; these are mentioned in the Inventory.

[8] Bradford, 171, 173, 175, 192, 196. The result was, the breaking up of the company of merchant adventurers, and the relinquishment, by the greater part of them, of any further care or aid for the colony. — Bradford, 196.

Mr. Lyford went from Plymouth and officiated at Nantasket, then at Naumkeug, or Salem, and thence to Virginia, where he died.

[9] Original "letters."

[10] Bradford, 187-8.

[11] Prince, 145; and Bradford, 156.

[12] Bradford, 158.

[13] Do., 167.

[14] Prince.

[15] Moore's Memoirs of American Governors, 139.

Chapter Twenty-Seven – 1625-1626

Human life is checkered at the best,
And joy and grief alternately preside. — Tracy.

During the year 1625, the affairs of the Plymouth colony were internally more encouraging than in any previous year. They had general health, were at peace with the Indians, and their planting had resulted in a good supply of corn. But externally, in respect to their connection with the merchant adventurers in London, their prospects were assuming a gloomy aspect. Many of those adventurers had entered into the agreement, at first, as a mere business speculation, and for large profits, and had found themselves disappointed. The losses at sea, including the loss of a large portion of what the new colonists had been able to return to them, with the unsettled and trying times, had discouraged or embarrassed others. While party spirit and contentions, greatly aggravated by the late Lyford difficulty, caused disaffection and deep chagrin in many more. The largest portion of them, therefore, discouraged, disappointed, or alienated, withdrew, and broke up the connection. [1] It is true that the case of the adventurers was hard, but harder had been that of the colonists. These had entered into the engagement on hard terms, at first. [2] Their losses by death had been many; and, after five long years of unexampled trials and efforts, still further aid was needed by them from abroad. In this state of things, those of the adventurers who stood firm to their original purpose, and were disposed to act further in the business, finding themselves left with a debt of 1400 pounds, now addressed the New Plymouth people accordingly: "The thing we feared is come upon us, and the evil we strove against has overtaken us, yet we cannot forget you, nor our friendship and fellowship together." "You and we are left to bethink ourselves what course to take in the future, that your lives and our moneys be not lost." "We hope you will do your best to *free our* engagements. Let us all endeavor to keep an honest cause, and see what time will bring forth, and how God in his providence will work for us. We are still persuaded you are the people that must make a plantation in those remote places when all others fail and return. And your experience of God's providence and preservation is such as we hope your hearts will not fail you, though your friends should forsake you (which we ourselves shall not do whilst we live, so long as your honesty so well appeareth)." [3] * * *

In return, fresh efforts were made by the colonists to meet the expectations of those friends in whose hands the claims and remaining business of that association were now left. All that these could obtain in the way of trade was immediately collected and forwarded by the returning ship. But here again were both adventurers and colonists to meet with another discouragement. This ship, after a prosperous voyage, even into the entrance of the English Channel, was captured with her freight of beaver and other furs and lading, by a Turkish man-of-war, and her men carried into captivity. In this state of their affairs, war threatening the country, and the plague raging frightfully in London, and all business at a stand, little could the colonists' agent do in procuring the means, and making purchases, even at exorbitant prices, for the next season's supply of clothing and goods for trade. Some first steps, however, were taken towards a final compromise with the remaining first adventurers.

In their church, under the continued direction and teaching of their elder, notwithstanding the check received from Lyford's untoward course, the number of members appears to have increased. [4]

This year also was there another marriage in the Elder's family, that of his other remaining daughter, Fear Brewster, to Mr. Isaac Allerton, the first, and for several years, the only assistant to the governor. He was in about his 36th year, had lost his first wife about five years before, soon after their landing from the Mayflower, was one of their principal men, much engaged in public affairs, and was subsequently confidential agent in England. [5]

Passing on to the year 1626, and early in that year, we find the first arrival of information of *two occurrences* which had taken place more than a year before, so long was it ere the news reached them. The first, and that which most intimately concerned them as a congregation, was the death of their pastor in Holland.

Sad to them, and unexpected, was this news. Sudden and discouraging was his death. He had been strongly attached to them, and they to him. Now in the prime of life, he had proved himself to be a man of marked ability, piety, and varied attainments. All along had he desired, and they of Plymouth expected him to come to them, with the remaining portion of their people in Leyden, and minister to the whole again, as he before had done; but want of means, and the opposing influence of those who had chief control among the merchant adventurers, had prevented. That expectation was now at an end. Their elder was now officially, as he had been before virtually, the chief teacher and guide of the pilgrim band.

Here it is matter worthy of inquiry, what were the religious characteristics of Mr. Robinson, with whom the Elder had been intimately associated for at least 13 years, in England and Holland, and with whom he had held most friendly correspondence now some four years more? Also, what were his and the Elder's position in relation to brethren of the Church of England? And what was their distinctive position in relation to the other separate congregations with whom they were classed? That they held, doctrinally, the great principles then held in the Church of England, has already been stated. Were there any doubts on this point, they must at once be dispelled by the following "seven articles which the Church of Leyden sent to the Council of England, to be considered of in respect of their judgments occasioned about their going to Virginia." These are the "seven articles" mentioned by Sir Edwin Sandys in his letter to Mr. Robinson and the Elder, Nov. 12, 1617, and lately brought to light. We present them here entire, with the original spelling and contractions, as an important addition to our history in this connection, and as a matter of curiosity to some of our readers, showing the manner in which the English language was written even by good scholars of that day: —

[STATE PAPER OFFICE, AMERICA AND WEST INDIES, VIRGINIA.]

Seven Artikes which ye Church of Leyden sent to y" Counsell of England to bee considered of in respeckt of their judgments occationed about their going to Virginia.

1. To ye confession of fayth published in ye name of ye Church of England & to every artikell theerof wee do wth ye reformed churches wheer wee live & also els where assent wholy.

2. As wee do acknolidg ye docktryne of fayth theer tawght so do wee ye fruites and effeckts of ye same docktryne to ye begetting of saving fayth in thousands in ye land (conformistes & reformistes) as ye ar called wth whom also as wth our bretheren wee do desyer to keepe sperituall communion in peace and will pracktis in our parts all lawfull thinges.

3. The King's Majesty wee acknolidg for Supreame Governor in his Dominion in all causes and over all parsons, and yt none maye decklyne or apeale from his authority or judgment in any cause whatsoever, but y' in all thinges obedience is dewe unto him, ether active, if ye thing commanded be not agaynst God's woord, or passive yf itt bee, except pardon can bee obtayned.

4. Wee judg itt lawfull for his Majesty to apoynt bishops, civill overseers, or officers in awthoryty onder hime, in ye severall provinces, dioses, congregations or parrislies to oversee y® Cliurclies and governe them civilly according to ye Lawes of ye Land, untto whom ye ar in all thinges to geve an account & by them to bee ordered according to Godlyncs.

5. The authoryty of ye present bishops in ye Land wee do acknolidg so far forth as ye same is indeed derived from his Majesty untto them and as ye proseed in his name, whom wee will also theerein honor in all things and hime in them.

6. Wee beleeve yt no sinod, classes, convocation or assembly of Ecclesiasticall Officers hath any power or awthoryty att all but as ye same by y® Majestraet geven unto them.

7. Lastly, wee desyer to geve untto all Superiors dew honnor to preserve ye unity of ye speritt wth all yt feare God, to have peace wth all men what in us lyeth & wheerein wee err to bee instructed by any. Subscribed by

JOHN ROBINSON.

and

WILLIAM BREWSTER. [6]

But were Mr. Robinson, the Elder, or theirs people, Brownists, or "rigid separatists," as many writers have called them? or did they say and teach — as did Robert Brown, or Mr. Smith, or other rigid separatists — that the Church of England was *no true church,* that it was *sinful* or *wrong to attend* its worshipping assemblies, or hear the preaching of the Word therein? [7] Though this has been in part answered, yet here again it is meet that they should speak for themselves. "For myself (says Mr. Robinson), I believe with my heart before God, and profess with my tongue, and have before the world, that I have one and the same faith, hope, spirit, baptism, and Lord, which I had in the Church of England, and none other; that I esteem so many in that church, of what state or order soever, as are truly partakers of that faith, (as I account many thousands to be), for my Christian brethren, and myself, a fellow member with them of that one mystical body of Christ, scattered far and wide throughout the world, that I have always, in spirit and affection, all Christian fellowship and communion with them, and am most ready in all outward actions and exercises of religion, lawful and lawfully to be done, to express the same; and withal, that I am persuaded the hearing of the word of God there preached, in the manner and upon the grounds formerly mentioned, both lawful, and upon occasion necessary for me and all true Christians, withdrawing from that hierarchical order of church government and ministry, and the appurtenances thereof, &c." [8] Such, then, were his distinctive views. "And," says Winslow, "if any joining to us formerly, either when we lived at Leyden, in Holland, or since we came to New England, have with the manifestation of their faith and profession of holiness, held forth therewith separation from the Church of England, I have divers times, both in the one place and the other, heard either Mr. Robinson, our pastor, or Mr. Brewster, our elder, stop them forthwith, showing them that we required no such things at their hands, leaving the Church of England to themselves, and to the Lord, before whom they should stand or fall." [9] The application to them of the terms "Brownists," "rigid separatists," he pronounces "another gross mistake." "Very injurious it is (says Bradford), to call those after his (Brown's) name, whose person they never knew, and whose writings, few, if any of them ever saw, and whose errors and backslidings they have constantly borne witness against." [10] And Robinson adds, again, on parting with them at Leyden, "Use all means to avoid and shake off the name of Brownist, being a mere nickname and brand to make religion and the professors of it odious to the Christian world." [11] Hence they have been called *semi-* (half) *separatists;* and Mr. Robinson, a "principal overthrower of the Brownists," "ruining the rigid separation," by "*allowing the lawfulness of communicating with the Church of England in the Word and prayer.*" [12]

Thus much, at least, justice to the cause of historic truth, justice to their late pastor, justice to the Elder, and to the distinctive views of themselves and people, seem to have been demanded, in order to show their position relative to the Established Church, and other separating congregations with whom, in many things, they sympathized.

But there was another occurrence, within a month after the preceding, the news of which came by the same ship from England, and which also deeply concerned the New Plymouth colony.

On the 27th of March, old style, 1625 (being on Sunday), died James the First of England; and he was succeeded by his only remaining son, the first Charles. [13]

During all the twenty-two years of James' reign in England, as well as during some twenty of the preceding years of Elizabeth, had Brewster been an observer of their public measures; and in some of them had he been personally interested. One of these measures, pressed to extremes by James, had caused the pilgrim movement, and the Elder's present position in the New World.

What his reflections now were (for he was a man of reflection), on hearing of the death of his earthly sovereign, and while casting his thoughts back, and reviewing the whole period, it would be interesting to know, and we might perhaps easily conjecture, but we have no recorded evidence. The evidence is clear, however, that towards that sovereign, in his legitimately approved acts, he had himself ever shown a spirit of loyalty; one arbitrary measure only excepted; and in respect to that, he had been willing to suffer.

Even while in Holland, self-exiled, and under the protection of the states, he and his pastor gave evidence how "grievous it was to them to live from under the state," away from the people and the institutions of England. And, in view of their removal from Holland to some other land, no tempting offers of gain, no inducements whatever, could draw him or his people from their desire and purpose to live under England's government and shield. With their own hands did pastor and elder write to those in authority, expressing all this, [14] and their willingness, not only to take anew "the oath of allegiance" (submission and obedience to the king as temporal sovereign, independent of any other power on earth), but "the oath of supremacy (say they) we shall willingly take if it be required of us" — acknowledging the king as civilly the head of the church. [15] The practical carrying out of the same was shown in the first and last words of the solemn compact on board the Mayflower. To the same effect was the late joint letter to the Weston people, urging them to fulfil the "worthy ends of the king's majesty and honorable council for New England, in the peaceable enlargement of his majesty's dominions, and the propagation of the Christian faith," as their bounden duty. Upon all this, therefore, would the Elder look back, in respect to king and country, with an approving conscience.

Even in respect to that, wherein was the offending point - that, where men, Christian men, thought, judged, and acted differently, in respect to obedience to sovereign authority enforcing by arbitrary will a certain church order and ceremony — even in this (whatever different minds might judge to be right or wrong), he would feel that himself had quietly submitted to the penalties; acting with no ill will to his sovereign, but with faithfulness to his God. [16]

But other things than these from the past would his memory bring up for review. With regrets had he seen the day when that sovereign, leaving the Protestant states to struggle for themselves, and violating his pledges to the Protestant cause, had negotiated long to unite his son to a princess of Spain, and finally contracted for him a marriage with a French princess, to bring into his court the influence of an opposite faith, at the same time neglecting his own Protestant daughter, suffering her dominion (the Palatinate) to be despoiled, and that daughter and her children to be driven for shelter wherever she could find it.

He had seen the day when his majesty could barter away for his own personal use, the treaty claim upon Holland, left by Elizabeth, of over £800,000, surrendering ingloriously, for one-third of that sum, those cautionary towns, and even that Flushing and its fortresses, of which he (Brewster) had once held the keys in the service of the Queen.

He had seen the day when his sovereign had resorted to the high-handed acts of committing to the Tower eminent statesmen, like his friend. Sir Edwin Sandys, for asserting the right of freedom of debate on matters of state in their places in Parliament. [17]

He had seen the time when the King, in places lately filled by such able statesmen as Elizabeth assembled about her, had, from mere humor or fancy of a fine person, raised suddenly to posts of highest honor and trust, and endowed with princely estates the low and the ignorant; [18] countenancing, also, in his court revolting intermixtures of profanity, excess, and licentiousness, with professions of religion.

All this, and far more, equally painful to contemplate, had the Elder witnessed in his late sovereign's course. Again, on the other hand, along the line of that course he had seen bright spots (for some bright spots there really were). Among these he could call to mind that act by which James yielded to the firm decision of Chief Justice Coke and his associates, and gave the first blow, which was a prelude to the final death blow, to the illegal power of the High Commission Court. And yet there had been another act, which shone conspicuously above all others in the King's life. At his suggestion, and under his authority, was undertaken and executed, by some of the ablest scholars in his kingdom, "the authorized translation of the Holy Scriptures into the English language:" a translation unrivalled in its faithfulness to the originals, in its majestic dignity yet simplicity of style — most wisely suited to reach the minds and hearts of the learned and unlearned; a work that has even done more than all others to develop the power, scope, and beauty of the English tongue. Of which work, though nearly 250 years have elapsed since its completion, there could even now, after all the researches of later times, be made but few improvements.

Yet, to glance no further at those acts in the life of James, which evidently, from all the circumstances, and from the volumes in his library, shared the thoughts and contemplations of the Elder, we shall allude to but one fact more. It was the apprehension of still more oppressive measures under the reign of his son. And how fully these apprehensions were realized, the history of Charles the First bears but too abundant testimony.

Returning again to affairs of immediate concern in the colony, we find them still *internally* improving. Their grounds, by diligent cultivation, yielded an encouraging harvest; and there was some surplus with which to trade with the natives. But in respect to their connection with the adventurers in London, all was becoming extremely embarrassing. Indeed, there was now an approaching crisis. One year more would end the seven years, when, according to the original agreement, all that belonged to the colony would be subject to a general division and distribution among the shareholders in England as well as themselves. Thus the lands they had cultivated, the houses they had built amidst so much suffering, and their whole stock, might, to a large extent, go into the hands of others. And, more than all, their name and character for integrity and honesty, as Christians, would be called in question, if all claims upon them were not fairly satisfied. It was a matter which deeply concerned all, governor and people, the Elder and his church. Determined to show all fidelity on their part, they sent a special agent, the Elder's son-in-law, Mr. Allerton, the first assistant of the governor, to England, with power and instructions to negotiate, and "make such composition with the adventurers" as he best could, and in all due form, with writings drawn, signed, and sealed, but subject to their own examination and approval on his return. [19] Under their own names and seals, also, they empowered him to obtain a loan, with which to purchase the needed supplies of clothing and goods. In this condition ends the sixth year of the New Plymouth Colony. [20]

[1] Brad., 196-200.
[2] See Ch. 17, note 19.
[3] Brad., 198-200.
[4] Bradford, 189.
[5] Prince and Bradford.
[6] See in the Collections of the New York Historical Society, Second Series, vol. iii., just published.
Mr. Bancroft, in presenting the copy of the original to this society for publication, remarks: "None of the successors of Prince seem to have been aware of the existence of this document. It escaped the notice of Bishop Wilberforce, to whom America is deeply indebted for the discovery of the original manuscript of Bradford's History of the Plymouth Colony, and of Mr. Anderson, who more distinctly announced to the world that the original manuscript of that long lost work was in the library of the Bishop of London.

"These Seven Articles, not inserted in Bradford's History," though "referred to on" pages 30 and 31, "seem to have slumbered unnoticed for more than two centuries, among the Virginia volumes in the State Paper Office in Westminster. The copy I send you was made for me by Mr. Sainsbury, a clerk in that office, in whose accuracy I have entire confidence." — Mr. Bancroft's Letter preparatoiy to said Articles, New York, Oct. 3, 1856.

[7] The language of the extreme separatists was: "We confidently deny that ever the English nation, or any one of our predecessors, were of the faith of Christ, or at any time believed visibly in a true constituted church, but were come of the race of the pagans, till Rome the mother came, and put upon us her false baptism, worship, and ministry, and so our case is simply paganish." "Your Church of England, being of Antichrist's constitution, is a false church — hath a false constitution, a false ministry, a false worship, a false government, and a false baptism, the door and entry into the church; and so all is false in your church." — Letter from two of Mr. Smith's Church, in Hunter's Appendix, p. 171.

And the very bitter language, (such as we like not to quote, did not historic faithfulness require it), used by that same Mr. Smith, even against Mr. Robinson and his people, because they would not go to the same extreme as himself, was such as this: "Be it known, therefore, to all the separation, that we account them, in respect to their constitution, to be as very a harlot as either her mother, the Church of England, or her grandmother, Rome is, &c." — Smith's "Character of the Beast." Bp. Hall's works, vol. vii. 385, ix. 409.

One reason of Mr. Robinson and people's removing from Amsterdam to Leyden, was the extreme rigidness, in some particulars, of Mr. Smith and others who were there before them. — Brad., in Young, 441, 446; and Winslow, in Prince, 87, 88. How different from all this was the language of Robinson and his people!

[8] Robinson's works. Treatise "Of the Lawfulness of Hearing of the Ministers of the Church of England;" also in Young's Chronicles, Notes 400-401.

[9] Winslow, in Young, 389, 400. "'Tis true (says he), Mr. Robinson was more rigid in his course and way at first than towards his latter end."

[10] Bradford, in Young, 444.

[11] In Young, 397-8.

[12] Prince's Annals, 87.

[13] Prince Maurice, of Orange, also died this same year.

[14] Winslow, in Young, 381.

[15] Bradford, 34, as well as the Seven Articles.

[16] This was the teaching of Luther; it was also the teaching of Robinson; see his "Just and Necessary Apology."

[17] Parliamentary Records of 1620-22.

[18] The case of Villiers, entitled Buckingham, is a striking illustration. We introduce the incident as narrated by the historian Rapin. Raised suddenly by the King from obscurity to a high office of state, with no other qualifications than an attractive person, and such qualities as struck the fancy of the sovereign, Villiers applied to the archbishop (Abbott) for instruction how to behave in his new position. The archbishop told him he had three lessons to give him: First, to pray without ceasing for the king's prosperity, and for grace to serve his master faithfully. Secondly, to labor continually to preserve a good union between the King, Queen, and Prince, Thirdly, to tell the King nothing but the truth. Then the bishop caused him to repeat *these three lessons* before him, to see if he retained them. The King, hearing of this, said the lessons were worthy of a bishop. And yet of this very bishop King James could afterwards say, he was too much of a Puritan for him.

[19] Capt. Standish, as agent, had made some beginning in this matter the year previous.

[20] Brad., 208, 210.

Chapter Twenty-Eight - 1627

"The wise and active conquer difficulties,
By daring to attempt them." — Rowe.

It is the spring of 1627. The New Plymouth colonists have found themselves involved, one and all, in difficulties differing from all through which they had hitherto passed. The London Association, on which they had depended for further aid, was broken up; the interest and credit of their own little colony were at stake; and a pecuniary crisis was before them. An agent dispatched to London with powers to bring matters to a settlement, and to assume the necessary responsibility, had with great efforts executed the mission, and returned.

The terms of the settlement were, that the colonists pay 1800 pounds sterling, in yearly payments of 200 pounds each, for nine years. On these terms they would be released from their former agreement; their lands, houses, and all their effects be secured to themselves. These terms, as favorable as could have been expected, were now at a general meeting, accepted and ratified.

But who, in their poor condition, would assume the obligations to meet these payments, and "discharge their other engagements, and supply the yearly wants of the plantation!"

In this emergency, Governor Bradford, and Elder Brewster, with some five others, came forward, and "jointly bound themselves, in behalf of the rest, for the payments." Great was the risk, but they shrank not from it. [1]

And now, having assumed the responsibility, how, under the circumstances, were the means to be procured"? All was in an uncertain condition amongst them. They had other large liabilities; and with great difficulty had they been able to meet their daily expenditures.

Yet these tried pilgrims were equal to the task. [2]

Put to the test, they devise the plan, not by tax, not by forced labor, which, as far as it had been tried, had failed, but by a plan laid deep in the first elements of man's nature, calculated to bring into action personal interest and privileges with the highest public good. It would enlist the hopes and desires of personal advancement with a sense of duty, justice, and the nobler emotions, in one combined, patient, and zealous effort. By this plan, the Governor and Elder, with the few others mentioned, proposed to receive into partnership with themselves, all the first colonists, with every young man of prudence among them, and give to each a share in all that belonged to the colony, with the right to each head of a family to purchase a share for his wife, and one for each child; also to divide at once to each shareholder equal portions of land, with title to his own habitation and improvements, on condition of his meeting his own specified share in the responsibility, by certain portions of the fruits of his industry; the chief ones in the movement reserving to themselves the management of the trade of the colony, in order to meet with its avails, the pledged engagement. Simple as this plan may appear, it had in it the simplicity of wisdom. It was received with general satisfaction, and adopted. Each shareholder drew by lot his or her portion of land, in addition to the homestead and small allotment before granted. Each drew also his share in the preciously valued domestic cattle in the colony. [3]

Under this arrangement the colonists passed from a state of dejection and fear to one of encouragement and hope. Fresh energies were awakened, new personal interests were enlisted, each went to his field of labor with the prospect, in clue time, of an unencumbered home; the forests gave way, the growing corn succeeded, while new channels for trade were opened, and ere long the happiest results crowned their united efforts. [4]

But we pass from this community of action and interest, in which the Elder had a twofold share, to an intervening occurrence in his own family. From

151

the list of the names of all of the colonists living to whom grants of land were now made, Mrs. Brewster's name is missing. [5] She had died, then, before this date. How long before (though since the arrival of her daughters) we know not. Yet, though no record gives the date, and no stone marks the place of deposit of her earthly remains, she lives in the remembrance of her descendants as a Christian mother, and the revered companion of the Pilgrim Elder — as one of the faithful band, who, from a home of plenty in England, accompanied her husband through all the self-sacrificing trials of the twelve years in Holland, the perils of the sea, and the still sorer trials of this new colony. At length, after having nurtured a worthy family, with enfeebled health, her spirit departed from this to a better world, leaving the Elder to finish singly his still longer pilgrimage on earth in the further service of his people and their God. Peace be to thy ashes, mother! and all due regard to thy memory! will every descendant of thine say. Though we have not seen thee, or the place of thy sepulture, may we meet thee in joy at the resurrection morn.

Early in this year came messengers and letters from the governor of the Dutch plantation, signed by Isaac De Rasieres, Secretary.

Some four years before this date, and some three years after the arrival of the pilgrim company, the Dutch from Amsterdam and other parts of Holland, had commenced a settlement at the mouth of the river Hudson, and called it New Amsterdam, after the chief city of their own country. [6]

Our Plymouth people had heard of them by way of the Indians, but could never meet with them, or in any other way learn anything from them until the present time.

But now had come congratulatory letters, in French and Dutch, with a friendly deputation, and kind tokens of regard, from their governor and council, proposing amicable intercourse and trade. These were answered in Dutch, in accordance with the same friendly spirit, with all due acknowledgments, and also with expressions of grateful remembrance of the years when many of themselves had received good and courteous treatment from their countrymen in Holland; "for which," says the answer, "we, and our children after us, are bound to be thankful to your nation, and shall never forget the same, but shall heartily desire your good and prosperity, as our own, forever." [7]

As the governor, with some few others, among whom was the Elder, became pledged for the payment of the debts, they became doubly interested in the trade of the colony. By that trade chiefly, in connection with any accruing produce of their lands, were the pledged payments to be met. Accordingly, for the conducting of that trade, while most of the people who were now partners in the new compact were engaged in planting, two prominent trading posts were established. One of these was at Manomet, called also Aptuxet, some twenty miles south of Plymouth. Here, on a small but navigable stream of the same name, was the singularly favorable point where coasting vessels, coming from the Sound of Long Island, New Amsterdam (afterwards

New York), and the Southern Colony, and passing up the Buzzard's Bay, could find a landing place nearest to the waters of Cape Cod Bay. Over this neck of land, called the Suez of New England, [8] was a land carriage of only about six and a half miles. Thus, in the transportation of all their light articles of traffic, was avoided the far longer and more dangerous passage around that singularly formed peninsula of Malabar and Cape Cod. [9] Here, at Manomet, then, in the wilds of the Indian country, with the Indian village near at hand, and the seat of a sagamore on the adjacent hill, they built their hewn plank trading-house and their coasting "Barque," placing there men to plant and trade in peace, to the mutual benefit of themselves and the native Indians.

There, too, was first made known to them, shortly after, that new medium of trade in place of money, the noted "Sewan" or "Wampum," [10] which proved to be especially beneficial. "It was not profitable at first," says Bradford, "till the *inland Indians* came to know it; and then we could scarce procure enough for many years together." "Strange it is to see the great alteration it in a few years makes among the savages; for the Massachusetts, and others in those parts, had scarce any, it being only made and kept among the Pequots and Narragansetts, who grew rich and potent by it; whereas the rest who use it not are poor and beggarly," [11] A striking evidence surely, from an eye witness, how greatly a circulating medium, be it what it may, promotes industry, improvement, and prosperity.

Thus, and at this place, were the beginnings of New England's commerce. Here, the very ground on which stood the pilgrims' first trading-house, can now be pointed out. On it may the traveller pause and reflect how things then were! how they now are! Now, on what sea, to what coast of the habitable globe, have not their descendants carried the products of their soil and industry, outstripping all other nations, with only England as a rival?

But there was also another trading post established nearly at the same time, some two hundred miles northeasterly from Plymouth, on the River Kennebec; hence the name of the place, Kennebec. From it was easy access to the natives far into the interior, as well as to the fishermen on the coast. Here had previously been some profitable trade; but now, having obtained from England chartered privileges, they erected their trading-house, and stationed men, as at Manomet; and here, with the surplus maize now raised in the colony, and with other commodities, and the use of wampum for money, were exchanges made for furs, skins, and other valuables; and all equally advantageous to themselves and the native Indians, especially those of the interior. [12]

Now, also, was there still another undertaking — the assuming of an additional responsibility. Families, and parts of families, of their friends were yet in Holland, pleading and despondingly waiting to come to them. The governor and some chief friends, with the Elder, seriously considered the matter, "not only how they might discharge the great engagements which already lay heavily upon them, but also how they might, if possible, devise means to help over some of those friends and brethren of Leyden." The matter being anxiously weighed, these men (knowing of no other way) resolved to run the risk of "hiring the trade of the colony for six years;" undertaking to pay, in that time, the eighteen hundred pounds, and the remaining debts of the plantation, amounting to six hundred pounds more; keeping in mind their purpose, as they informed some few of their friends, of providing also for the coming of those friends from Leyden; and then to restore the trade again to the company as the term should expire. To the main resolution, laid before a general meeting and discussed, consent was given, and articles of agreement were signed. With increased energy these men, quaintly called in the agreement, "undertakers," carried their purpose into effect. And in time, by patient perseverance through all difficulties, by self-denial, and with some assistance from England, the whole was effected. [13] The result was, that in the time, not only was the amount of the first obligations, £2400, discharged, but over £2600 more were expended in removing their brethren thither — a proof of strength of attachment, and of faithfulness to each other, unexampled in the annals of any people. [14]

We have already noticed the opening of a correspondence with them, and the commencement of friendly intercourse for purposes of trade, by the Dutch colony at New Amsterdam.

On the 4th of October of the present year, came another letter from the secretary, De Rasieres, informing the governor of his arrival in the barque Nassau, at Frenchman's Point, on the headwaters of Buzzard's Bay, near the Plymouth colony's trading station at Manomet. Sent for at his request by the colony boat, he arrived in her at Plymouth, "with sound of trumpets," and honorably attended. Appropriately received and entertained for some days, he, with a skilful eye and master's hand, draws up, by way of report, a description of the location, the circumstances, prospects, and institutions, civil and religious, of the pilgrim colony. This report, unknown to our colonists, but made at the time by this intelligent and unbiassed foreigner, and lately brought to light from the archives at the Hague, has furnished valuable items in their history, nowhere else to be found.

"New Plymouth (says he) is on a large bay to the north of Cape Cod, or Mallabear, west from the north point of the cape, which can be easily seen in clear weather. Directly before the commenced town lies a sand bank, about twenty paces broad, whereon the sea breaks violently with an easterly or northeasterly wind. On the north side lies a small island, where one must run close along in order to come before the town; the ships running behind that bank, lie in a very good roadstead." "At the south of the town flows a small river of fresh water, very rapid, but shallow, taking its rise from several lakes in the land above. "Where it empties into the sea, there come so many herring, in April and the beginning of May, as is quite surprising."

"The fish (caught in a singular manner) each man takes according to the land he cultivates, and deposits three or four in each hill, where he plants his maize, which grows therein luxuriantly; if they lay not fish therein, the maize will not grow, such is the nature of the soil."

"Their farms are not as good as ours, because they are more stony, and consequently not so suitable for the plough. But they have better means of living than ourselves." "They apportion their land according as each has means to contribute to the 18,000 guilders promised to those who sent them out; whereby they have their freedom without rendering an account to any one; only if the King should choose to send a governor general, they would be obliged to acknowledge him sovereign chief."

"Respecting trade, and payments from the produce of their fields (he continues), the maize which they do not require for their own use, [15] is delivered to the governor at three guilders (6 shillings) the bushel, who, in his turn, sends it in sloops to the north, for the trade in skins amongst the savages; reckoning one bushel of maize against one pound of beaver skins." "When division is made according to what each has contributed, they are credited for the amount yearly towards the reduction of their obligation. With the remainder, they purchase what next they require, and which the governor takes care to provide every year,"

"The tribes (of Indians) in their neighborhood are better conducted than ours, because the English give them the example of better ordinances, and a better life; and who also, to a certain degree, give them laws, by means of the respect which they from the very first have established amongst them." [16]

View from Plymouth Burial Hill

155

"Their government is after the English form. The governor has his council, which is chosen every year by the entire community, by election or prolongation of term. In the inheritance they place all the children in one degree, only the eldest son has an acknowledgment for his seniority of birth."

"They have stringent laws and ordinances in respect to violation of the marriage vow, and the like, which laws they enforce very strictly indeed, even among the tribes that live amongst them."

"The town itself, of New Plymouth, lies on the slope of a hill, stretching east towards the sea, with a broad street about a cannon's shot (800 yards) long leading down the hill; with a (street) crossing in the middle northwards to the rivulet, and southwards to the land. The houses are constructed of hewn planks, with gardens inclosed behind, and at the sides with hewn planks, so that their houses and courtyards are arranged in very good order; with a stockade, against a sudden attack; and, at the ends of the streets, are three wooden gates. In the centre, on the cross street, stands the governor's house, before which is a square inclosure, upon which four 'patereros' are mounted, so as to flank along the streets."

But the part of De Rasieres' description most material to our purpose, relates to their place of worship, and the order of their assembling; bearing in mind that the minister mentioned was Elder Brewster, and that this was the order of things twice on the Sabbath.

"Upon the hill they have a large square house, with a flat roof, made of thick, sawn planks, stayed with oak beams, upon the top of which they have six cannons, which shoot iron balls of four and five pounds, and command the surrounding country. The lower part they use for their church, where they preach on Sundays, and the usual holidays.

"They assemble by beat of drum, each with his musket or firelock, in front of the captain's door; they have their cloaks on, and place themselves in order three abreast, and are led by a sergeant without beat of drum. Behind comes the governor, in a long robe; beside him, on the right hand, comes the preacher, with his cloak on, and on the left hand, the captain, with his side arms and cloak, and with a small cane in his hand; and thus they march in good order, and each sets his arms down near him. Thus they enter their place of worship, constantly on their guard, night and day."

Thus wrote "Isaack De Basieres," [17] messenger and secretary of the colony of New Amsterdam — a wise observer and reporter of what he saw and heard at New Plymouth: — an account more specific in some particulars, than is anywhere else to be found on record.

[1] Mass. Hist. Coll., 1st series, iii. 46, 47, 48; and Bradford, this year.

[2] Says Bradford, "To look humanly on the state of things as they presented themselves, it is a marvel it did not wholly discourage and sink them. But they gathered up their spirits, and the Lord so helped them; as now when they were at lowest, they began to rise again, and being stripped (in a manner) of all human helps and hopes, he brought things about, otherwise, in his

Divine Providence, as they were not only upheld and sustained, but their proceedings were both honored and imitated by others;" p. 208, &c.

[3] The number of acres now allowed was twenty each; the number of shareholders was 156. The value of a certain red cow was, according to the currency of that time, compared to the present, about $160.

[4] See Bradford, 217; Prince, 161, 166.

[5] See the list in Hazzard, and Baylie's, i. 262.

[6] The regular settlement at New Amsterdam (after its capture by the English named New York) is said to have been in 1623, though the Dutch had carried on trade in those parts some years earlier.

[7] Brad., 222, 225. See the Letters, also, in the Mass. Hist. Col., iii. 51, 53, dated March 19 (N. S.) and August 14, 1627.

[8] Russell's Plymouth, and in Young, 305.

[9] Brad., 221, and in Young, 306-7, and notes; and Mass. Hist. Coll., viii. 122, 123.

[10] This Sewan, Wampum, or Wampumpeague, as a kind of Indian money, was made of the beautifully polished portions of the shell of the small clam, called *quahog;* some say also of the periwinkles. It was both of the purple and the white shell, of convenient size, and graceful shape, with a drilled opening in the centre, to be strung like beads. The purple was of twice the value of the white. A fathom of this stringed money was valued at about five shillings. Three purple shells or six white ones passed for an English penny. Of the like material were made some of the most valuable ornaments of the natives. — Mass. Hist. Coll., i. p152, iii. 54, 231; Thatcher, 70; Young, 305-7.

[11] Bradford, 234.

[12] Bradford, 233; Thatcher, 70, 72.

[13] The chiefs of the colony (says Baylies), almost deprived themselves of the common necessaries of life to get their brethren over, and to support them until they were able to support themselves."

[14] The various sums found mentioned in Prince, are — (pages 168, 192, 201)—

£1800
600
1400
550
500
200
_____
£5050 paid in these six years, besides £50 a year for company clothing.

[15] "All the while, this people were (still) forced to pound their corn in mortars;" not having means to grind by the help of wind or water. — Hubbard, Mass. Hist. Coll., ii. v. 99.

[16] "Even to this day," says Hubbard, "the hopefullest company of Christian Indians live within the bounds of Plymouth colony," —Mass. Hist. Coll., ii. v. 98.

[17] De Rasieres is said to have been a descendant of French Protestant ancestry, who had fled from persecution in France, and settled in Guilderland, on the river Waal, and hence they were called Walloons. He came on from Holland the year before to New Netherlands, and on his arrival had become chief commissary, next in rank to the governor, and secretary of that colony. Soon after his return from Plymouth, owing to certain factions, he returned to Holland, and addressed this communication to one of the leading directors of the Dutch

"West India Company, S. Blommaert. It found its way into the royal library at the Hague, where it was lately discov-

ered, and was soon translated and published in the New York Hist. Soc. Coll.,
vol. i., new series, p. 357, &c. The

preacher mentioned was Elder Brewster.

Chapter Twenty-Nine - 1629

I hear the tread of pioneers,
Of nations yet to be,
The first low wash of waves where soon
Shall roll a human sea. — Whittier.

Passing on through the year 1628 into that of 1629, we find the Elder all along performing ably and constantly all the duties of his position, "beloved and honored among the people, taking great pains in teaching and dispensing the Divine Word." [1] Their active counsellor, and one of the chief in all that concerned their civil and temporal interests, he yet manifested no cessation of effort on account of advancing years.

Near the beginning of July (1629), there came incidentally to New Plymouth one Mr. Ralph Smith, a clergyman, lately from England. Elder Brewster, always declining to be any other than their Elder, and Mr. Smith, being a "grave man," and an accredited minister, was kindly entertained, and chosen, after some trial, to be their Pastor," [2]

This connection, bringing some relief to the Elder, continued for about six years. But Mr. Smith proving (to use the words of Cotton), "to be, though a grave man, yet of low gifts and parts," the Elder, as a far abler man, would still be often called upon to expound the Scriptures, as well as rule in their church, as before. Having an *ordained* Pastor, however, they could now have the Christian ordinances.

Elder Brewster, relieved in part from his long accustomed labors, could now arrange more effectively his private concerns, and more deliberately mark occurrences outside of the little colony. Other colonies there were which had attracted, or were now to attract, special attention.

We pause not here to inquire what may long before have been his thoughts respecting the colonies of South America, near to which some of their own company had once advocated their removal, where golden fruits and golden mines had attracted a world-wide notice. Nor would we stop to inquire what may have been his and his people's views respecting the French settlements in Canada, stretching far into the interior, shutting in, as it were, the prospects of the English on this continent. There were other nearer, and, in some respects, kindred colonies; one, long since commenced, others now about to be commenced, the success or failure of which was a matter of deep interest. Of the Dutch colony we have already had a passing notice.

Respecting the colonizing spirit of his own nation, he could look back to the times of Elizabeth, when such bold spirits as Sir Walter Raleigh, and afterwards the far-famed Capt. Smith, for love of adventure and fame, went forth to explore, and plant the English standard in parts unknown. Others, too, had gone forth in pursuit of wealth, a larger number still, to retrieve broken fortunes, and some to be chiefs or leaders in new enterprises. Yet all these latter attempts to colonize, though sustained by wealth and power, and some by men of ablest talents, all these, with one exception, had Brewster seen come to a miserable end.

Respecting this one, it was in the very year when himself and pilgrim band were leaving England, exiles for their own church system, that men were on their way, chiefly for adventure, to plant themselves on the shores of *Virginia,* supported by one of the most powerful companies of the time in England. But of their failures, sufferings, and almost entire extirpation by savage foes, and by their own recklessness; of their times of despair, and revived hopes, and preservation by fresh aid and large additions, we speak not further than to state again that, while the Virginia colonists were afterwards suffering most, the pilgrim company were also enduring the greatest privations. While the former became fitted to their more southerly location, the other, tried and inured to hardship, and cemented together by the strongest bond that earth can witness, became fitted to be the *pioneers* on the stern shores of New England.

Connected with that Virginia company, and one of its chief promoters, and most earnest in making it the means of advancing the cause of religion, was Sir Edwin Sandys; at the same time, he showed himself the warm friend of the Elder, exerting himself to promote his and his people's purposes in their removal and settlement. [3]

In Virginia, also, for a time, was George Sandys, the worthy brother of Sir Edwin, and doubtless an acquaintance of Brewster, an active and laborious agent for that colony. Being an accomplished man of letters, he, in the year of King James' death, and of the accession of the first Charles, after devoting "the days to his majesty's service," wrote the first English poem in the New World. In other words, he translated the Metamorphoses of Ovid into English verse; a work of merit, though he modestly termed it "the sweet-tongued Ovid's counterfeit." In its dedication to his king, he offers it as a production "lim'd by that unperfect light, which was snatched from the hours of night and repose;" "for the day was not mine," says he; "a double stranger (it is) sprung from the stock of the ancient Romans, but bred in the New World, of the rudeness whereof it cannot but participate, especially having wars and tumults to bring it to light, instead of the Muses." [4]

Nearly at the same time was there another person, named Brewster, of some note in the Virginia colony, whether a relative or acquaintance of the Elder, we know not. Cavalierly treated, however, by the acting governor, and by the power of martial law in time of peace, it required an appeal to the council in England to extricate him from a fatal dilemma. To this end returning to England, he appears not again to have visited the shores of that colony.

Without even glancing at the *history* of this settlement, it is sufficient here to remark, that between it and New Plymouth there was early and frequent intercourse; ships on the coast were passing and repassing; [5] while the success of the Plymouth people appears finally to have given no small encouragement to those in Virginia. When dangers threatened, or calamities befell the one, as in the great massacre of 1622, there was great sympathy felt, if there could not be direct aid, by their northern neighbors. Nor was sympathy all. Between them, as colonies of the same nation and blood, enduring similar trials, many were the acts of kindness, not hindered by the fact that in church organization and order the one was connected with the Church of England, from which the other had separated. [6]

But there were now beginnings of other colonies nearer home, and still nearer in habits of thought, in which the Elder and Plymouth people felt a peculiar interest.

Growing agitations in England, on subjects and rites, civil and religious, were the moving causes. Charles the First, and those who acted with him, had now determined on enforcing *conformity* more rigidly, systematically, and indiscriminately, than had ever been done before. Consequently, many ministers, and among them not a few learned and able men, who had been suspended and oppressed for non-conformity, were, with their people who thought with them, disposed to leave their country, and find liberty in other lands.

Added to this, was the increasingly bitter conflict between King and Parliament, now agitating the nation. The lines of division, which had some beginning in the days of Elizabeth, but had become still more distinctly marked in the late reign of James, were now assuming a threatening aspect. The agitation was beginning to reach the heart of the nation. The opposing elements were diversely combining and mustering their forces. On the one side was the King, vacillating, at one time claiming and exercising above all law, the highest stretch of arbitrary power, at another time yielding, and then forfeiting his word. With him were the court with courtly advisers civil and ecclesiastical, and the hitherto larger, but now lessening portion of the nation. On the other side was the Parliament, with a daily increasing portion of the people, petitioning for, and finally demanding concessions, and defined limitations of the royal prerogatives.

In the conflict, argument met argument; will met will; the strongest passions were moved; the long gathering storm was seen slowly rising; thoughtful men were becoming fearful; the warring elements, it was believed, must soon meet; and if so, terrible must be the contest. In this state of things it was, that many were disposed to escape, while they could, from the coming struggle: some to the continent, others to the far off wilds of the west. If from the causes first mentioned resulted the settlement of Virginia, from the latter combination of causes were planted additional colonies in New England. [7]

In these additional settlements, of which Massachusetts was the principal, a deep interest was felt by that at Plymouth. With its chief rulers and ministers, as well as many of its people, was Elder Brewster now brought into acquaintance and correspondence.

And even earlier than this, it would seem, had he become personally interested in another settlement farther north, the germ of New Hampshire, at Portsmouth.

In this year (1629), is the name of Wrestling Brewster found in Portsmouth, and there soon after settled with a family. It has been stated by various writers that the Elder's son, of this name, died young — "died in his youth" — "died without a family." How, indeed, he could have removed thither, and become located, and there left a family, and no writer had knowledge of it, we are unable to explain; but facts, of late brought to light, seem to show that such may have been the case. [8]

[1] Bradford, 256.
[2] Bradford, 263.
[3] G. Chalmer's Annals of Virginia, and our preceding statements.
[4] First edition, London, 1626; in the invaluable collection of Peter Force, Esq., of Washington City; a collection nowhere equalled, it is believed, in all that pertains to the first colonial settlements of North America down to the time of the American Revolution.
[5] Chalmers, 38.
[6] Brad., 123-5, 151-154, 218-219.
[7] See the period, Charles the First, Pictorial History of Eng. "It was the concussion of religious opinions, chiefly, that first peopled New England."
[8] The statements and facts are these: Governor Bradford, in the Appendix of his History, page 451, speaking of Elder Brewster's family (those that had died, and those that were living in 1650), has this brief statement: "His son Wrestling died a young man, unmarried." Subsequent writers, in varied language, have said the same. He was numbered in the Elder's family, at Plymouth, on the division of cattle, in 1627. That he died young is admitted; but in relation to his dying *unmarried*, other facts prove, either that the governor was here mistaken, or that there was another person, of the same name, about the same age, in this country at the same time. The proofs of this are:

1st. A deed of land in Portsmouth, New Hampshire, commencing in the words following: "Portsmouth, sixth day of December, Anno Domini one thousand six hundred twenty and nine, and in the highly favored fifth year of the raigne of our soveraign Lord Charles the first. King of England, and Scotland, and France, and Ireland, and defender of the faith, &c. &c.," (by which) "Joseph and Hannah S. Pendleton" (convey to) "Wrestling Brewster eighty acres of land, for £8, adjoining to land previously belonging to said Wrestling."

These lands have descended by inheritance in the Brewster family in Portsmouth, who claim to be descendants of this Wrestling Brewster, until within the memory of the present generation.

2d. There are parts of a family record, still preserved, showing that said Wrestling Brewster was *married*, in 1630, to Emla Story; that they had a son, John Brewster, born Jan. 20th, 1631, and a daughter, born May 3d, 1636, and named Love Lucretia (the names of the Elder's second son. Love, and of his eldest son's wife, Lucretia) — a most significant fact surely.

3d. There have been preserved, among the old papers belonging to said family, bills, receipts, and accounts, relating to this Wrestling Brewster's transactions in business.

All these documents and papers are in the possession of Dr. George Gaines Brewster, of Portsmouth, New Hampshire, from whom the author obtained the use of such as pertained to the present purpose.

With the evidence before us, the writer is inclined to the opinion that Wrestling Brewster of the pilgrim company and the Wrestling Brewster of Portsmouth, N. H., were the same person; and that his removal to that place, and marriage there, were in some way unknown to the governor. That, dying soon after the year 1636, and having received all the patrimony that would come to him, as was the case with the Elder's daughters and their children, no notice would be taken of him or his in the settlement of the Elder's estate.

See also note 4, on page 38.

Chapter Thirty – 1632-1633

"The axe rang sharply 'mid these forest shades,
Which from creation toward the sky had tower'd
In unshorn beauty." — Mrs. Sigourney.

From the date in the last chapter to the beginning of the year 1632, no marked occurrence appears in the Elder's life, requiring particular notice. His studies, duties, and labors were evidently continued with unabated efficiency as last mentioned.

The body of the colonists were likewise pursuing their onward course, laboriously, but improvingly; while the chief ones, who had assumed the heavy indebtedness of the whole undertaking, were extricating themselves from embarrassment, and meeting their liabilities, though suffering heavy losses, by some of their unfaithful agents. [1]

But in this year (1632) were the increase and prosperity greater than in any former year. Many, desiring to escape from the increasing troubles in England, and encouraged by the success that was beginning to attend the emigrating enterprise, were now arriving in this and the neighboring colony. Consequently, the products of their fields were now in increasing demand; their cattle had a ready sale at high prices; goods from abroad became more plentiful; more lands were required for cultivation. The town, in which they had thus far lived compactly, could no longer contain them with their new additions. Fears of the savage natives in their vicinity had diminished. The more enterprising now penetrated the surrounding forests, seeking out new locations, and more enlarged farms. [2] There were, indeed, some occurrences unfavorable to the first settlement, particularly the removal of many in order to secure better lands. Across the harbor, on the north side of the Plymouth Bay, and in fair sight of their first homes, was commenced the next principal settlement. There, bordering on the bay, and nearest towards Plymouth, were the lands allotted to the brave Captain Miles Standish, including what is called "Captain's Hill" (a place of no little interest). This new town received the name of Duxbury, doubtless from the town of the same name, the seat of the captain's connections in England.

Adjoining the captain's land northerly, and bordering on the Bay of Duxbury, including what from that day to this has been called "the Nook," lay the farm allotted to their venerable Elder Brewster. Bordering upon his, was that of his eldest son, Jonathan. Here, on his own allotted acres, could the Elder with his other son, be often seen aiding in the labors of clearing away the forests, perhaps never before cleared since their first growth, after the earth's creation.

Here was erected a new dwelling for himself, in his widower state, and his son Love; and here, also, as in the first and older settlement, as his other duties would permit, would he aid in planting their newly cleared fields. Most favorable for this purpose was the location, proving to be on lands among the best in the colony. [3]

In this growing settlement, too far distant for constant attendance upon public worship at Plymouth, was soon organized, though with many objections and hindrances, another church of the same order. Of this church also, it appears Brewster became, as in Plymouth, the ruling elder. [4]

Thus, while attending to family and other duties, as an active pioneer in the New World, was he continuing his accustomed duties as the only ruling elder of the colony.

And clear evidence is there, that though advancing in years, no small portion of his time was devoted to reading and study, as well as to meditation and devotion. His principal residence was yet in Plymouth.

We now turn to another incident of which we have particular record. In a former chapter, on the visit of De Rasieres, the secretary of the Dutch colony to New Plymouth, we had a view of the assembling of the pilgrim congregation on the Sabbath morning, and their marching in order to their place of worship on Fort Hill. We now have an opportunity to take an observation within (probably in the same place), and to notice some particulars of their mode of *teaching,* and *order of worship.*

It was on the occasion of a visit from the governor of the Massachusetts colony to the governor and chief men of the Plymouth colony; and the account of it is from Governor Winthrop himself.

"On Thursday, October 25th, 1632, came Governor Winthrop, with Mr. Wilson, pastor of Boston, and other friends, to Plymouth. Governor Bradford, with William Brewster, their ruling elder, and some others, came forth to meet us without the town." "They conducted us to the governor's house, where we are entertained together, and are feasted each day at several houses." "On the Lord's day was the Sacrament, in which we partook. In the afternoon, Mr. Roger Williams proposes a question; Mr. Smith, their pastor, speaks briefly upon it; and then Mr. Williams prophesies (that is, explains); afterwards, the governor of Plymouth (who had studied the Hebrew and antiquities), speaks on the question." "After him, Elder Brewster (a man of learning) speaks; then two or three of the congregation." "Then the Elder desires Governor Winthrop and Mr. Wilson to speak on the same, which they did. [5] This ended, the deacon, Mr. Fuller, [6] puts the congregation in mind of the duty of contributing for the poor, and the support of public worship, when the governor, and all the others, go to the deacon's seat, deposit their gifts, and return. After which, the exercises are brought to a close." [7]

The peculiarity in this public speaking, one after another, by members of their church, says Prince, "they had from Mr. Robinson, their former pastor, in Leyden, founded on the primitive practice of the church at Corinth, according to St. Paul. But, growing in knowledge, and, I suppose, (says he), in the apprehension that such a practice was peculiarly accommodated to the age of inspiration, to which they never pretended, they afterwards gradually -lay it aside."

Should it seem to be entering into particulars too minutely to introduce here those apparently small matters, and some others that may follow, the remark may be met by that maxim, worthy of being kept in mind: "That small things in the beginnings of communities, civil or ecclesiastical, are of far higher importance, and more worthy of note, having more influence in after times, than far greater matters, when a people or nation has become established." What the influence of precedent is in legislation, such is the influence of even small acts or habits adopted in the origin of a people. They often form the peculiarities or habits in after generations, even when the origin of them has been forgotten, or the original practice has been discontinued.

While the chief men of the older and of the younger colony were thus cultivating friendly feelings and relations, and consulting on matters of deep interest to them both, events were transpiring on their northern borders, in England, and on the continent, causing many anxious thoughts and fears.

On their northern borders, the king and court of England had, by a late treaty with France, given up to that power the Canadas, including also Nova Scotia, Port Royal, and Cape Breton. These portions of the New World, most valuable for trade, fisheries, and naval stores, were thus yielded up, merely to settle the question respecting one-half of the queen's dowry.

One of the sad fruits of these proceedings to the Plymouth people, was the treacherous robbery of their trading post at Penobscot. Under pretence of distress, and for repairs, a French vessel put in at that place. Finding that the chief men of the post were absent, and only three or four servant men left in charge, the Frenchmen, violating all the principles of hospitality, with the greatest apparent politeness, commenced by admiring the arms, and the manner in which they were arranged, asking if they were loaded; then, taking them down from their places, they threatened death to the abashed servants if they resisted, and compelled them to help to carry on board the vessel the goods, beaver, and stores, amounting to 500 pounds sterling; and then left with a taunting message for the Plymouth owners, among whom was the Elder. To all of them it was a sore loss and hindrance in payment of their assumed responsibilities. [8]

Turning to England, the agitating and absorbing theme still was, the contest between the King and royalist party on the one side, and the Parliament and their supporters on the other. In this contest, the minds of all were becoming more and more involved, and the opposite parties more and more alienated. Prejudices and passions on both sides arousing the strongest elements of man's nature, caused some to gird themselves the more resolutely for the contest, and others to escape from it to the new colonies, to build new states; notwithstanding the efforts of the government to prevent it. Many, therefore, were the hopes and fears, of the effects on the new settlements.

On the continent, especially in Germany, and even to the borders of Holland, under the protection of which the pilgrim band had passed so many years, and where yet were not a few of their dear friends, had ruthless wars against human rights, liberty of conscience, and of the Protestant cause, been again raging with overwhelming power and awful cruelties.

Again, and avowedly, had it been the purpose of the Emperor, Ferdinand II., and his general-in-chief. Count Tilly, as it before had been that of Philip II., of Spain, to exterminate the Protestant power, drive its adherents from the continent, or force them to renounce their faith.

In their distressed and weakened state, Gustavus Adolphus had come forth from Sweden, with his small but heroic army, to their rescue. With a rapidity almost incredible, he had met and routed, in battle after battle, the Emperor's veteran forces, and their great commander; until he had restored nearly the whole of Central Germany to their rights, and liberty to worship God, whether Catholics or Protestants, in the way which they should choose. He was hailed everywhere by the Protestants, as, under the Divine Hand, the great deliverer of their country. Thus proceeding, he proclaimed wherever he came liberty of conscience and of worship to all. Catholics and Protestants; making no distinction, his maxims being, "Every one is orthodox who conforms to the laws;" and "that to keep men from going to hell was not the calling of princes, but that of the ministers of religion."

On taking a Catholic town, to those who would induce him to treat its burghers with harshness, his answer was: "I am come to loosen, not to rivet afresh the fetters of bondage. Let them live as they have lived heretofore; I give no new laws to them who know how to live as their religion teaches." [9]

Progressing thus, victorious over the hearts of the people, as over the arms of the enemy, on the 6th of Nov. of this very year (1632), in the hour of victory over the mighty Wallenstein, he fell on the field of battle, sorely lamented all over Protestant Europe, and even in the new colonies on the far off shores of New England.

All these victories, as well as the subsequent reverses, were, to all our colonists, matters, next to their own, of absorbing interest. [10]

While these events, of so much interest to them, were transpiring in England and in Germany, trains were being laid — not only for bringing into exercise the controlling power of the king and his ecclesiastical advisers over the colonies, but, more than all (and what these colonists now began to fear) — trains or plans for increasing the French power; thus threatening to make the northern parts of America French instead of English — as truly French as South America was Spanish. [11]

Passing on now to the summer of 1633, we come to the next recorded event, personally affecting the Elder; it was the death of his daughter, Fear Allerton, She had been married to Mr. Isaac Allerton about seven years. Called hence thus early in life, she left an only son, Isaac Allerton, jun., who afterwards became a resident with his Grandfather Brewster, and was probably, in part, fitted by him to enter the college at Cambridge, Mass., where he was a graduate in the year 1650.

We have next to notice an occurrence of some historical interest, which engaged the particular attention of the Plymouth church, and brought out their views on one point in respect to one of the Christian Sacraments,

It was, to say the least, an unpleasant occurrence, causing differences of opinion, and no little agitation of feeling, in the Plymouth company.

Associated for the last two years as teacher with Mr. Smith, their pastor, was one Mr. Roger Williams, who had begun to advance some opinions which they had never entertained, but to which they had been opposed even while in Holland. These were, the extreme of separation from the Church of England, "pronouncing it sinful to attend its worship, or have with it any fellowship; also renouncing any authority of the magistrates in matters of church order, and advocating a different mode of baptism, and some other minor points." Finding himself opposed in sentiment to the pastor and Eider, and to the greater part of the people, he asked to be dismissed to the Salem people, where he had before officiated. The subject became matter of public discussion. He was a man in many respects highly gifted, zealous, eloquent, and as such had been recommended from highly respectable sources in England, but in some things eccentric, exclusive, and extreme. As might be expected, some became attached to him and his views. Asking for a dismission to Salem, and the matter coming to a public discussion in their church, some were in favor of, and others opposed to, his leaving. The counsel of Elder Brewster was called for in the emergency, and given, which was to grant the desired dismission, grounded on the considerations that Mr. Williams' continuance with them "might *cause divisions,* that he might (as he feared would

166

be the case) run the same course of rigid *separation* (as it was then called), Anabaptistry, which Mr. John Smith, the Separatist, of Amsterdam, had done." And this afterwards came to pass, as the Elder feared and foresaw.

From the great respect for the Elder, and confidence in the wisdom of his counsel, the Plymonth church consented to Mr. Williams' dismission, and liberty to go to the people of Salem.

This act, with the remark of the Elder, has by some been censured, but with no good reason. Such censurers forget the maxim, fair, just, and universally applicable, *that every organized body has the right to dismiss from its connection any who may cause division, or who may disagree with its standards.* Nor was it uncharitable, in discussing the subject in their church assembly, to give the reasons of their action in the case, especially as the dismission was asked for, and was attended with no personal injury. He went from them in peace, with those who chose to go with him. The consciences of those from whom he differed were to be as much respected as his who differed from them. In this, the action of the Plymouth people appears to have been blameless.

As to the treatment Mr. Williams afterwards received from the Massachusetts colony, that is altogether another question, one which we are not here called upon to discuss. Had the only question with them been respecting the great principle of toleration, for which Mr. Williams was a distinguished advocate, and for which his name may deservedly be held in honorable memory, it would be easy to vindicate him as being in the right.

But when we take into account his extreme and exclusive views of *separation*, his uncharitable language at this time to those who differed from him in opinion; his disrespectful acts, as well as treatment, towards the magistrates of Massachusetts; the steps he took to change the rites and church order of that people, with whom he was next associated, the question assumes another aspect. And with this statement we leave the point at issue — favoring neither extreme.

---

[1] Bradford, 284, 290.

[2] Bradford, 302, 303; also, Mass. Historic Collection, iii. 7; and Winsor's Duxbury.

[3] Mass. Hist. Coll., 2d series, vol. vii. Appendix, pp. 74-5.

Some years ago was found in the garden of this farm, a small silver spoon, bearing the initials "I. B." Being valued as an ancient relic of the Brewster name, Mr. M. Soule, the present owner of the land, presented it to the wife of the author.

Who were the Elder's indented servants, we know not; but in the year 1636, we find his record: "Sold to Jonathan Brewster, as servant, J. Bundy, for five years."

[4] Winsor's Duxbury.

[5] Alluding to Acts xiii. 14, 15.

[6] Mr. Fuller was the physician of the colony.

[7] Prince, Mass. Hist. Coll., 2d series, vol. 7th, appen., 70, 71.

[8] Mass. Hist. Coll., 2d series, vii. Appen. 62; connected with the general history of the times.

[9] Kohlrausch's Hist. Germany, 337.

[10] This is evident, not only from the history of the colony, but from the volumes on the subject in the Elder's library.

[11] Of this the records of the time bear full testimony. This led to what was here colloquially called the French war.

Chapter Thirty-One – 1634-1636

"The world is full of meetings such as this,
A thrill, a voiceless challenge and reply,
And sudden partings after." — Willis.

In this year, 1634, were two occurrences in Elder Brewster's family, presenting a strange contrast; yet they are such as do at times meet in families less numerous than his: a marriage and a death.

The marriage, the last in his family, was that of his second son, Love Brewster, on the 15th of May, to Miss Sarah Collier, lately from England. Her father, Mr. William Collier, had been one of the company of merchant adventurers, so often mentioned in these pages. He had not, like some of that company, engaged in that enterprise solely for purposes of gain, but from a good motive, and to promote a good work. Nor had he deserted the cause in the time of its deep depression and perplexities. On the contrary, he had continued steadfast; and had only the year before this, come over and cast in his lot among this people. A man of wisdom and experience, already had he been chosen one of the governor's assistants, and was possessed, probably, of more property than most others of the colony. [1] The marriage of his daughter, with a son of the Elder, appears to have been satisfactory to both families. On the Elder's part there was a covenant endowment, or pledge to the bridal pair, that his house in Duxbury, in which they were to reside, and one-half of his estate and lands, *should be theirs,* after his own decease. With such prospects did the young couple commence the married life. [2]

The death referred to (and how near it was to the date of the marriage we cannot say, except that it was soon afterwards) was that of his daughter Patience, or Mrs. Prince, the last daughter, and the last female of the Elder's own family. Already bereaved of his wife and his other daughter, in the loss of this only remaining one in the prime of life, he must have felt a saddening void nothing earthly could fill. She had been married (in 1624) to Mr. Prince, who is this present year elected governor of Plymouth. She now leaves to his care three children, daughters, under circumstances deeply affecting to parent and grandparent. [3] None but those similarly situated can realize the feelings of desolation which, even cheerful and resigned as the Elder usually was, this additional bereavement must have caused. About this period it appears to have been, and under the impression of all that he had passed through in life, and perhaps in reference to the loss, in their early years, of

168

these endeared ones, that he wrote across the title-page of one of the Latin volumes [4] in his library this sentence, affixing thereto his name: —

It is the Hebrew, partly translated into Latin, of a portion of the 4th verse of the 144th Psalm, Englished thus: —

"Man is all vanity;" and the same is illustrated in the words that follow, "His days pass away as a shadow."

Thus bereaved, the Elder's lingering affections, though greatly weaned from earth, would now naturally rest more upon his sons, with the one of whom just married he not long after took up his residence. [5]

We have at length arrived at a period in the life of this venerated man, and in the settlement of the Plymouth colony, when small matters may be passed by, as no longer affecting his position or character. And after mentioning a few additional transactions, we may draw towards the close of our narrative.

He is now in his 74th year, and yet, for years to come, we find him still in the active performance of his appropriate duties, as the Ruling Elder at Plymouth and at Duxbury — nay, in the whole colony. In Duxbury he likewise appears to have been their spiritual teacher, from their first organization until the calling of their first minister, in 1637. [6]

Nor was this all. The dates and subjects of the volumes in his library, show that, even at this period of life, his thoughts, reading, and investigations were not confined to what related to his official duties alone. His mind took a wider range. It acted upon all the various agitating questions of the time, not only respecting their own colony, but those around them, and in connection with the Indian tribes, and respecting changes abroad, that required corresponding action at home. Hence, with remarkably robust health, as well as mental vigor, he continued to be the wise and experienced counsellor, the conciliatory medium in matters of debate, and active assistant in matters of legislation.

On the appointment of a special committee, for revising their former acts and establishing a code of laws for the colony, in the autumn of 1636, he was selected as one of its prominent members. [7]

Important was the occasion of this appointment. Up to this period, in the words of Judge Baylies, "The Plymouth colony may be considered to have been but a voluntary association, ruled by the majority." It "had adopted no constitution, or instrument of government, except the compact signed in the cabin of the Mayflower." That compact specified no controlling principles but allegiance to the King, and the power in the majority to elect such officers and enact such laws and constitutions as should, from time to time, by such

169

majority, be deemed expedient. Scarcely had they, up to this date, availed themselves of their delegated powers, under their patent, to enact laws. A few laws only, and such as were of the most urgent necessity, had been established. All matters of general interest were decided at general meetings of the whole, called *courts,* in which the governor presided. These courts decided matters judicially, except when committed to a jury. With the acknowledged royal authority, there appears to have been, tacitly, a general acknowledgment of that of the laws of England in general, but practically, here was, under the King, a pure "democracy." [8]

Such was the civil rule.

But the fact is to be borne in mind that New Plymouth was settled by a church. At first the ecclesiastical government had chief influence. "The power of their church was, in effect, superior to the civil; but in terms, it was confined to cases of discipline, or the infliction of censure only, or final exclusion. As to the maintenance of their ministers, the attachment of the people insured that, without the coercion of law." In short, it was their union as a religious society, more than all else, that kept them together. It was true of the Leyden emigrants, as their pastor and the Elder had said, "We are knit together as a body in a more strict and sacred bond and covenant, of the violation of which we make great conscience, and by virtue of which we do hold ourselves straitly bound to all care of each other." Failings they had, but what colony ever had fewer? [9] In this body, after they left Leyden, through all the first period, the Elder was the centre of influence — the guiding spirit. And afterwards, he had coordinate rule in effect with their pastors.

Such had been the state of things hitherto. But, in the words, of Judge Baylies, "as the settlements expanded, as trade increased, as strangers came in in pursuit of gain, without any reference to the ordinances of religion, and who, regardless of their spiritual good, pursued their temporal interests, the authority thus founded became impaired; the selfish principles of man, interwoven in his system, became predominant." "Disputes would occur; wrongs would exist; and such authority would be questioned and found inadequate." The period now arrived when all perceived the necessity of defining the limits of the power, and prescribing the actual duties of the magistrates; of securing the civil rights and privileges of the people; of establishing fundamental and organic laws, civil and criminal, and of providing for their execution; thus "placing their government on a stable foundation." This was the important work of their committee. This they accomplished, and the laws which they proposed were duly enacted.

The first Tuesday in June was made the legal day of election of governor and seven assistants, to "rule and govern the plantation as prescribed by law," "The election was confined to the freemen." To be a *freeman,* the individual must be "at least 21 years of age, of a sober and peaceable conversation, orthodox in the fundamentals of religion, and have a certain ratable estate."

But to enter into particulars respecting the specified duties of the governor, of the assistants, of the construction of their courts and juries, the choosing of inferior officers, with their duties, the mode of legislation, and the laws enacted, would be foreign to our purpose, even though the Elder was one among the originators, as well as promoters of the system adopted.

Finally, it was provided that all "be done, directed, and made, in the name of our sovereign lord the King," each freeman, as well as officer of every grade, acting under oath of fidelity to the King, and to the laws and interests of the colony." [10]

In this state of things, the Indians around them began, ere long, through their influence, to adopt a mode of government in some respects similar, and to follow their example in morals, laws, and judicial courts, with the proper officers. [11]

[1] Brad., 308, and note; Baylies, i. 214, and Winsor's Duxbury.

[2] Court Record of this date, with that of the settlement of the Elder's estate.

[3] Prince, Bradford, and Life of Gov. Prince.

[4] The Harmonized Commentary on the History of the Four Evangelists, in the library of Yale College.

[5] Plymouth Rec. of settlement of his estate; and Winsor.

[6] Baylies, i. 278, and Winsor's Duxbury.

[7] Felt's Ecclesiastical Hist., i. 290.

[8] Baylies, i. 154, 241, 225, 227, 233.

[9] President Dwight's Travels, i., Letter xii.

[10] See the laws, &c., and Judge Baylies' Memoir of New Plymouth, i. 227-240.

[11] The following is a curious specimen of a "Warrant" issued by an Indian magistrate, and directed to an Indian constable, which will not suffer by a comparison -with our more verbose forms: —

"I, Hihoudi, you Peter Waterman, Jeremy Wicket, quick you take him, fast you hold him, straight you bring him before me. Hihoudi." — Thatcher, 146.

Chapter Thirty-Two – 1636-1643

"Learning is more profound
When in few solid authors 't may be found.
A few good books, digested well, do feed
The mind." — R. Heath.

During the next seven years — from 1636 to the close of 1643 — were many incidents, in which it might be shown that the Elder had a personal, or by no means a remote interest. Indeed, so interwoven were his life, labors and character from the first, with the interest and progress of the colony, that whatever concerned that concerned him. But we pass those incidents, to notice here the position of his remaining family, and yet more particularly his *literary* acquaintances and associations.

The eldest of his three sons had become one of the well-informed, active, business men of the colony, and an enterprising agent in extending the new settlements, and in opening sources of trade, especially on the yet wild shores of the Connecticut. Again, he was one of the public-spirited, Christian men of the new town of Duxbury, and one of its deputies to the colony or legislative court. When occasion required, he was a counsellor before the judicial tribunals. In after years, he held yet more elevated positions in the colony of Connecticut. Removing thither near the close of 1648, or early in 1649, to the new settlement of New London, he was made keeper of its records, a deputy with the younger Winthrop to their colony court, and an associate judge; to him were also committed other public trusts. Having established, by appointment, a trading post on the banks of the Thames, on lands purchased of Uncas, the chief of the Mohegans, and thenceforth called Brewster's Neck, he there, at length, resided until his death, near the year 1661. [1]

The next son. Love, devoted himself to the cultivation of the paternal acres in Duxbury, forming there (with his father) a family home, and, as far as the new country would afford, an abode of comfort, social and cheerful; and where, in due time, a portion of the estate became his own and his children's inheritance. [2]

Respecting the other son, "Wrestling, of whom there are conflicting statements, we have already spoken. [3]

But who were the Elder's literary associates? Among such the mental powers are most developed; mind meets mind, thought meets thought, cultivated mental energies meet corresponding energies.

As had been the case in England and in Holland, so was it to some extent in the New World, his associates included some of the able men and scholars of the day.

Among such, for a time, at Plymouth, was Roger Williams, of original mind, liberal education, a pupil of Chief Justice Coke, eloquent, though erratic; but of whom we have before had occasion to speak more particularly. [4]

The pastor at Plymouth, at this time, was Mr. Raynor, educated at Magdalen College, Cambridge, ordained to the ministry in the Church of England, and characterized as a man of great humility, worth, and piety. [5]

Another and more eminent man was Dr. Chauncey, from Trinity College, Cambridge, where he had taken his degrees in the arts and in divinity; and where, for his attainments in the languages, he was made professor of Hebrew, and afterwards lecturer in Greek, and held other corresponding positions. He was also the friend of Archbishop Usher; but, for his Puritan tendencies, falling under the displeasure of Laud and the High Commission Court, he left for New England. Being solicited, he officiated for some time as teacher at Plymouth; yet entertaining opinions decidedly in favor of baptism only by immersion, and unwilling, by any compromise, to continue permanently with this people who differed from him in that particular, he removed thence to Scituate. Notwithstanding, on account of his learning, he was chosen not long after to the presidency of the New England Cambridge College (now Harvard University). [6]

The Rev. John Norton, who officiated also for a time at Plymouth, was a scholar of the first standing at the University of Cambridge, and curate for some time of Starford, Hertfordshire. Declining a fellowship in the university, and "marrying a lady of estimable qualifications and character," he came to New England, and to Plymouth, and finally succeeded Mr. Cotton in Boston. That he was a writer of pure and elegant Latin is sufficiently evident from his Latin treatise, on the questions of Appolonius, for the divines of Zealand. Of him, as the author of various other works, the church historian, Fuller, says: "Of all the authors I have perused, none to me was more *informative* than Mr. John Norton, one of no less learning than modesty." [7]

Likewise the Rev. Ralph Patridge, who had been for twenty years a minister of the established church, and eminent for scholarship and piety, but who, for non-conformity (according to his own words), was "hunted like a partridge upon the mountains," fled to New England, and was now, during all these years, the pastor of their church in Duxbury, and the near neighbor and associate of the Elder. [8]

Such, with Governors Bradford and Winslow, who, though not educated at a university, were yet men of extensive reading and knowledge of other languages, and, for that day, were no mean writers; — such, even in this far-off wilderness, were some of the chief scholars and literary associates of Elder Brewster. [9]

But that we may have a further and more just idea of his own attainments as a scholar, we must examine the character of his library. A library, procured and used in circumstances like his, could be no untrue index of his mind. Gathered when books were comparatively scarce and costly, and preserved through all the trying scenes, losses, and deprivations, to which he had been subjected, his was surely most creditable to its possessor. Portions of it appear to have been lost on leaving England; gifts from it had probably been made to friends, and to members of his family; yet with some additions from time to time, the inventory, at the close of his life, shows it to have consisted of over *four hundred volumes;* [10] a choice treasure, indeed, to the colony, as well as to its owner.

Yet to say that it consisted of four hundred volumes gives but a very indistinct idea of its value or character. To say, also, that of these four hundred volumes sixty-four were in Latin, with some in Greek and Hebrew, while it gives a clearer, furnishes still a very unsatisfactory estimate. [11]

On examining the works enumerated, and separating them into classes according to the subjects of which they treat, we find, *first,* that of the *sixty-four* volumes in Latin, &c., no less than thirty-eight were versions of the Sacred Scriptures, or expositions and illustrations of them, critical and practical; and of these, not a few were huge *quartos* and *folios,* of from 1200 to 1500 closely printed pages each. They were such as Beza's Greek and Latin

Version of the New Testament with Notes; a work appraised, even in the inventory, at a sum amounting to $20, present currency; Malaratus' Latin edition of the New Testament, and Notes, at the same rate of valuation, 824; Tremelius and Junius' edition or translation in Latin of the "Holy Bible," including also Beza's translation of the New Testament, with Notes, in all nearly 1600 folio pages, $18.

The commentators, annotators, and illustrative writers were such as Beza, Musculus, Peter Martyr, Erasmus, Calvin, Chrysostom, Piscator, Stephanus, Scultetus, Parens, Molerinus, not to mention various harmonies, and other works of similar character. Taking these into view, and the fact that these were among the best editions and expositions at that period, and that there were yet very few like them in the English language, we are enabled to form some distinct idea of the Elder's reading and acquirements in this department of Christian literature.

Along with these were other Latin works, such as the Syntagma of Vigandus, the work of Polanus, two volumes folio, the Clavis, or Key to certain portions of Scripture, by Flacius Illyricus, in folio, and others, illustrating or setting forth various points of doctrine; also treatises on church order and polity, history, natural philosophy, and the languages, giving a further view of the culture of his mind, and acquirements, not only in biblical, but other various departments.

And we are to add to these, next, the three hundred and forty volumes or treatises in the English language. Of the English works, nearly sixty volumes were large folios and quartos, and of like class and character with those which we have just noticed in Latin, such as the Refutation of the Remish Translation of the New Testament, published by himself, in some 1600 pages folio, with kindred works in divinity, systematic and practical; also controversies with the Roman Church; discussions on the Reformation; on the controversies of the times in England and Holland; on toleration, controversies between themselves and the extreme separatists; church and civil history, philosophy, advancement of learning, views of the times, doings at court and in Parliament, with numerous other writings of the day, civil, religious, devotional, political, and colonial, as well as those pertaining to the arts, trade, and e very-day life. Such is a very brief view of his library. [12]

It was at a time, too, when English literature was acquiring character, and making a rapid advance on a broad and solid basis. The English mind was breaking loose from the fetters of arbitrary systems, and the dominant power of half civilized customs, and struggling forth into the open fields, not only of adventure, but of original investigation and discovery in science and arts, and of discussion of principles of government and law. Pre-eminent among original thinkers Bacon arose, a *sun* in the firmament of science and literature, to send forth, with some darkening shades, its enlightening and expanding beams over all succeeding ages.

Of his works, valuable portions were in the Elder's library, occupying evidently a share of his thoughts and meditations. And if, at such a period, and amidst such workings of mind, extremes and extravagancies sometimes followed, and errors were committed, it can be no matter of wonder; it would be something above human were it otherwise. They were explorers, preparing the way for others.

Subsequent periods have brought forth works in all departments of science, law, government, divinity, history, poetry, fiction, such as have become the glory of the English name, but the chief beginnings were in the age of which we are speaking.

[1] On this tract, lying between the Thames and the Poquetanock Cove, and on the plain near its centre, was set apart a burial place, where evidently rests his dust, and by his side that of his wife, surrounded by the remains of their children, and children's children, to the present generation. Lately, the crumbling stones marking the place have been exchanged for a noble monument, erected to his memory, and that of his wife Lucretia — a testimony honorable to the descendants by whom the work has been accomplished. —See Hist. of Duxbury, of New London, and Conn. Court Records.

[2] Plym. Court Records, and Winsor's Duxbury.

[3] Near the close of chap, xxix.

[4] At the close of chap. xxx.

[5] Bradford and Morton.

[6] Baylies, i. 313, 314; also, Felt; Bradford and Mass. Hist. Coll., iv. 111, 112; x. 31.

[7] Baylies, i. 314, 315; Mass. Hist. Coll., 2d series, vi. 640, 641. et caetera.

[8] Felt, Winsor's Duxbury, and Bradford.

[9] We have noticed the earliest literary production of George Sandys in the Virginia colony, and we should not here pass unnoticed the first classical Latin poem on New England (Nova Anglia), by William Morell, Episcopal minister of Gorges' settlement, Weymouth, but who resided at Plymouth about a year, where he wrote in 1623, and, on his return to England, published this poetical description, the translation of which is not worthy of the original, — See Mass. Hist. Coll., i. 125-139.

[10] Plymouth Court Records, book Wills, vol. i. 53-59.

[11] And this is all that writers have said of it, only adding that the inventory of the same was on record.

[12] It had been designed to place the entire inventory of the Elder's library in the appendix; but the additional expense it would occasion, and the difficulty in ascertaining the true titles of some of the works, will prevent the execution of that design. Very few of those *identical* volumes which he possessed can now be discovered. The principal one which the writer has seen, is in the library of Yale College, with the. Elder's name, written with his own hand, across the title page, as we have before mentioned.

Chapter Thirty-Three

The soul, immortal as its sire,
Shall never die.   — Montgomery.

We now approach the close of Elder Brewster's long and not uneventful life. His last years were passed in the enjoyment of the high esteem and reverential regard of the whole colony — nay, of all the colonies. His was also the blessing of remarkable health, kept up to the last by temperate habits, continued mental exercise, active industry, and even labor in the fields.

His closing years were marked by great serenity and peace. Eventful and agitating as had been the scenes through which he had passed, and fearful as were the prospects abroad of the future, he ever trusted in God, and was not dismayed.

He had seen forty years in the sixteenth century, and forty-three, at least, in the seventeenth; and had thus witnessed nearly three long and most remarkable reigns of English sovereigns, and their memorable acts. In the times of Elizabeth, the period of great men, of thrilling events, and heroic deeds, he received his early training. Through alternate periods of peace, and of trials, public and private, in his own country and in Holland, his mental energies had been matured. In this western world, through suffering and endurance that passed description, he had lived to see a Christian colony planted; the savage foe to a large extent appeased, conciliated, and in several cases encouragingly influenced by Christian instruction and example. From that one poor settlement had others arisen, now numbering eight towns. Instead of one small church, he could now behold eight Christian folds, with their pastors. In room of the small number of fifty souls, spared through the first season, were now eight thousand, with a constitution, established laws, and a government defined. A neighboring colony, first encouraged by its example, now rivalled their own; while other infant colonies were rising in strength, and already uniting with them in confederacy, for protection against native and foreign foes. [1]

Along with their churches, he had witnessed the establishment of schools, to be the glory of New England; and not only these, but a college, and its graduating classes, showing their purpose, that freedom, education, and religion, should go hand in hand. [2]

Thus could he look over the past scenes of his life and times; the conflicts, the sad errors, as well as heroic acts of the age; the faults, as well as sterling virtues of his own people; and could look forward with hope that, though they themselves had "sown in tears," their children "would reap in joy."

And now his days were drawing to a close. His work on earth was done. Not sadly, but peacefully, and in the full possession of his faculties, his spirit was called to depart. [3] It was a privilege to mark the closing scene. Interesting particulars come to us from one evidently present, and who had been his

176

junior companion for nearly half a century. "I am to begin this year," he says, "with that which was a matter of great sadness and mourning unto them all" — the "death of their reverend Elder, and my dear and loving friend, William Brewster: a man that had done and suffered much for the Lord Jesus, and the Gospel's sake, and had borne his part, in weal and woe, with this poor persecuted church above thirty-six years, in England and Holland, and in this wilderness, and done the Lord and them faithful service in his place and calling." "Upheld to a great age, notwithstanding the many troubles and sorrows he had passed through, he had this blessing added to all the rest, to die in his bed in peace, in the midst of his friends, who mourned and wept over him, and administered to him what help and comfort they could, and he again, while he could, *recomforted* them. His sickness was not long. Until the last day he did not wholly keep his bed; and his speech continued until a little more than half a day, when it failed; and at about 9 or 10 that evening, without a pang, as a man fallen into a sound sleep, he sweetly departed this life unto a better." [4] How true, in such a case, are the words of Young —

"The death-bed of the just, undrawn
By mortal hand, merits a Divine.
Angels should paint it; angels ever there.
Dare I presume?
            . . . I pause —
Is it his deathbed? No, it is his shrine.
. . . .
You see the man; you see his hold on heaven,
Sweet peace, and heavenly hope, and humble joy
      . . . beam on his soul.
What more than human peace!
His comforters he comforts; . . .
      . . . unreluctant gives, not yields
His soul.
Whence this?
His God sustains him in his final hour;
His final hour brings glory to his God;
'He sleeps,' [5] . . .
            . . . In Jesus sweetly sleeps,
To waken at the resurrection morn."

Let us approach the place, and view the scene where the venerable pioneer passed his closing years, and where his immortal part took its departure to the "spirit land."

North of Plymouth, some three miles by water, and nearly eight by land, is the picturesque point or neck of land, extending southerly into Plymouth Bay. As we draw near, from either direction, there looms up conspicuously before us, the noted "Captain's Hill;" an elevation, oval-shaped, rising to the height of 180 feet. Ascending this hill, we have from its summit, on all sides, a view, which for variety, extent and beauty, has in this part of the country no equal.

Far away over the waters, eastward, may be discerned in a clear atmosphere, skirting the horizon, the highlands of Cape Cod. "We can almost see its sickle-shaped harbor, where the pilgrims first entered, and formed their compact; and where for five long weeks lay moored their sea-worn barque.

Nearer, and within clear view, we trace where the last of their exploring expeditions, after coasting the whole southern circuit of the Cape Bay, approached in their frail disabled shallop, in the raging storm, to enter the waters of the Plymouth Bay. No lighthouse, or fair twin lights were there, as now, on the "Gurnet's Point," to guide them inward in safety. We trace where they pressed onward amidst fears and perils and bare escape from the roaring breakers. Still nearer before us is the memorable Clark's Islet, under whose lee they found shelter. Further south, rises to view the green point of Manomet. Nearer, on the right, is the outer, and next the inner Plymouth Harbor, where at length

Old Brewster Place, near Plymouth, taken from Captain's Hill

the "Mayflower" entered, and found her winter's moorings, and whence these emigrants landed, and built, amidst sufferings and deaths, the first town of New England. [6]

Returning to our stand-point, we see at our feet, including the hill, with all to the right or south, the lands allotted to the brave Capt. Standish.

Descending the hill a few paces *eastward* and *midway* between its northern and southern extremities, we have full before us, extending to the water's edge, and around northerly, including the so-called "Nook," the grounds allotted to the Elder. On them, prominent before us, stands a gray, decaying farm-house, with its appendages; not that built by the Elder, but evidently its representative, and near the site of the original. [7]

Here but lately had been the haunts of the red man; here, in full view of scenes that could not fail to bring vividly to mind the past of their own fresh history, the Elder passed his closing years. Here he drank in more and more the spirit of that Word, and the grace of that Redeemer, in whose faith he had lived; here he gave his last counsels; here bid adieu to all of earth.

We draw near the scene. We join in thought the sympathizing company. The death of one so greatly loved and revered could not but be deeply felt throughout the colony. "It was the sorest loss that had hitherto befallen them." [8] From all the scattered settlements they came, testifying their sense of their bereavement, and accompanying the remains to their final resting-place. They speak of the departed, of his early and matured piety, his sound learning, his acquaintance with men and life, from the peasant to the court; also, of his gentle manners, discreet, calm, social, innocent life and conversation. They call to mind his humility, undervaluing himself rather than others; and yet his firmness of purpose and unconquerable perseverance in what his judgment and conscience approved; how he shunned no responsibility laid upon him, shrunk from no personal sacrifice for those with whom he sympathized, sharing in all their deprivations, and yet, withal, manifesting no repulsive austerities, no spirit of dictation. Their memories could bring up to view the many cases of his deep and effective sympathy for those reduced to want, or afflicted or oppressed. As their ruling elder, they could call to mind his mode of government — firm, yet never severe; and his manner and ability as a teacher, affectionate, persuasive; in effect, powerful, in all, eminently successful. In short, there could be but one conclusion, peculiarly fitted had he been to be their spiritual guide, in all that they had passed through. [9]

With such reflections, we must suppose, and with arrangements partaking of primitive simplicity, they accompanied the remains in long procession, winding around on the bay's western shore to the Plymouth Burial Hill. [10] There doubtless had been deposited, more than seventeen years before, the remains of his beloved wife, and subsequently those of his two daughters. There, too, in years gone by, in the basement of that fort, he had led their devotions; there his voice, now silent, they had often heard proclaiming the life-giving word. Now they were performing for him the last sad offices of love. Few were the rites of sepulture. No monument ever marked the place; but his memory remains less perishable than the adamant.

The solemnities ended, the chief part of the assembly, with the "two only surviving sons, returned from the burial, to the house of the governor."

The Elder having left no *will,* different views were entertained by the two sons in respect to the division of the estate. At the house of the governor, in the presence of the ministers of Duxbury, Marshfield, and Plymouth, and of the present and subsequent governors, Bradford, Winslow, and Prince; also, their military chief. Miles Standish, and a numerous company — the two brothers, after a frank and friendly statement by each of the entire facts of the case, entered into an amicable arrangement for the harmonious division of the estate between them, "to the great satisfaction of the whole assembly:" a matter of note in the colony, and an example of peaceable proceeding worthy of the descendants of the Elder. [11]

[1] Bradford, 416.

[2] Cambridge College, or Harvard University, first named after Cambridge University, England, where most of its founders had been educated, was established in 1638; being the oldest in the United States. Its first graduating class took their degrees in 1642. Zealously sustained by nearly all the first settlers of New England, it furnished, for a long time, most of their educated men, for the ministry, and the other learned professions. The Elder's grandson, Isaac Allerton, was here graduated, in 1650.

[3] Bradford gives the date of the Elder's death thus: "*About* the 18th of April, 1643." Morton, secretary of the colony, wrote in the church "Records, April 16th, 1644."

We should take Bradford's date to be the correct one, had not he himself said again afterwards, "He died, having lived some 23 or 24 years here in this country." Now, even 22 years and 5 months would bring us to April, 1644, as Morton recorded it. This latter date seems to receive some further confirmation, also, from the fact that the Court Records show the inventory of his estate to have been taken on the 10th and 18th of May, 1644, and the letters of administration to have been granted at the next annual meeting of the court, "June 5th, 1644."

Again, as to his age, Bradford says: "He was near fourscore years of age (if not all out) when he died." Morton writes that the Elder was "aged 84 at his death."

As Bradford's words indicate that he did not speak from exact knowledge, and Morton speaks positively, and had been twenty years in the colony when the Elder died, and was for many years the keeper of the records, we are inclined to give his dates the preference. Consequently, deducting the age 84 from the year 1644, leaves 1560 as the year of Elder Brewster's birth.

Church Records and Court Records, compared with Bradford, 408, and Appendix, 451, and Morton's Memorial.

[4] See Bradford, 408.

[5] Young, Night the 2d.

[6] Of the beauty of this landscape, an idea may be formed from the annexed view of its eastern portion, and from its position as marked on the map of Plymouth Bay, p. 241.

[7] See the engraved view of the old Brewster Place.

[8] Hubbard, Mass. Hist. Coll., 2d ser. vi. 663, 664.

[9] See Bradford's Corresponding Historic Reflections, pp. 413, 414, 91, 12, 412.

[10] This last is satisfactorily ascertained by necessary inferences from several expressions in the record of the settlement of his estate.— Vol. i. of Deeds, &c., pp. 198, 199.

[11] See settlement of the Elder's estate; record referred to last. Though a minor consideration, it may be added that the estate, as divided between the two sons, consisted of his house, &c., in Duxbury, with one hundred and eleven acres of upland, besides marsh lands belonging to him, and also his share in the undivided lands as one of the purchasers of the patent and plantation of New Plymouth. In addition to this were his books, household furniture, farming utensils, and cattle, appraised at £150 00s. 7d. currency of that day.

Chapter Thirty-Four

I like most its history; for who understands any phenomenon if he is not master of the course of its development? — Goethe.

We have traced the life, and taken a glance at the *times* of the Pilgrim elder. We have gone back to the period when he was living and acting. We have marked the surroundings and the development of principle that influenced the man, that moulded his character, that moved him to act, or led him to endure. Standing as at one of the great starting points in this portion of the world's history, we have viewed men agitated, changing, yet many of them clinging to the domineering sway of ages past, and all of them unconscious how largely "old things were to pass away," and equally unconscious what were to be "the new." There standing, we have viewed the instrument or instrument? prepared. We have seen the first movement, as "a little cloud gathering, small as a man's hand," even over Scrooby's fenny soil. We traced thence its course, as moved or forced by winds adverse or favoring, from England to Holland, and from Holland to this western world. ^Here, increasing slowly at first, until joined by others, it at length spread forth far and wide across this entire hemisphere.

In this view, we have marked with deep reverence the evident providences of God, traced by discipline at every point, bringing good out of evil; providences which, without presuming to scan, we gratefully acknowledge as facts standing out in bold relief on the pages of this portion of our history. And we mark one, and not the least of those providences, in the *precise period* of the pilgrim movement.

Had this portion of the new continent been thrown open and taken in possession *earlier*, before the Reformation, how unmistakably different would have been its destination, history, and character! Hither 'would then have been transferred the rank growths of despotism, and ignorance alike of real religious and political rights and duties. Hither would have come the debasing maxims, superstitions, and corruptions, which degraded the fairest portions of Europe, to be here fixed, we know not how firmly or how long.

On the other hand, had this movement been at a *later* period, when the demands for room in the Old World had become more pressing, when the causes and facilities for emigration had greatly increased, and the prospects of immediate gain more sure and tempting, how then would this new land have been flooded with the inrolling tides of emigrants of *diverse nations, races,* and *languages,* of opposite *customs, conflicting laws, interests, prejudices, and institutions!* While *no one people would have been here* of enlightened views, and sufficiently established, to quietly receive, and happily mould the heterogeneous masses into one united whole.

Or if some conquering power might, in such case, have forced its sway over the rest, how would its *arbitrary dictates* and military rule, instead of the mild laws of this Republic, have been even now going forth as of old: "The King and our Council, unto all the people, nations, and languages of our kingdom, do send our *royal decrees.*"

Nay, had the pilgrim movement been even *one generation later,* such were the claims, so extended were the settlements of the French, so strong their chain of posts, and their influence among the Indian tribes, from New Foundland to the farthest lakes, that, instead of a New England, as now, *this would have been an Acadie or a new France.* [1]

But what, at length, was *the special purpose* of the pilgrim movement? and what the corresponding development? Here is historically the important point around which all the rest centres.

It was a twofold purpose, as the facts show. They left England for Holland to escape persecution. In Holland they found indeed what they thus sought, protection and toleration; but they found there, also, after twelve years of exertion in overcoming difficulties, that they were but an *isolated company;* and what was more, that their posterity would evidently *soon degenerate,* would lose their English name and character, and become absorbed in the Dutch. This became to them matter of profound grief. [2] To avoid this, and find an asylum, and found a civil commonwealth by themselves, in some unoccupied portion of the earth, was the immediate design. That design, put in execution, led to the memorable results.

Already had they chosen and become accustomed to be guided by their own officers in their church system; and were therefore prepared for the same course in their civil organization. What some few enlightened statesmen and philosophers were speculating upon in theory, respecting constitutional liberty and law by the free choice of the governed, this brave, earnest-souled people were working out in practice. [3] Not all at once could the problem be solved, but step by step. Yet as circumstances favored, they had minds to seize the opportunity; therein exercising man's right and duty under their earthly sovereign, and in unquestioning obedience to the teachings of the Divine Word.

Before they crossed the ocean, a civil organization under the King was clearly in view. [4] But the first move, the *germ,* was in the *compact* formed

182

ere they landed from the Mayflower. Thenceforth were its principles developed more and more; the germ, planted in the favoring soil of the New World, became the tree; the tree in due time sent forth its branches; these, linked with others of kindred growth, multiplied and spread. Hence the development of this broad republic.

Not then the individual man merely, not the founding of a little colony only, is it, that here attracts the attention, but the germ of a nation; the rising of a power and of institutions on a new and wide theatre, which have changed the face of a continent, which seem destined to affect the whole race.

But there was another, and in the minds of the pilgrims a still greater purpose in the movement. It was to found their church, where they and theirs after them, with all who should unite with them, might, without hindrance or danger of a degenerate end, worship God in mode and with a ministry after their own choice; and also be the means, "though they should be but as stepping stones for others in the great work," of carrying the blessings of the Gospel to the native savage heathen. [5]

Here was the chief moving *cause*. For these combined purposes especially, they left Holland for this far-off wilderness. For these they labored, endured, suffered. Brave hearts, earnest, devoted, heroic souls, had they, those pilgrim fathers, strong in faith and hope, thus to go through all they did, so patiently, so perseveringly, so unflinchingly.

We say not that they were without faults; but who had less? We pretend not that they understood the broad principles of religious toleration in their full extent and clearness; but what community then understood them better? They were in advance of their brethren in England, much in advance of what was afterwards manifested by their sister colony of Massachusetts, with whom, in this respect, they have been unjustly classed. [6]

"To judge them fairly (to use the words of Prescott), we must not do it by the lights of our own age. We must carry ourselves back to theirs, and take the point of view afforded by the civilization of their time. Thus only can we arrive at impartial criticism in reviewing generations that are past. We must extend to them the same justice we shall have occasion to ask from posterity, when, by the light of a higher civilization (should we not say Christianization'?) posterity shall survey the dark or doubtful passages of our own history, which hardly arrest the eye of a contemporary."

Accordingly, whatever may be our distinctive views or opinions of church polity, whatever our estimate of some of their peculiar practices, yet over all, and above all sectional or denominational considerations, how much is there in which we may all unite in yielding to those fathers our high regard and veneration.

We trace, indeed, some dark lines in the onward course of development in some portions of their descendants — defections from the humility, unity, and some of the most dearly cherished principles of those first founders. Yet we trace also as characteristics the mighty elements of energy, perseverance, zeal, with an unextinguished impress of their religious character. We trace the development of most valued principles, and of a power of expansion without limit, along with institutions which are the glory of our land. [7]

But, finally, the movement itself stands out prominently before us as one of a peculiarly marked character. Many were the enterprises near that period, many the leaders influenced by various motives, for the founding of new settlements, new colonies, new states, in new portions of the earth. Not a few adventurers came to the stern coasts of New England; but of them all there was but *one only designated pilgrim band,* but *one* Elder Brewster. [8]

Imperishable is their memorial. Theirs were deeds and sufferings which have laid hold of men's feelings and sympathies with a force unrivalled, undiminished. Though soon surpassed in numbers and wealth, and finally absorbed by the younger Bay colony, the interest in this *first* colony remains the deepest, the *prestige* of Plymouth continues pre-eminent. Thither, more than elsewhere, the pilgrim visitor directs his steps. Where those pious founders trod, labored, prayed, he pauses and reflects with a more than classic interest. "To abstract the mind," said the stern Dr. Johnson, when standing on the Isle of Iona, "to abstract the mind from all local knowledge would be impossible if it were endeavored, and be foolish if it were possible. Far from me and my friends be such frigid philosophy as may conduct us indifferent or unmoved over any ground which has been dignified by wisdom, bravery, or virtue. That man is little to be envied whose patriotism would not gain force upon the plains of *Marathon,* or whose piety would not grow warmer among the ruins of *Iona;*" may we not add, or amidst the scenes of the struggles and endurances of the Pilgrim founders of New Plymouth?

[1] For the grounds of this latter statement, see Bancroft, or Hildreth, at the period mentioned. As things *were,* the northern English colonies were but *just able,* after long contests, to keep their possessions. Nor was the struggle much less severe on the part of the Virginia colony, to maintain itself against the combined attacks of the Indians and French.

[2] Winslow, in Young, p. 381; and Bradford, 24.

[3] More had written his Utopia; L'Hopital had made known his liberal views in France; Bacon was now meditating and preparing, though he never completed his New Atlantis.

[4] Bradford, p. 66.

[5] Winslow in Young, 382; and Bradford, 24. This was also the specified purpose of the Virginia colony; and the same was the case in the other subsequent colonies. In this work the Plymouth colony did much, but chiefly by example, counsel, and Christian intercourse within their boundaries.

Some five years later (in 1549), was organized the first society in England, of which the recorder of London, Wm. Steele, Baron, and afterwards Lord Lieutenant of land, was for a long time the first president; and by the aid of which the two distinguished Elliots, father and son, as well as others, became successful missionaries. — See Mass. Hist. Coll., vol. i. pp. 168, 226; and 3d series, vol. iv. pp. 161, 196, 200, *et al.*

[6] "The Pilgrims (says Mr. Bancroft, truly) carried with them to the New World, the moderation which they had professed in their dealings with the court. There is a marked difference in this respect between the government of the Old Colony, as that of Plymouth was called, and the government of Massachusetts." "The pilgrims Great Plymouth were never betrayed into the excesses of religious persecution." "Mr. Anderson, in his History of the Church of England in the Colonies (vol. i. pp. 453, 454), of his first edition, has seen fit to attempt to refute the remark. But in this he has only committed a double injustice in consequence of a mistake of his own, in confounding the two colonies of the Massachusetts Bay and New Plymouth." "Should this notice reach the eye of Mr. Anderson (he adds), I hope he will take pains to see for himself the error of the statements which his misapprehension has led him to make, and prove his substantial candor by the correction which historic truth requires." — New York Hist. Coll., 2d series, vol. iii. close of the Letter on the Leyden Articles.

In the Plymouth colony, persons belonging to the Church of England, and those who were inclined to the views of the Baptist persuasion, lived with them undisturbed: except such as openly interfered with, and would subvert their own church organization and order. Strangers and visitors of other religious belief, were hospitably received and entertained by them for months together; to the great increase of their own deprivations and self-denial. The restriction was, that none but their own church members should be voters, or eligible to office; though this restriction was at times dispensed with and finally removed.

[7] Said Burke of them, in their subsequent development in connection with other colonies: "Nothing in the history of mankind is like their progress. For my part, I never cast an eye on their flourishing commerce, and their cultivated and commodious life, but they seem to me rather ancient nations, grown to perfection through a long series of fortunate events, and a train of successful industry, accumulating wealth in many countries, than the colonies of yesterday, than a set of miserable outcasts, a few years ago, not so much sent as thrown out on the bleak and barren shore of a desolate wilderness, three thousand miles from all civilized intercourse."

[8] This is not only true in respect to the Elder, in the eminent sense here implied, but equally true historically in another sense. He was their *only* Elder from the formation of their Society; his successor at Plymouth, Mr. Thos. Cushman, not being chosen until some five years after his decease, that is, in 1649. — Bradford, in Young, 456, and Thatcher, 67.

Appendix No. 1 - List of Passengers in the Mayflower

Being the *names* of those who came over first, in the year 1620, and were the founders of New Plymouth, which led to the planting of the other New England Colonies. This list of their "names" and families, was preserved by Governor Bradford at the close of his History, and is here presented in the order in which he placed them. The value of such an accurate list cannot be too highly estimated. — See his History, Appendix No. 1.

Mr. John Carver — who was chosen their first Governor on their arrival at Cape Cod. He died the first spring. Katherine, his wife — she died a few weeks after her husband, in the beginning of summer.

Desire Minter — afterwards returned to her friends, in poor health, and died in England.

John Howland — man servant, afterwards married the daughter of John Tillie, and had ten children.

Roger Wilder — man servant, died in the first sickness.

William Latham — a boy, after more than twenty years visited England, and died at the Bahama Islands.

A maid servant — who married, and died one or two years after.

Jasper More — who died the first season.

Mr. William Brewster — their Ruling Elder; lived some twenty-three or four years after his arrival.

Mary, his wife— died between 1623 and 1627.

Love Brewster — a son, married, lived to the year 1650, had four children.

Wrestling Brewster — youngest son. (See note at the close of Chapter Twenty-Nine.) [1]

Richard More and Brother, two boys placed with the Elder - Richard afterwards married, and had 4 or more children. His brother died the first winter.

Mr. Edward Winslow — Mr. W. afterwards chosen Governor, died in 1655, when on a commission to the West Indies.

Elizabeth, his wife — died the first winter. Mr. W. left two children by a second marriage.

George Soule and Elias Story – two men in Winslow's family. G. Soule married and had eight children. E. Story died in the first sickness.

Ellen More — a little girl placed in Mr. Winslow's family, sister of Richard More, died soon after their arrival.

Mr. William Bradford — their second Governor, author of the history of the Plymouth Colony, lived to the year 1657.

Dorothy, his wife — who died soon after their arrival. Gov. Bradford left a son in England to come afterwards — had four children by a second marriage.

Mr. Isaac Allerton — chosen first assistant to the Governor;

Mary, his wife — who died in the first sickness;

Bartholomew — son, married in England;

Remember and Mary, daughters. Remember married in Salem, had three or four children; Mary married in Plymouth, had four children;

John Hook — servant boy, died in the first sickness.

Mr. Samuel Fuller — their Physician: his wife and child remained, and came over afterwards; they had two more children.

William Butten — servant, died on the passage.

John Crackston — who died in the first sickness;

John Crackston — his son, who died some five or six years after,

Capt. Myles Standish — who lived to the year 1656; chief in military affairs;

Rose, his wife — died in the first sickness: Capt. Standish had four sons living in 1650, by a second marriage.

Mr. Christopher Martin and his wife, Solomon Prower and John Langemore (servants) - all died soon after their arrival.

Mr. William Mullins, his wife, Joseph, a son - these three died the first winter;

Priscilla — a daughter, survived and married John Alden;

Robert Carter — servant, died the first winter.

Mr. William White — died soon after landing;

Susanna, his wife — afterwards married to Mr. E. Winslow;

Resolved, a son — married, and had five children.

Peregrine, a son — was born after their arrival at Cape Cod, he cannot therefore be numbered among the passengers proper — married, and had two children before 1650.

William Holbeck and Edward Thomson – servants, both died soon after landing.

Mr. Stephen Hopkins, and Elizabeth, his wife - both lived over twenty years after their arrival, and had a son and four daughters born in this country;

Giles, and Constantia - by a former marriage - Giles married, had four children. Constantia married - had 12 children.

Damaris, a son, and Oceanus, born at sea - children by the present marriage.

Edward Doty, and Edward Litster, servants, E. Doty by a second marriage had seven children; after his term of service - went to Virginia.

Mr. Richard Warren — his wife and five daughters were left, and came over afterwards. They also had two sons; and the daughters married here.

John Billington — he was not from Leyden, or of the Leyden Company, but from London. (Bradford in Y— 149.)

Ellen, his wife;

John, his son — who died in a few years;

Francis, the second son — married, and had eight children,

Edward Tillie, and Ann, his wife - both died soon after their arrival.

Harry Samson and Humility Cooper, two children, their cousins, Henry lived, married, had seven children; Humility returned to England.

John Tillie and his wife - both died soon after they came on shore;

Elizabeth — their daughter, afterwards married John Howland.

Francis Cooke — who lived until after 1650; his wife and other children came afterwards; they had six or more children.

John, his son — afterwards married — had four children.

Thomas Rogers — died in the first sickness;

Joseph, his son — was living in 1650, married and had six children.

Mr. Rogers' other children came afterwards, and had families.

Thomas Tinker, wife, and son - all died in the first sickness.

John Rigdale and Alice, his wife - both died in the first sickness.

James Chilton, his wife – both died in the first sickness;

Mary — their daughter, lived, married, and had nine children; another married daughter came afterwards.

Edward Fuller, his wife - both died in the first sickness.

Samuel — their son, married — had four children.

John Turner,

Two sons, names not given; all three died in the first sickness. A daughter came some years afterwards to Salem and there married.

Francis Eaton,

Sarah, his wife — she died the first winter; by a third marriage he left three children.

Samuel, a son — married and had one child.

Moses Fletcher, John Goodman, Thomas Williams, Digerie Priest, Edmond Margeson, Richard Britterige, Richard Clarke - These seven died in the general sickness; the wife of D. Priest and children came afterwards, she being the sister of Mr. Allerton.

Peter Brown — lived some fourteen years after, was twice married, and left four children.

Richard Gardiner — became a seaman, and died abroad.

Gilbert Winslow — after living here a number of years, returned to England.

John Alden — "a hopeful young man," hired at Southampton, married Priscilla Mullens, as mentioned, and had eleven children.

John Allerton, Thomas English.

William Trevore and — Ely - two seamen — are commonly, but incorrectly reckoned in the number of the first company of passengers for the Colony; Bradford himself says: "Two other seamen were hired to stay a year; * * when their time was out they both returned."

Accordingly, he says of the Mayflower company: "These being about a hundred souls, came over in the first ship." Afterwards he adds: "Of these one hundred persons who came over in this first ship together, the greatest half died in the general mortality, and most of them in two or three months' time."

Omitting those two hired sailors who returned, and counting the person that died and the child that was born while on the passage as one passenger, we have the exact number — *one hundred* of the Pilgrim Company, "who came over in the first ship." And, as *fifty-one* died the first season, this enumeration makes good those other words of the historian, that, "the greater half died in the general mortality" — See his *Appendix*, pp. 450, 455.

[1] The Elder's remaining children came over afterwards: The author proposes to publish hereafter a full Genealogy of the descendants of the Elder.

Appendix No. 2 - List of Passengers That Arrived, After One Year, in the Second Small Ship "Fortune;"

Being parts of families, with others, left in England or Holland the year before. They arrived at New Plymouth, on the 11th of Nov. 1621.

John Adams,

William Bassite (Bassett, probably two in his family),

William Beale,

Edward Bompasse,

Jonathan Brewster — the oldest son of Elder Brewster.

Clement Brigges (Briggs),

John Cannon,

William Coner.

Robert Cushman — for several years the Leyden Company's agent in England. He returned in the Fortune to act still further as agent for the Company — was of great service in various ways; but died before coming again to settle in the Colony.

Thomas Cushman — son of Robert, about twelve years old — came with his father in the Fortune, became an exemplary man in the Colony, and succeeded Elder Brewster in the eldership, in 1649.

Stephen Dean,

Philip De La Noye (Delano),

Thomas Flavell and Son.

Widow Ford and three children — William, Martha, and John.

Robert Hickes, William Hilton, Bennet Morgan, Thomas Morton, Austin Nicholas, William Palmer (probably two in his family), William Pitt, Thomas Prince, or Prence — married the Elder's daughter, Patience; was afterwards Governor.

Moses Simonson (Simmons),

Hugh Statie (Stacy),

James Steward (Stewart),

William Tench,

John Winslow — brother of Mr. Edward Winslow.

William Wright. — See in Bradford, 105, 106, and in Young, p. 235.

Appendix No. 3

The following is an alphabetical list of those who came over in the "Ann," and "Little James." The vessels parted company at sea; the "Ann" arrived the latter part of June, and the "Little James" some week or ten days later; part of the number were the wives and children of persons already in the Colony.

Anthony Annable — afterwards settled in Scituate.

Edward Bangs — settled in Easthara.

Robert Bartlett, Fear Brewster, Patience Brewster - daughters of Elder Brewster.

Mary Bucket,

Edward Burcher,

Thomas Clarke. This Thomas Clark's grave-stone is the oldest on the Plymouth Burial Hill.

Christopher Conant,

Cuthbert Cuthbertson — was a Hollander.

Anthony Dix,

John Faunce,

Mauasseh Faunce,

Goodwife Flavell — probably the wife of Thos. Flavell, who came in the Fortune.

Edmund Flood,

Bridget Fuller — apparently the wife of Samuel Fuller, the Physician.

Timothy Hatherly,

William Heard,

Margaret Hickes and her children - the wife of Robert Hickes, who came in the Fortune.

William Hilton's wife and two children - He had sent for them before his death.

Edward Holman,

John Jenny — had "liberty, in 1636, to erect a mill for grinding and beating of corn upon the brook of Plymouth."

Robert Long,

Experience Mitchell,

George Morton — he brought with him his son Nathaniel and four other children.

Nathaniel Morton — son of George M., and afterwards Secretary of the Colony.

Thomas Morton, Jr. — son of Thomas M., who came in the Fortune.

Ellen Newton,

John Oldham — a man of some note afterwards.

Frances Palmer — wife of Wm. Palmer, who came in the Fortune.

Christian Penn,

Mr. Perce's two servants,

Joshua Pratt,

James Rand,

Robert Rattliffe, Nicholas Snow — settled in Eastham.

Alice Southworth — (widow, afterwards the second wife of Gov. Bradford.)

Francis Sprague — settled in Duxbury.

Barbara Standish — i. e. second wife of Capt. Standish, married after her arrival.

Thomas Tilden,

Stephen Tracy,

Ralph Wallen.

Those who came in the first ships, the Mayflower, the Fortune, the Ann, and Little James, are distinctly called the *old comers,* or the *fore-fathers.* — See Hazzard's State Papers, I., pp. 101-103; and Young's Notes (p. 352) of his Chron. of the Pilgrims.

Appendix No. 4

At a general Court held on the 22d of May, 1627, a division of the cattle belonging to the Colony, proportionably to each share-holder, was concluded upon, and also twenty acres of land to each. This division being put upon record, it is believed that the record presents the name of every family and person then belonging to the Colony proper. The names taken from the Record are as follows: —

Francis Cooke, Hester Cooke, his wife, John Cooke, Jacob Cooke, Jane Cooke, Hester Cooke, Mary Cooke.

Isaac Allerton, Fear Allerton — his wife, a daughter of Elder Brewster, Bartholomew Allerton, Mary Allerton, Sarah Allerton.

Cuthbert Cuthbertson, Sarah Cuthbertson, Samuel Cuthbertson, Mary Priest, Sarah Priest.

Myles Standish, Barbara Standish, his wife, Charles Standish, Alexander Standish, John Standish.

Edward Winslow, Susanna Winslow, his wife, John Winslow, Edward Winslow, Resolved White, Peregrine White.

John Howland, Elizabeth Howland, his wife, John Howland, Jr., Desire Howland.

John Alden, Priscilla Alden, Elizabeth Alden, John Alden.

William Brewster, Love Brewster, Wrestling Brewster, Jonathan Brewster, Lucretia Brewster, his wife, William Brewster and Mary Brewster, - children of Jon. and L. B.

Thomas Prince, Patience Prince, daughter of the Elder, Rebecca Prince, Humility Cooper, Henri Sampson.

John Adams, Eleanor Adams, James Adams.

John Winslow, Mary Winslow.

William Bassett, Elizabeth Bassett, William Bassett, Jr., Elizabeth Bassett, Jr.

Francis Sprague, Anna Sprague, Mercy Sprague.

Stephen Hopkins, Elizabeth Hopkins, his wife, Giles Hopkins, Caleb Hopkins, Deborah Hopkins.

Nicholas Snow, Constance Snow.

William Palmer, Frances Palmer, his wife, William Palmer, Jr.

John Billington, Helen Billington, Francis Billington.

Samuel Fuller, Bridget Fuller, Samuel Fuller, Jr.

Peter Browne, Martha Browne, Mary Browne.

John Ford, Martha Ford.

Anthony Anable, Jane Anable, Sarah Anable, Hannah Anable, Damaris Hopkins.

Richard Warren, Elizabeth Warren, his wife, Nathaniel Warren, Joseph Warren, Mary Warren, Ann Warren, Sarah Warren, Elizabeth Warren, Abigail Warren, John Billington.

George Sowle (Soule), Mary Sowle, Zacheriah Sowle.

Francis Eaton, Christian Eaton, his wife, Samuel Eaton, Rachel Eaton.

Stephen Tracy, Triphasa Tracy, Sarah Tracy, Rebecca Tracy.

Ralph Wallen, Joyce Wallen, Sarah Morton.

William Bradford, the Governor, Alice Bradford, his wife, William Bradford, Jr., Mercy Bradford.

Manasses Kerapton, Julien Kempton.

Nathaniel Morton, John Morton, Ephraim Morton, Patience Morton.

John Jenne, Sarah Jenne, his wife, Samuel Jenne, Abigail Jenne, Sarah Jenne.

Robert Hicks, Margaret Hicks, Samuel Hicks, Ephraim Hicks, Lydia Hicks, Phebe Hicks.

Moses Simonson (Simmons),

Philip De La Noye (Delano),

Experience Mitchell,

John Faunce,

Joshua Pratt,

Phineas Pratt,

Edward Bompassee,	John Shaw,
John Crackstone,	Robert Bartlett,
Abraham Pierce,	Thomas Prence,
Thomas Clarke,	Joseph Rogers,
Clement Briggs,	Thomas Cushman,
Edward Doten (Doty),	William Latham,
Edward Holdman (Holman),	Stephen Deane,
Richard More,	Edward Bangs.

Appendix No. 5 - Extracts from Webster's Speech at the Pilgrim Festival, New York, 1850

"Gentlemen: There was, in ancient times, a ship that carried Jason to the acquisition of the Golden Fleece. There was a flag-ship at the battle of Actium which made Augustus Caesar master of the world. In modern times there have been flag-ships which have carried Hawke, and Howe, and Nelson, of the other continent, and Hull, and Decatur, and Stewart of this, to triumph. What are they all, in the chance of remembrance among men, to that little bark, the Mayflower, which reached these shores in 1620? Yes, brethren, that Mayflower was a flower destined to be of perpetual bloom! Its verdure will stand the sultry blasts of Summer and the chilling winds of Autumn. It will defy Winter. It will defy all climate and all time, and will continue to spread its petals to the world, and to exhale an everlasting odor and fragrance to the last syllable of recorded time." * * * * * *

"Gentlemen, brethren of New England, whom I have come some hundreds of miles to meet this night, let me present to you one of the most distinguished of those personages who came hither on the deck of the Mayflower. Let me fancy that I now see Elder William Brewster entering the door at the further end of this hall; a tall erect figure, of plain dress, with a respectful bow, mild and cheerful, but of no merriment that reaches beyond a smile. Let me suppose that his image stood now before us, or that it was looking in upon this assembly. 'Are ye,' he would say, with a voice of exultation, and yet softened with melancholy, 'are ye our children? Does this scene of refinement, of elegance, of riches, of luxury, does all this come from our labors? Is this magnificent city, the like of which we never saw nor heard of on either continent, is this but an offshoot from Plymouth Rock?

"Quis jam locus * * * *
Quae regio in terris nostri non plena laboris?"

Is this one part of the great reward for which my brethren and myself endured lives of toil and of hardship? We had faith and hope. God granted us the spirit to look forward, and we did look forward. But this scene we never anticipated. Our hopes were on another life. Of earthly gratifications we tasted little; for human honors we had little expectation. Our bones lie on the hill in Plymouth churchyard, obscure, unmarked, *secreted,* to preserve our graves from the knowledge of savage foes. No stone tells where we lie. And yet, let me say to you who are our descendants, who possess this glorious country and all it contains, who enjoy this hour of prosperity and the thousand blessings showered upon it by the God of your fathers, we envy you not, we reproach you not. Be rich, be prosperous, be enlightened, * * if such be your allotment on earth; but live, also, always to God and to duty. Spread yourselves and your children over the continent, accomplish the whole of your great destiny, and if it be that through the whole you carry Puritan hearts with you, if you still cherish an undying love of civil and religious liberty, and mean to enjoy them yourselves, and are willing to shed your heart's blood to transmit them to your posterity, then will you be worthy descendants of Carver, and Allerton, and Bradford, and the rest of those who landed from stormy seas on the Rock of Plymouth.'"